"An extraordinary book...thoroughly absorbing and accurate in its presentation of the entire range of UFO related phenomena. It arranges the material in such a way that anyone not familiar with the hard facts can easily judge for themselves what the story is. Both as a reference book and as good reading, I highly recommend this book. It may not please religious fanatics or die-hard 'scientists' steeped in 19th-century materialism (the majority, alas!), but it does present a balanced and excitingly accurate picture of 'the problem' relating to the reality of UFOs."

—Hans Holzer
      Author of *The UFOnauts,*
      The Secret of Healing, and many other books

"Dr. Lewels is a very courageous soul. His research, although highly controversial, is conducted with respect and sensitivity. The information he has clearly presented is designed to offer a new perspective to a very old subject—what is a human?
The God Hypothesis is a powerful catalyst for growth, and growing pains often bring pain as well as strength. This work is a gift from heaven to an earthbound race who have forgotten their roots. Now is the time to remember who we are, where we have come from and where we are going."

—Robert Stanley
      Unicus Magazine

"Finally, a book that seriously addresses the question of what the possibility of an alien presence does to religion.
It's an exciting, pioneering look at what is almost certainly about to become the burning question of the age, indeed, of all ages.
Lewels addresses the issues of belief and meaning with incisive intelligence and an intellectual dynamism that is as refreshing as it is exciting. Altogether, an important, useful and timely effort by an articulate and pioneering thinker."

—Whitley Strieber,
      author of *Communion,*
      Transformation, Breakthrough and *The Secret School*

"Lewels has written an important book.
He is a prominent and distinguished figure in his El Paso
community who has courageously marshalled data from many
sources to confirm that the Earth and its citizens are being visited
by beings whose origins are not known.
Clearly written, his book should contribute to overcoming the
official denial of this extraordinary phenomenon, which carries
such vast implications for all of our lives.
Furthermore, Lewels is not afraid to link science with spirituality
and to discuss the profound spiritual and
religious implications of alien encounters.
This work will surely put further
'rips in the fabric' of the strictly materialist world view
that still dominates so much of Western thought."

—Dr. John E. Mack, M.D.
    Professor of Psychiatry,
    Harvard Medical School,
        author of *Abduction: Human Encounters With Aliens*

"Dr. Lewels has attempted a synthesis
of everything from the Bible, reincarnation, past life therapy
and NDEs to quantum physics, the holographic universe, and the
latest in UFO abductions
to develop his synthesis, a very ambitious task.
In a sense, he has developed a
"Unified Field Theory of Physics and Spirituality,"
which is an attempt beyond what Einstein tried. Einstein only
sought to show that a single theory could explain the energy in the
universe—Dr. Lewels is arguing for a single theory to explain both
energy and meaning in the universe."

—Rev. Dr. Barry H. Downing,
    Pastor of the Northminster Presbyterian Church,
    Endwell, New York
        Author of *The Bible and Flying Saucers*

The God Hypothesis

Joe Lewels, Ph.D.

Wild Flower Press

The God Hypothesis

Extraterrestrial Life

and

Its Implications for Science and Religion

Joe Lewels, Ph.D.

Wild Flower Press
P.O. Box 190
Mill Spring, NC 28756

Library of Congress Cataloging-in-Publication Data
Lewels, Joe. 1944—
The God Hypothesis:
extraterrestrial life and its implications for science and religion/
Joe Lewels.

ISBN 0-926524-40-2
1. Unidentified flying objects—Religious aspects.
2. Space theology.
I. Title.
BL65.U54L48 1997
001.942--dc21
96-40867
CIP

The New Millenium Library
Volume I

Cover Artwork: Maynard Demmon
Manuscript editor: Brian Crissey

Printed in the United States of America.

Address all inquiries to:
Wild Flower Press
an imprint of Blue Water Publishing, Inc.
P. O. Box 190
Mill Spring, NC 28756
U.S.A.

Blue Water Publishing, Inc.,
uses all recycled paper.

DEDICATION

This book is dedicated to
those who have experienced "alien" encounters
and to
those who have dedicated their lives to discovering
the truth behind the UFO mystery.

May God grant you
the courage to face the truth when you find it,
and
the wisdom to know how to use it
for the benefit of your fellow human beings.

The God Hypothesis

Contents

INTRODUCTION

by Rev. Barry H. Downing

UFOs have been hovering above world consciousness since World War II, and researchers believe UFOs have been visiting us for centuries. The popular view of UFOs is that they are space visitors from another world. In scientific terms, this is called the extraterrestrial hypothesis.

It is called an hypothesis because we do not have proof of what UFOs are, and, in fact, the official hypothesis is quite different. It comes from most government leaders of the world, and many scientists. That hypothesis is that UFOs are a modern myth, a space age creation of the human imagination. This official view is publicly supported by the United States government and its military leaders. The myth hypothesis was developed by the late psychologist C.J. Jung, who in 1959 published *Flying Saucers: A Modern Myth of Things Seen in the Skies*.[1] Scientists like the late Carl Sagan have strongly argued for this view of UFOs, saying that in our modern age, in which science has displaced the old religion and its faith in angels, UFOs—technological angels—have come flying in to take their place.

---

1. Jung, 1959.

But the more popular hypothesis—the extraterrestrial hypothesis—has for some time had its serious scientific proponents, like Jacques Vallée, and the late J. Allen Hynek.

Independent organizations were formed to study UFOs scientifically, like the Mutual UFO Network (MUFON), the Fund for UFO Research (FUFOR) and the Center for UFO Studies (CUFOS). The members of these organizations busied themselves taking soil samples where UFOs had apparently landed, interviewed pilots who had reported UFOs, studied radar patterns of UFO sightings, and interviewed those who said they had been abducted by aliens.

Scientists who joined these organizations often risked their professional credibility, but the evidence seemed to be mounting that UFOs were something real, even that the abductions were something real. A scientist of the stature of Harvard's Dr. John Mack published his findings in his book *Abduction: Human Encounters with Aliens.*[2]

All of this seemed to point to the emerging triumph of the extraterrestrial hypothesis at the expense of the "official" hypothesis of our government, that UFOs are a myth.

But the more "real" the aliens became, the less valid the extraterrestrial hypothesis seemed. For the extraterrestrial hypothesis presumed the aliens are a bunch of space folks, if not from Mars, then at least from another galaxy. It would only be a matter of time before they landed and said, "Take me to your leader." But this has not happened. As the alien abduction evidence began to mount, the questions mounted: Who are these folks, and what do they want?

In some abduction cases, the humans confronted the aliens, and asked them, "Who are you, and why are you here?" The composite answer is something like this: "We have been around for thousands of years. The Earth belongs to us, and we have made you what you are."

This view of the aliens puts quite a different perspective on things. This seems to be more the language of angels than aliens. Jacques Vallée in his book *Dimensions: A Casebook of Alien Contact,*[3] concluded that UFOs are a force that shapes and controls human culture—they are a godlike force. John Mack discovered a huge spiritual dimension in the reports of many of the abductees he interviewed. Scientists like

2. Mack, 1994.
3. Vallée, 1988.

Vallée and Mack found themselves speaking the language of theology as well as the language of science.

As this new scientific interpretation of the UFO evidence began to take shape, it appeared that we needed a new hypothesis to explain the UFO evidence, and Dr. Joe Lewels calls it "The God Hypothesis."

Needless to say, this is an inconvenient hypothesis for many reasons. For one thing, it enables those who subscribe to the myth hypothesis to say to serious UFO researchers, "We told you so—we knew you were doing religion all along." Many scientists who support the extraterrestrial hypothesis have worried that those like Vallée, Mack and Lewels have lost their scientific minds and gone out on a New Age limb with Shirley MacLaine.

Furthermore, it means scientists have moved into religious territory, without asking religious leaders for permission. What is going on here is very ironic. It was scientists like Copernicus and Galileo who started the war between science and religion in Western culture, destroying the old Christian cosmology. Then Darwin came along and destroyed the biblical idea of creation. Science seemed to have vaporized the power of religion, leaving religion to serve only as cultural art and entertainment for the gullible.

Dr. Lewels comes to us with training as a journalist to report what he sees on the front lines of scientific UFO research. He believes that what UFO researchers have discovered will do more to revolutionize our idea of God and religion than the works of Galileo, Copernicus and Darwin combined.

But here is the strange part. It was science that pushed religion, like Humpty Dumpty, to a shattering fall. Now scientific research is putting God and spirituality back together in a way that is scientifically credible, but also in a way that will not bring joy to most orthodox religious leaders.

The task that Dr. Lewels undertakes is difficult. He reminds one of a cowboy trying to rope an octopus—there are a lot of loose ends.

The God Hypothesis has three major sections. In "Section One: Paradigm Shift," Dr. Lewels deals with his personal changing awareness of UFO research, and what this might mean for his understanding of reality. He does an excellent job introducing concepts like quantum physics and the holographic universe. In modern science we have gone from an atomic universe to a quantum universe. Our old view of the universe was that it was like a collection of billiard balls, large ones formed the suns and planets, small ones formed atoms. The universe at both the macro and micro level was a series of billiard ball collisions.

Then came quantum physics, which concluded that the universe is a sea full of energy waves. The universe is like a large pond in which everything is connected, and one little pebble dropped in the pond, or one prayer offered, sends ripples through the whole universe. The world of quantum physics is a spiritual universe.

"Section Two: Toward a New Reality," then explores how everything from UFO encounters to the Law of Karma and out-of-body experiences may make sense both scientifically and spiritually. In a quantum universe, the paranormal may in fact be normal.

Finally, in "Section Three: Our Hidden History," he explores ways in which the UFO reality may have influenced Western religious history, beginning with Moses and the Exodus, and including Jesus and his resurrection. Biblical images of Apocalypse, along with ecological stress, and warnings from the aliens to change our ways, complete the journey.

The God Hypothesis is a joy to read, but we are in a new land here. There are no road signs to help us understand where we are, where we should go next, or how we can return home, even it we wanted to.

Of this I am sure: If tomorrow the United States government were to announce, "Sorry, we have been lying to you. UFOs exist, and they are some kind of intelligent reality from another world," then all the issues Dr. Lewels raises in *The God Hypothesis* would immediately move to the front and center of our scientific and religious attention. That in itself may be the main reason that we should not expect our government to make any such announcement, even though it would be true.

Of course, Pharaoh was not about to give the God of Moses any free publicity either, even in the face of indisputable evidence, so, until something undeniable flushes our public institutions out of their collective paralysis on these issues, perhaps the best thing you can do to prepare yourself for that day is to spend some time reading this delightful and important book.

Rev. Dr. Barry H. Downing is pastor at the Northminster Presbyterian Church in Endwell, NY, and is the author of The Bible and Flying Saucers.

Section One:

Paradigm Shift

CHAPTER 1   # THE GOD HYPOTHESIS

The discovery of life beyond Earth would transform not only our science but also our religions, our belief systems and our entire world view. For in a sense, the search for extraterrestrial life is really a search for ourselves—who we are and what our place is in the grand sweep of the cosmos.

—Time magazine, February 5, 1996, on the discovery of two new planets outside the solar system.

New Worlds Discovered

In October 1995, a team of Swiss astronomers at the Geneva Observatory in Switzerland confirmed what most scientists had already concluded—that planets, much like those in our own solar system, exist elsewhere in the universe. They discovered a planet circling the star 51 Pegasi, lying 45 light years from Earth, in the constellation Pegasus. Within two months, an American team of astronomers had discovered two more planets and were confident that, given the enthusiasm among astronomers to search for more, at least ten more would be discovered in the next two years. With these discoveries came a growing realization within the scientific community that, at some point, someone will discover a planet having the right combination of characteristics necessary to bear life—possibly intelligent life.

Then, less than a year later, scientists from NASA and three universities dropped a bombshell on the world with their announcement that they had discovered potential evidence for life on Mars in the distant past. They believe they have discovered microscopic forms of fossilized bacteria, billions of years old, buried in a meteorite that came to Earth from the red planet 13,000 years ago. The discovery sent reporters in search of both astronomers and theologians for comments on its meaning. Indeed, astronomer Kurt Anderson of the New Mexico State University, when asked by journalists about the importance of the find, said that if the meteorite is proved to contain traces of extraterrestrial life, it would probably have a greater impact on philosophy and theology than on astronomy.[1]

Humankind is growing up. As giant antennae scan the skies searching the heavens for radio signals from distant, extraterrestrial (ET) civilizations, even the most conservative scientist and theologian is being dragged (sometimes kicking and screaming) toward the consensus view that we are probably not alone in the universe. And such a consensus view has far-reaching ramifications for humankind. For if humanity is ready to accept this, we are on the verge of a new era of understanding that will, indeed, transform both science and religion and will turn our entire world view on its head. It could be the beginning of an era in which the human race learns and accepts its true place in a hierarchy of intelligent beings that exist throughout the universe. It could be a time during which we reach a state of maturity necessary to take our place as citizens, not of a country or even of a planet, but of an entire galaxy.

This relatively recent "consensus view" of reality represents the leading edge of mainstream scientific and religious thought. It is the view that *Time* magazine, the major media, the largest universities, the largest scientific associations, your church and many of your neighbors can cautiously agree upon. It is the view that makes them feel comfortable—comfortable because, by adopting it, they can postpone something which they understand may be the inevitable. They gain comfort in seeing it as an event that will no doubt happen in the far distant future, and that they, themselves, will not have to confront. That something is the total transformation (as *Time* magazine so clearly puts it) of their scientific and religious belief systems—their entire world view. Few people today are really ready to take such a step. The consensus view holds that it may be centuries before we make contact with other intelligent civilizations and, because of the distances involved, such communication can be conducted at a safe distance, with no chance of ever meeting our neighbors face to face. In

---

1. Crowder p. 2A.

4

such a scenario, dealing with the issue of how to incorporate this new knowledge into our understanding of science and religion can be done at leisure. Since there is no proof yet that such civilizations exist, the consensus view argues that it would be foolish to start worrying about it now. "After all," they say, "it has taken our best minds many hundreds of years to achieve the level of understanding that we have today. How can we simply throw all of that away?"

Transformation

Yet, there is an alternate view that is gaining strength daily throughout the world. It is the view that this stunning transformation of human society is already upon us—a transformation that has already changed the lives and perceptions of millions and millions of people in every country in the world. This is the understanding that extraterrestrials are already here and that they have always been here. It is the knowledge that the human race is intimately related to the amazing beings that travel the skies and the galaxies in ships of light. It is also the understanding that their renewed activity during the past fifty years or so is not coincidental, but has profound implications for the future of the human species—for the message they are communicating is a dire warning that humanity has gone too far in its self-serving and self-destructive ways. To survive, humankind will have to change. The human species will have to transcend the trap we know as the physical world and reach out beyond, to the higher realms of the nonphysical. There is strong evidence that at least some of these beings are attempting to aid us in this effort—serving as midwives, if you will, to the birth of a new species of humans gifted with profound psychic abilities that allow them to "see" beyond the boundaries of the physical world.

For those who have experienced first hand what it is like to be in the presence of these beings, the transformation is shocking, mind shattering and sometimes life shattering. For others, who, like myself, gain this knowledge through research, the transformation may be gradual, sometimes taking half a lifetime. But whichever way it happens, once the knowledge is received, the person is transformed. No longer can he accept the consensus view of the scientific community regarding what it considers the "impossibility" of traveling among the stars. No longer can he accept the church's teachings regarding the nature of God and of the universe. Such a person is caught in no-man's land—that place between science and religion where all the rules have been changed and for which there is no guidebook.

It is my hope, as one who has been through this difficult transformation, (in fact, one who continues on his transformative journey) that this book may help serve as such a guide. To be sure it is an incomplete guide, for the enigmas of the Unidentified Flying Object and of "alien" visitations are extremely complicated and all-encompassing. The researcher quickly learns that one cannot delve too deeply into these mysteries without getting entangled in an intricate web of related, paranormal phenomena including out-of-body experiences, angelic or demonic-like apparitions, psychic abilities, past-life memories, and precognitive visions. He also finds that it is impossible to try to understand these phenomena without becoming deeply involved in such diverse fields as the study of the origins of the human race, ancient civilizations, ancient and current religions, the latest findings in quantum physics, neurophysiology, and psychiatry, to name but a few.

For this reason, it is the generalists and the independent researchers who have the advantage in this daunting undertaking. Only those who are able to freely cross the borders into diverse fields of knowledge have a chance to gain the enormous perspective necessary to understand the true nature of the problem. To understand why this is so, one merely needs to ask the question, "Who has the best credentials necessary to research and understand God?" Certainly there is no one field of study that can prepare someone for such a task. But, in the end, that is exactly what ufology is all about, for it is, in fact, the study of our place in the universe and the ultimate purpose for our creation.

The serious researcher of the UFO mystery finds inevitably that the enigma is like a large onion. Every time a layer of understanding is uncovered, there are new layers to be explored that provide deeper, more subtle and more astonishing answers. And gradually, he begins to understand that at the core of the onion lies the one, all-encompassing mystery that each of us has to deal with individually and for which there can be no perfect guidebook. It is the mystery of the universal consciousness that mystics (and now quantum physicists) have come to know as the "All That Is." It is the mystery of God.

Extraterrestrials in History

From the most ancient writings of the first known civilizations, those of that area of the Middle East known in ancient times as Mesopotamia, we know that the idea of extraterrestrial visitors was commonplace. Their legends tell of the beings who came down from the heavens to create humankind, to mate with humans and to teach them the sciences. Indeed, every culture and civilization on Earth, from the deepest jungles of the rain forests to the plains Indians of North America, has its legends of such visitations. Every religion in the world is based on the interaction of humans with extraterrestrials, either in physical form or through mental communication. These beings were believed, in all cases, to reside primarily in a vague area sometimes referred to as "the heavens." In ancient times they were called gods and were associated by different cultures with various star systems— Orion, Sirius, and the Pleiades, among others. Examples of ancient UFO events are too numerous to list here, but a few examples should suffice to familiarize the reader with the quality of the reports available to UFO historians.

From the annals of Thutmose III, regarded by historians as one of the greatest of all the rulers of ancient Egypt, comes this report:

> The scribes of the House of Life found a circle of fire that was coming in the sky...it had no head, and the breath of its mouth had a foul odor. Its body was five yards long and five yards wide. It had no voice. Now after some days had passed, these things became more numerous in the sky than ever. They shone more in the sky than the brightness of the heavens, and extended to the limits of the four supports of the heavens.[2]

Ancient Indian texts describe many strange events involving aerial phenomena, including abductions of people and celestial wars conducted by the gods who traveled in flying machines known as "vimanas" that had awesome destructive powers:

> Varanasi burned, with all its princes and their followers, its inhabitants, horses, elephants, treasuries and granaries, houses, palaces, and markets. The whole of a city that was inaccessible to the gods was thus wrapped in flames by the discus of Hari,

---

2. The Annals of Thutmose III c. 1450 B.C.

and was totally destroyed. The discus then, with unmitigated wrath, and blazing fiercely...returned to the hand of Vishnu.[3]

The unseen dwellers of the woodlands watched this sad and shameful deed as the all-powerful Rasksha abducted the poor and helpless dame. He set her upon his winged chariot which shone as bright as gold, and moved as fleet as the god Indra's heavenly steed! ...Then the chariot rose in the skies, high over the hill and wooded vale.[4]

Historians of Alexander the Great, whose feat of conquering all the known, civilized world, recorded events in which UFOs played important events in battles. In 329 B.C., while Alexander and his army were crossing the river Jaxartes into India, two "shiny shields" were reported to have dived repeatedly from the sky onto military columns, causing soldiers to disperse. Then in 322 B.C., during Alexander's siege of the Phoenician city of Tyre, soldiers observed in amazement a large "flying shield" flying in formation with four smaller ones. As they circled over the city, the large one is reported to have emitted a beam of light that shattered the city walls and allowed Alexander's troops to enter and take the city. Then, they shot off and disappeared into the sky.[5] Examples such as these which describe what the ancients believed to be the actions of gods, abound in the historical record.

Although the Greeks, at the height of their glory, had no trouble with the concept of extraterrestrial civilizations, they still believed UFO events were the manifestations of the gods. One of their leading thinkers, Democritus, taught that it is only natural to assume that what has happened here on Earth would also have happened throughout the universe. It seemed obvious to him that the laws of nature that applied on Earth were universal and would also apply on other worlds. Yet, they too saw the beings who interacted with humans from behind a curtain of invisibility as gods, rather than as aliens from other planets. It seems that we want very much to believe that beings from other planets are very much like ourselves, at the same level of scientific and spiritual development—someone we can relate to, someone we can understand. Even Democritus was not ready to deal with the

3. Mahabharata c. 400 B.C.
4. Ramayana c. 300 B.C.
5. Brookesmith, 1995, p. 14.

concept of beings who might be millions of years more advanced in science and spirit. Such beings could only be thought of as gods.

Much later, as the "one God and many angels" concept took hold, beings that traveled the sky in flying shields, often described as "bright clouds," were relegated to a lower status and demoted to the rank of "angels." They were believed to be created beings, above our level, but not as powerful as God. They were said to be merely the messengers of God. And gradually, over the last 500 years or so, as science gained strength and became the primary arbiter of what is real and what is not, it demoted such phenomena to the category of myth, denying their existence altogether. However, theologians and scientists did find some common ground. Both agreed that the Earth was a lonely outpost in the cosmos and that humanity was unique. To the Church this meant that our relationship to God was special. To science it meant that a freak accident, the chance mixture of the right chemicals under the perfect conditions, created life on this particular grain of sand in the vast universe. Such an accident, which required an extremely rare mixture of elements and conditions, could easily be thought of as unique. So for the past several hundred years, those of us in the Western world have been taught by science an "isolationist" view of reality in which we Earthlings evolved from the muck into sentient beings, secluded, if not forsaken, from the rest of the cosmos.

For the religions of the Judaeo-Christian world, the discovery of extraterrestrial life would also endanger the dogma they have taught for centuries and to which they have become firmly committed—that the origin of life is unique and that it was the result of a divine act. If life is found elsewhere in the universe, the uniqueness of the human race, and thus its divine origin, is called into question. As natural historian, Paul Davies wrote in *Time* magazine on the discovery of planets outside the solar system:

> Historically, the Roman Catholic Church regarded any discussion of alien life as heresy. Speculating about other inhabited worlds was one reason philosopher Giordano Bruno was burned at the stake in 1600.... The existence of alien beings, especially if they were further advanced than humans intellectually and spiritually, would disrupt this cozy view.
>
> Christianity faces a peculiar problem in relation to the Incarnation. Was this event unique in the universe, as official

9

doctrine insists, or did God take on alien flesh too? Is Christ the Saviour of humans alone, or of all intelligent beings in our galaxy and beyond?[6]

In spite of its past record of denying the possibility of life elsewhere, there is some evidence that even the Catholic Church is beginning to soften its official position in favor of the growing consensus view. When the news of the Mars meteorite find was released, Pope John Paul II happened to be vacationing with a group of philosophers and astronomers from the Vatican Observatory. (That the Vatican even has an observatory is an indication that the Church has given much private thought to this issue for quite some time.) Although no official Papal statement was forthcoming, a Vatican expert on meteorites, Jesuit Guy Consulmagno, was quoted in *Newsweek* magazine expressing elation at the prospect of life elsewhere in the cosmos:

> Finding life on other planets is a vindication that God is not limited by our imagination. As our understanding of creation grows, our understanding of God gets bigger. It may be that God became incarnate in other forms elsewhere in the universe. If we were to make contact with other intelligent life, we'd have to tell our own sacred story, listen to them tell theirs, and learn.[7]

If this cheerfully optimistic statement truly represents the official view of the Church, then it is obvious that there has been a major change in Church policy since the days of poor Giordano Bruno. But if so, it belies the immensely serious theological issues that have yet to be addressed with regard to the issue of alien life forms, particularly if those life forms have a view of God that does not coincide with that of the Church. And such open-minded views may not be consistent among theologians of the many world religions and denominations. Indeed, if the existence of intelligent life elsewhere were to be acknowledged, fundamentalists of many religions would find it difficult to reconcile their deeply held views with this new reality. Muslims would have to decide if aliens should be considered infidels and whether or not to wage a holy war against them as they have with other non-Muslims. Christians and Jews on the other hand would

---

6. Davies, 1996, p. 58
7. Woodward, 1996, p. 58.

10

have to confront the possibility that other worlds might have no knowledge of or interest in their concepts of Jehovah and Jesus Christ. So for now, the religions of the world are happy to speculate, along with scientists, about some future discovery of alien life on distant planets, but none is willing to officially address the possibility that UFOs might be real and that extraterrestrials are already here. At least not yet.

A Fly in the Ointment

For scientists and theologians seeking to cling to their consensus views, the going would be fairly easy but for a fly in the ointment, so to speak. There is still one troubling and pesky issue that will not go away and leave this consensus view of reality in peace. It seems that the skies are still full of strange "things" that cannot be accounted for, not even in a modern, highly technological society. The "flying shields," as they were referred to by the Romans and the Egyptians, are still here. And humans are still having visitations by nonhuman entities who refuse to obey the laws of physics. They walk right through bedroom walls, communicate telepathically and carry their victims off to other dimensions, just as reported in the Bible and other ancient texts. Because today's scientific methods of studying such phenomena provide much better and much more detailed information about these events, and because, in an age of mass media, these stories are widely disseminated, they cannot be completely ignored. As these stories became public, more and more people began to step forward to testify about their own, similar experiences. Among the millions of witnesses are those of unimpeachable credentials, many with scientific backgrounds. Ultimately, even two U.S. presidents have spoken publicly about their sightings of UFOs (Jimmy Carter and Ronald Reagan), while one presidential candidate (Barry Goldwater) proclaimed his belief in the phenomenon. To some extent, scientific and religious leaders have been forced to respond to the growing public awareness of the UFO enigma.

UFO Theories

For the few theologians who have responded at all to the UFO mystery, the solution has, for the most part, been a simple one. Many believe that UFOs are uniformly Satanic—a product of the "fallen angels" who parted with God in ancient times. Their appearance in modern times is also simple to explain—they are a sign that the end is near. As proof, they site the Book of Revelations which speaks of strange signs in the sky as omens that foretell the second coming of Christ. To those who support this view, alien abductions are simply cases of demonic possession and must be dealt with through prayer and a closer association with the Church. Although the major religious institutions have yet to make official pronouncements on the issue, numerous individuals have ventured opinions.

Thomas Kulp, a Greek Orthodox priest, has warned that "there is no single UFO incident on record that cannot be explained as a demonic deception or apparition.... Ever since the Garden of Eden," he says, "the demons have been engaged in continual warfare against the human race, ever striving to drag us down to their own level, causing us to stray from the path of truth that alone leads to eternal salvation."[8]

Two books written by fundamentalist Christians have argued similarly that UFOs are evil. Clifford Wilson (*UFOs and Their Mission Impossible*) and John Weldon and Zola Levitt (*UFOs: What on Earth is Happening?*) claim that the devil and his angels occupy UFOs and are wreaking havoc on Earth. This, they say, is a sign that the end is near. The same conclusion was reached by two authors, one a Roman Catholic and the other a Protestant, in their book, *Unmasking the Enemy*.[9] For Nelson Pacheco and Tommy Blann, the UFO phenomenon is merely the latest chapter in the eternal struggle between good and evil. They believe that demons are simply disguising themselves as ETs in order to be accepted by humans. Their conclusions were made after reviewing UFO literature and finding ample evidence that the phenomenon has a sinister side in the many reports of cattle mutilations and abductions. Citing the aliens' seeming disregard of human free will, Pacheco argues that the answer is obvious. "I don't know how anyone can study UFO abductions and still have doubts about whether what's happening is good or evil.... [These beings] set themselves up as the true savior of humankind in order to undermine traditional Christianity."[10]

8. Kulp, 1996, p. 32.
9. Pacheco, 1994.

The Devout Nonbelievers

For mainstream scientists, devoted to upholding their consensus view of reality, UFOs are a variety of things. They are honest mistakes of perception made by normal people who are not educated enough to be able to identify perfectly explainable phenomena; they are hoaxes perpetrated by those silly folks who are always seeking publicity; they are natural, yet unexplainable, phenomena; they are the result of some new psychological syndrome caused, in all probability, by chemical reactions in the brain; they are the hallucinations of the mentally ill; they are the result of the fanciful imaginations of those who desperately want to believe in "little green men in flying saucers"; or they are the product of a culture that has been indoctrinated by three quarters of a century of science fiction stories in the mass media. Each of these theories assumes that people are basically unintelligent, uneducated yokels who are easily fooled into believing that the Earth is being invaded from outer space. And such an abundance of handy explanations conveniently absolves scientists from any obligation to address the phenomenon seriously. Instead of investigating, the mainstream scientist simply takes the most suitable theory off the shelf and states it as an obvious fact.

An excellent example was the view of the late Dr. Carl Sagan, who was firmly committed to the SETI (Search for Extraterrestrial Intelligence) program and to the idea that intelligent life exists elsewhere in the universe. But when it came to UFOs and the alien presence, Sagan turned a blind eye. "Anecdotal evidence," he stated emphatically "is not enough." That is, the eyewitness testimony of millions of otherwise credible people is not enough reason to take the phenomenon seriously. He conveniently omitted mention of the volumes of cases where physical traces have been found and the excellent photographic evidence that exists. When invited by ufologist Budd Hopkins and Harvard psychiatrist John Mack to participate in some of the best abduction investigations, he simply did not respond. For mainstream scientists, even a televised flying saucer landing on the White House lawn may not satisfy their need for proof.

However, under scrutiny, none of the above-mentioned, mainstream theories stands up in the face of the abundance of evidence

---

10. Huyghe, 1994, p. 101.

which includes multiple witnesses, physical evidence, excellent photos and videos, and official, classified government documents. These theories are the assumptions of the uniformed—those who have never seriously investigated UFO cases or of those who, in light of the overwhelming evidence, are not ready to experience the transformation necessary to develop a paradigm that could fit such a concept into their lives. Few scientists are willing to chuck everything they have ever been taught and start anew. Fewer yet are willing to become outcasts from the consensus view by venturing into the forbidden sciences—the punishment is simply too severe.

The Alien Invasion Theory

Among serious researchers, the prevailing theory of UFOs and alien abductions is that the Earth has been under study for some time, possibly a hundred years or so, by highly advanced beings from another planet, or possibly several planets, in our galaxy. The areas or origination most often mentioned are the constellation Orion, the Sirius complex, the Pleiades and Zeta Reticuli. Although the exact purpose of such a study can only be speculated, it is believed that the beings take great care not to interfere with human culture. For various reasons, they find it more useful to interact with us in a surreptitious manner, cloaking themselves in invisibility, leaving few traces and erasing the memories of those with whom they are having contact. This is variously seen as a sign that the beings are merciful and kind by some researchers or diabolical and sinister by others. Ufologists are pretty much in consensus that human genetics is high among the areas of interest that the aliens have in the human race. From the many cases of abduction that have been well researched, an incredible scenario has emerged which tells the story of strange creatures kidnapping men, women and children by the thousands, some think millions, for the purpose of extracting sperm and ova and using human DNA to mix with alien DNA in the creation of a hybrid species. Fertilized, and thus hybridized, ova are then placed in the fallopian tubes of their captive women so that the fetuses may be gestated for a period of six to eight weeks. At that time, the woman is recaptured, the fetus removed and the hybrid is grown, like a plant in a glass container, an artificial womb if you will, until it is ready to emerge as a "newborn" baby. (See Figure 1 on page 15.)

Those who espouse the "alien study" theory believe that the purpose of this project is to improve the aliens' own race, which is unable to reproduce and which is dying out. The "alien study" theory easily turns into an "alien invasion" theory among those who react fearfully to their findings. To these researchers, the hybrid race that is being created by the extraterrestrials is ultimately meant to replace humankind as part of a great, galactic scheme to take over the Earth.

Parallel Universe Theory

The view that the aliens, rather than being extraterrestrial, originate in another dimension or perhaps in a parallel universe, has been given credence by the discovery in quantum physics, discussed in a later chapter, that the universe is holographic in nature and may be made up of many invisible, but overlapping dimensions. In such a scheme, aliens arrive in our dimension by simply tuning in the right frequency, thus opening a dimensional doorway which allows them

FIGURE 1. *Glass tanks holding hybrid fetuses are often shown to abductees. (Illustration by David W. Chace, reprinted by permission.)*

access to our reality. Certainly, many witness accounts of close encounters with alien craft and with alien beings support this theory. Both the beings and the craft are reported to be able to materialize out of thin air and to vanish just as easily. The beings pass through solid materials as if they were merely holographic projections, rather than physical creatures. But this still does not answer the question of where they reside. Do they live on planets, either in our dimension or in another? Or do they principally exist in a nonphysical form, only occasionally making excursions into our reality?

The leading proponent of this theory is researcher Dr. Jacques Vallée, who in his book, *Dimensions: Alien Contact and Human Deception*,[11] argues that the UFO phenomenon has been interpreted in different ways throughout history by different cultures, often altering the shape of human affairs and directing events from their hidden dimension. He defines his perspective as different from his colleagues as follows:

> My own private conjecture, which deviates considerably from the accepted dogma among UFO believers, is that we are dealing with a yet unrecognized level of consciousness, independent from man but closely linked to the Earth, which has its own relationship to cosmic forces.[12]

Vallée's exploration of the beings' interrelationship with humans throughout the ages and their involvement in Earth's religions elevated UFO research to new levels of understanding, thus permitting ufology to take an important step toward dealing with the phenomenon in a broader, less restrictive perspective.

The God Hypothesis

Thanks in part to Vallée, a growing number of serious UFO researchers are coming to the conclusion that the answer to the UFO mystery is much more complex than previously thought. Even the "alien research project" theory has become too simplistic for them. Why would a highly advanced alien civilization need a hundred years or even 50 years to study us? Couldn't they have learned everything they needed to know in a much shorter time? And if they really

---

11. Vallée, 1988.
12. Vallée, 1988, p. xvii.

wanted to take over the Earth, it seems that they could have done so a long time ago. In addition, the phenomena being reported by witnesses who have encountered these beings go far beyond abilities that could easily be ascribed to mere "aliens." The use of mental telepathy for communication, the ease with which they seem to be able to move between our physical reality and other, unknown dimensions, their seeming ability to be able to interact with humans while they are "out of their bodies," and the nature of the information they are sharing with the people they contact, all argue for a broader, deeper explanation.

It seems that the word "alien" is too simplistic for a being who is able to transcend time and space as well as physical reality. What do you call a being who can exert mental control over humankind, who can create new life forms, who can manipulate us in our physical bodies or take us out of our bodies and interact with us just as easily? Certainly these are not merely aliens from another planet, who are basically just like us, just more advanced. This is the description of something else—something more profound. In searching for terms, those who have experienced the beings often refer to them as angels or demons. Perhaps ancient humans would have called them gods. But all of these terms are loaded with emotional, connotative meaning that cannot be separated from the words, no matter how hard we try. Whitley Strieber, one of the more famous abductees, simply refers to them as the "visitors." But are they really visitors? What if they belong here as much as we do? What if we are the visitors? Others, including myself, tend to use the word "extraterrestrial." This is a term with less emotional baggage, yet it still implies that they originate somewhere other than on Earth. Of this, we cannot be certain at this time. Even the term, "non human" may not be correct, as we shall see in later chapters, for it is possible that we are intimately related to them.

Whatever they choose to call the beings, those who lean towards what I will call "the God Hypothesis" believe that they have been around much longer than a mere 100 years. They have come to the conclusion that they have always been here, that they were involved in the creation of the human race, that they are involved in the process of human evolution and that they have been responsible for most, if not all, of the world's religions. Such a dramatic conclusion borders on being a theological statement, rather than a scientific finding, yet to some ufologists, the distinction between science and theology is simply not clear cut. They have found themselves caught between the two and find that they cannot speak of one without referring to the other.

A Theologian Speaks Out

The foremost proponent of the God Hypothesis is a man who is uniquely qualified to speak on such matters because of his interdisciplinary training. Dr. Barry Downing is a Presbyterian minister in Endwell, New York, who holds degrees in both divinity and physics. He has served on the board of the largest UFO organization in the world (The Mutual UFO Network) for many years and is an expert on the UFO phenomenon. Dr. Downing long ago reached the conclusion that UFOs and the beings who fly them have been responsible for many of the religious beliefs of mankind, including Judaism and Christianity. In 1968 he published what serves today as the most authoritative work on the God Hypothesis, a book titled *The Bible and Flying Saucers,*[13] and in 1988 he authored a followup article specifically on the God Hypothesis.[14]

When I first heard of Dr. Downing and his bold assertions regarding the nature of UFOs, I was as impressed with his courage as I was amazed by the conclusions he had reached. I found it incredible that the minister of a mainstream Christian church would have reached the conclusion that ETs in flying saucers were the source of the many miracles of which the Bible speaks. I found it equally impressive that, after reaching this conclusion, his Christian faith remained intact and his congregation didn't boot him out on his ear. That he is still the minister at the same church nearly 30 years later and that he is more resolute than ever in his convictions, bestows great credit on him and on the Presbyterian Church, in my opinion. Perhaps it is simply that the congregation finds his sermons so amazing that they hate to let him go.

Downing's book is a scholarly examination of the Bible through the eyes of a modern-day scientist, which he is. In so doing, he rediscovers the hidden meanings behind many of the miraculous events of both the Old and the New Testament including such things as the mysterious "cloud" in which the God, Jehovah, appeared to the Jews,

---

13. Downing, 1968.
14. Downing, 1988.

the parting of the Red Sea during the Exodus and the amazing circumstances surrounding the arrival and departure from this Earth of Jesus Christ, as depicted in the New Testament. He concludes that highly advanced technology could have been responsible for these events—a technology wielded by incredible beings known as "angels" in religious lore. But Downing finds that this "demystification" of religious doctrine, rather than denigrating the concept of God, lends support to those who believe the Bible is based on factual accounts. In his view, however, the Bible accounts should be taken as literal truth in that they are descriptions of actual events which were written by people who had no better way of describing or understanding such advanced technology.

Ultimately, Downing concludes:

> It is my assumption that the alien/angelic reality was involved in the development of both the Old and New Testaments, as well as perhaps providing stimulation to other religious leaders like Mohammed, or the development of the Hindu Vedic tradition.... They also were responsible for the experience at Fatima and the experience of Joseph Smith, founder of the Mormon Church.... UFO alien reality and what the Bible calls the angelic divine reality, are the same reality.[15]

But far from being a UFO cultist, Downing holds a theological position that remains firmly in the camp of the traditional Christian faith. He explains this seeming contradiction in this way:

> My theory does put the Christian view of God at risk. And here is how. I am convinced that modern UFOs are fully capable of having brought about the biblical religion. That is, whatever the UFO reality is, it has the power to control our minds and our physical reality so totally, that it could have performed every miracle the Bible lists. If UFOs carry the angels of God, then this is fine. They are acting for God, and the traditional Judaeo-Christian view of God is validated by UFOs, not contradicted by them.[16]

In the years since the publication of his book, a number of the leading UFO experts have quietly begun to discuss and take seriously Dr. Downing's provocative point of view, but few are willing to speak

15. Downing, 1994, pp. 8-10.
16. Downing, 1993, p. 43.

about it openly for fear of stirring the wrath of the religious community. They also find it difficult enough to gain credibility within the scientific community and with the public at large as it is, without being accused of being "anti religion" by some or of trying to create a UFO cult by others. And while some might lean toward seeing the phenomenon in Biblical terms, few have the faith that all UFOs bear good angels. Some see sinister and evil aspects to the abduction phenomenon and are quick to criticize Downing for his Pollyanna views. One such researcher is John White, a UFO researcher who hosts an annual UFO conference in New Haven, Connecticutt. In a 1992 article titled "Aliens Among Us—A UFO Conspiracy Hypothesis in a Religious Mode," in the *MUFON Journal*, White challenged Downing's conclusion:

> I find Downing's position flawed because the Bible recognizes "fallen" angels who retained their superhuman capacities, but turned from their allegiance to God. Since then, their paranormal abilities have been used for evil, rather than good[17]

White argues further that good angels don't use deception, nor do they wound the psyches of those they contact. Angels also show respect for human rights and do not engage in rape, mind control, unauthorized surgical invasions and unauthorized impregnation of people. In short, White sees a grand conspiracy to take over the Earth:

> I get a strong sense of conspiracy by the abductors—a vast subversive plot of long duration and careful coordination which aims at nothing less than the complete enslavement of the human race...[it is] a battle between the forces of light and the forces of darkness for the salvation or damnation of humanity and the planet. [18]

Indeed, White raises a good point. If UFOs can carry the angels of God, then they can also carry what have been called in the past, "demons" or "incubi." In fact, the premise of this book is essentially that many of the legends of angels, gods and demons originated in the UFO phenomenon, but that our understanding is increased by refusing to use religious terminology. Now is the time to redefine and reex-

---

17. White, 1992, pp. 7-8.
18. White, 1992, pp. 7-8.

amine the terms used by our ancestors to refer to these beings and to shed the legacy known as "religious dogma" with which we have been burdened. Failure to do so allows us to be dragged into a swamp of conspiracy theories no different than those of the Red scare of the 1950s. Attempting to deal with UFO phenomena strictly from a traditional Judaeo-Christian viewpoint can too easily result in a heightened state of paranoia. Such a view readily sees aliens behind every social ill and as the masterminds of a grand conspiracy in which international bankers and politicians are manipulated for the purpose of creating one world government and enslaving humanity. It is this kind of paranoia that causes people to grab their guns and ammunition and head for their underground bunkers. Dwelling in such fears is counterproductive to our search for truth and prevents us from seeing the UFO enigma in its truly cosmic perspective.

This book will attempt to take a more neutral road by trying to give the reader a broad perspective with which to interpret for himself UFO data—particularly those things we tend to see as evil. Ultimately, the reader may come to realize that the universe is, in fact, a paradox in which good and evil are the same—just different sides of the same coin. Such a view will require the reader to consider the possibility that there is a nonphysical dimension that exists in parallel to the physical world and that rather than being like a machine, the universe is instead more like a vast intelligence that exists in perfect balance between positive and negative forces. But regardless of the reader's spiritual or religious inclinations, it is hoped that this book will serve to advance the discussion of the religious and spiritual implications of the UFO phenomenon—a discussion that is becoming more essential with every passing day.

Dr. Downing summarized quite well the state of ufology's approach to religion at the annual symposium of the Mutual UFO Network in 1994. The religious issue, he said, is "like a sleeping gorilla" that researchers keep tiptoeing around in fear that he will wake up. With this statement, this author agrees wholeheartedly. But to this, I might add that perhaps the day has come to rouse the gorilla from his long slumber. If so, it will be an event that will truly be of Earth-shaking proportions, for it will herald an age in which our understanding of both science and religion will undergo a vast and profound transformation.

CHAPTER 2

A PERSONAL TRANSFORMATION

Coincidences that are so unusual and so psychologically meaningful they don't seem to be the result of chance alone are called "synchronicities." Such coincidences are actually flaws in the fabric of reality.

—physicist David Peat in his book, Synchronicity: The Bridge Between Matter and Mind.

A Strange Star in the Sky

It was a chilly February night in southeast Alabama in 1969, but the clear, star-filled sky beckoned to us as we lifted off the runway in our single-engine Cessna, pointing the nose of the plane toward the Gulf of Mexico and the Florida border. Colonel Bob Jones (real name withheld), Editor in Chief of the U.S. Army *Aviation Digest* magazine sat in the left seat, while I, an Army captain and his assistant, flew the right seat position, handling the radios and the charts that would guide us from Cairns Army Airfield at Ft. Rucker, Alabama, on a three-hour, triangular course through the night sky and back to our home field. Our mission that night was simply to complete three hours of flying time so that we could qualify for our monthly flight pay. Nothing could be more routine—or so we thought.

The Colonel and I had both recently returned from the Republic of Vietnam where we served as aviators with secondary assignments as public information officers for our units. We were both experienced pilots and observers, having flown—and survived—our share of combat missions, often under enemy fire and in extreme weather conditions. Upon returning from Vietnam in October 1968, with only nine months of service left, I found myself working side by side with Bob as the chief editors of the official publication of Army aviation. Compared with Vietnam, the assignment was like being on extended vacation, and the little flying we did was often boring and tedious in comparison to the combat missions we were used to.

We had been airborne for no more than 10-15 minutes when I became aware of an unusual, orange ball of light ahead of us, but at a much higher altitude. "What in the heck is that?", I thought to myself. In my mind I began to run through all of the possibilities. A planet? A star? A plane or helicopter? A weather balloon? A satellite? A reflection in the window? I thought of all of these, but none made any sense. The object did not seem to be a planet or a star—it seemed too low. Yet, I knew it couldn't be an aircraft, for it remained still in the night sky and did not have blinking red and green lights. It was nothing I had ever encountered, yet I felt foolish mentioning it to my boss.

What seemed like a long time went by before the silence was finally broken. Bob elbowed me gently and asked, "Have you been watching that thing up there?" He pointed to the strange, luminous ball of light hanging in the sky.

"Yeah," I replied, "I'm sure glad you said something about it, because I wasn't going to."

"What the heck is it?" he asked, clearly agitated.

"Darned if I know. I was hoping you could tell me." Together we again went through all the possibilities, but the object didn't fit any of the categories. We continued to watch it until it was time to change our course, leaving the mystery behind us.

"Boy, that was strange," he said after we made our turn and the object was no longer visible. And I agreed. But what more could we say about it? We continued our flight, checking our gauges and our radios, making our routine calls to the air traffic controllers and enjoying the smooth and peaceful night.

We had been on our new course heading, our eyes averted to the instruments, for perhaps 15 minutes, when Bob pointed to the sky in front and to the right of us and said excitedly, "There it is again." And he was right. Ahead of us, still at approximately the same altitude, the mysterious globe had suddenly reappeared. It would have to have traveled at a fantastic speed to arrive at its present position in such a short time, yet it appeared totally motionless in the sky above.

24

"Was it following us?" I asked myself, as a strange chill climbed up my spine and made the hair on the back of my neck stand on end. We remained strangely silent for some time, neither of us knowing exactly what to say about this peculiar turn of events. We watched it without much conversation until we made our next course change and we lost sight of it once more.

Up until the moment that we had seen it again, I had been thinking that as soon as I got home I was going to look up the positions of the stars and planets to see what the celestial object might be. But now I knew that would be a fruitless exercise, for no star or planet moves so quickly across the sky and then stands motionless. In all of history there was no precedent for such an event or natural phenomenon that I knew of, unless, of course, one included the mysterious star of Bethlehem that the Bible said guided the wise men to the birthplace of Christ and then stood motionless above the sacred spot.

"Hmmm," I wondered to myself, "what if this is what they saw?" Then I let the thought drop. It was too disturbing to hold for very long.

Looking back on that night, I find more interesting the things that were not said and were not done by us, considering the positions of potential influence we both held, than how we actually reacted. Never once did we discuss notifying the air traffic controllers that we were observing an unidentified flying object. (In truth, we never saw it flying.) Never once did we consider asking them if the object was visible on radar. Never once did we discuss the possibility of making an official report to higher authorities. (Neither of us presumably wished to be considered foolish.) We never discussed writing about our experience in the magazine we produced, even though it would have made a highly interesting and perhaps enlightening story for our readers. And finally, neither of us ever mentioned the subject again, not to each other nor to any of our co-workers or fellow aviators. In fact, with the exception related in the narrative below, I don't remember ever telling anyone about it for nearly 25 years. The fact was, and remains today, that UFOs are a taboo subject among military and commercial pilots as well as among air traffic controllers.

Yet, the memory of that night still weighs heavily on me, for it was the night that I began to realize there are strange, unidentifiable objects traveling our skies with impunity, operating by their own rules, answering to no human masters. That knowledge, that there may be higher levels of intelligence than that of humans, left me with a longing to know more about this amazing phenomenon and with an increased awe of this strange and complex universe we live in.

Opportunities Missed

In the years ahead, the issue of Unidentified Flying Objects kept intruding into my life, only to be brushed aside like a bothersome insect on each occasion. Only three years later, I found myself in the Ph.D. program at the school of journalism at the University of Missouri. Because of my work experience as a writer and editor, I was lucky enough to land the much coveted editorship of the *Freedom of Information Digest and Reports*, publications of the Freedom of Information Center. The Center was a non-profit organization, headquartered at the school of journalism, dedicated to researching and reporting on First Amendment issues. With a worldwide readership made up primarily of media executives, editors, publishers, television producers and reporters, the Center's files and resources were frequently used to help the media with legal and constitutional problems they were facing. In its role as activist, promoting freedom of speech and press, the Center's lobbying efforts were instrumental in achieving passage of the Federal Freedom of Information Act (FOIA), which permitted access to government files for the first time, under certain conditions.

During those years, while studying media law in class and writing and editing numerous articles on First Amendment issues, I became an expert on government censorship. Later, while employed by the U.S. Department of Justice in Washington, D.C., during the period of the Watergate break-in and subsequent cover-up, I received first-hand experience in government secrecy and bureaucratic lying.

It wasn't long after starting my job as editor that an interesting case came across my desk. It was the case of a citizen's group called Ground Saucer Watch, based in Phoenix, Arizona, which had filed a complaint against the Central Intelligence Agency (CIA), seeking access to its UFO files. The agency had previously denied even a passing interest in the subject of UFOs, yet under duress imposed upon it by the FOI Act, the agency revealed that in fact had voluminous files on the subject. Later, another group calling itself Citizens Against UFO Secrecy (CAUS) filed FOI lawsuits against not only the CIA, but also against every other federal intelligence-gathering agency, seeking all documents pertaining to UFOs. After years of battling in the courts, the group ultimately obtained thousands of pages of documents, most of which had been heavily censored in the name of national security. Until this time, intelligence agencies had publicly dismissed the subject of UFOs as simply being inconsequential and as having no military or intelligence value. In fact, when the Air Force closed its now-famous Project Bluebook in 1969, it was with the authoritative statement that UFOs "pose no serious threat to national security." However, when faced with substantial penalties under the FOI Act, each of the agencies refused to release their files, using as their excuse a provision in the law that permits the withholding of information that could "endanger the national security of the United States."

"How," I asked myself, "can the government have it both ways?" Either UFOs are not important or they are. And if they are, then the public should be told. Ultimately, each agency was required to release many documents, but each document was so heavily censored that in most cases only the date and the name of the agency was revealed.

This case stirred my curiosity. I considered writing an article for the publications I edited. I even briefly contemplated making this issue the topic of my dissertation. But again, I did nothing. The topic was too controversial for someone who cared a great deal about being seen as credible. The subject was too bizarre to even mention to my adviser as a possible topic. I let the idea drop.

By 1973, my dissertation, a sociological study of how the Mexican-American civil rights movement used and manipulated the media to achieve its goals, had been published as a book, and at age 28 I was offered the chairmanship of the department of journalism at the University of Texas at El Paso. Within a few short years, I received tenure, an associate professorship and chairmanship of the larger department of mass communication. My efforts to become a credible scholar and to climb the academic ladder were succeeding. And once again, UFOs entered my life unexpectedly. This time it came in the form of another academician, Dr. J. Allen Hynek, founder of the Center of UFO Studies (CUFOS), and former consultant to Air Force Project *Bluebook*, the official UFO investigating agency of the U.S. Air Force. Dr. Hynek was the chairman of the department of astronomy at Northwestern University and had been invited to speak on campus on the subject of UFOs.

Although Hynek had for years served as the Air Force's official debunker of UFOs, being responsible for the now-famous swamp gas explanation for a series of remarkable sightings with hundreds of witnesses in Michigan, (resulting in demands for an official Congressional investigation by then-Congressman Gerald Ford) he eventually quit the project and denounced the Air Force's attempts to cover up the UFO issue. By the time he reached El Paso around 1976, he was one of the foremost advocates for UFO research in the country. Coincidentally (or maybe not) he was interviewed by our campus radio station, KTEP-FM, which was part of my department. Also, coincidentally, he needed a ride to the airport. I immediately volunteered for the job.

As we left the university that afternoon, I felt the need to confide in him about that strange night in Alabama and about my concerns that a government cover-up of UFO information was not in the best interests of humankind. Seemingly impressed, he said, "We need people like you in our organization. Would you consider joining CUFOS and serving as our representative in the El Paso area?"

"I am flattered by the offer, but I'll have to think it over," I replied. And then I added, "Tell me, Dr. Hynek, is there anything, any information, that you were not able to divulge during your lecture or the radio interview? Are there aspects of the phenomenon that you don't feel comfortable revealing to the public at this time?"

Dr. Hynek's brow furrowed as he considered carefully his answer. After a long pause, he looked up at me over his spectacles, took a deep breath and said, "This is very confidential because it's not something I can prove." He paused again as if weighing each word carefully in his mind. Finally, he went on, "I know an Army colonel who does not want to be identified who swears that our military captured a crashed flying saucer in 1947 near Roswell, New Mexico, just a three-hour drive from here." Again, he paused, searching my face for a clue to my reaction to this explosive information. "I've heard about that case, but I had no idea that it could be true" I told him, obviously impressed by the source of his information. Apparently satisfied with my response, he continued, "That's not all. He also swears that alien bodies were recovered." Once again he awaited my response. But this time, all I could do was stare at him in wide-eyed amazement. That was new information to me, and in 1976 it was an explosive revelation.

In truth, I don't remember the details of the rest of our conversation at the airport that afternoon. I was stunned to say the least. The seriousness with which he confided the information to me and his embarrassed uneasiness as he spoke, led me to believe that he not only was telling me the truth, but that he possessed knowledge that would challenge the foundations of science and religion if it were commonly known.

Yet in spite of all of this, the amazing nature of his revelations and his offer to include me in his network of investigators, I ultimately declined the invitation. The subject was simply too controversial for an academician and journalist with aspirations for climbing the academic ladder.

Another Chance Encounter

For the next 17 years, UFOs were always in the back of my mind. I took every opportunity to read what books I could find on the subject, and I was forever attentive for unusual objects in the sky. But for the most part, my life consisted of my career and of raising, together with my wife, our three children. I left the academic world and entered the business world as a financial consultant, and the topic of UFOs was still taboo. Although it was a subject that burned deeply in my consciousness and I yearned to have someone to talk to about it, there was no one I knew who had the same curiosity. Then, one night, all of that began to change. While channel surfing in the comfort of my den in suburban El Paso, I stumbled across a televised interview with five or so of the most credible UFO researchers. It was November of 1992, and much had transpired in the field of UFO research of which I was not aware. One of the panel members, a woman by the name of Linda Moulton Howe, caught my attention for several reasons. First, she had excellent journalistic credentials. With a master's degree in communication from Stanford University and with years of experience as a documentary producer for the CBS station in Denver, she impressed me as being someone I could relate to, someone who was well versed in the principles of objective reporting. She had also won regional Emmy Awards for her work. Secondly, she struck me as being extremely articulate and bright. And thirdly, she was an expert in an area of UFO research I knew little about—cattle mutilations.

Linda's involvement in UFO research began in 1979 when, as Director of Special Projects for the Denver, CBS-affiliated TV station, she was called upon to do a story on mysterious cattle mutilations occurring throughout the state of Colorado and which were being attributed in the press to the work of satanic cults. Knowing little about the subject, she was in no way prepared for what she found. In her book, *An Alien Harvest*,[1] Linda relates how her investigation began. "Within a month of talking to dozens of ranchers, law enforcement officials and fellow journalists who had investigated the intense mutilation activity in 1975-1976, I heard one 'off the record' UFO story after another. A Wyoming rancher said that an orange, glowing disk the size of a football field had approached him one night in 1976 while he was watering a field of barley. That same year the rancher found two of his cows mutilated."

Arriving on the scene of freshly mutilated horses or cattle, she found mystified and frightened ranchers, sheriffs and veterinarians who could arrive at no reasonable conclusions for what they were seeing. The mutilated animals, often found in remote pastures, far removed from any roads, bore surgical cuts that seemed to be made by laser-like instruments. Their sexual organs, their rectums, their tongues and sometimes their eyes and some internal organs had been removed with surgical precision. Yet there was no, or very little blood, on the animals or on the ground; there were no predator teeth marks or tracks in the vicinity; and sometimes there were no tracks made by the animal itself!

Then, there were the stories of mysterious lights in the night sky, told by nervous ranchers and law enforcement officers, unwilling to be quoted or interviewed for television. "The description of orange or white glowing lights and/or beams of light shining down from something silently hovering above the pastures was a common theme among people I interviewed," she explains. Eventually, she located ranchers who had actually seen small gray, non-human entities in broad daylight taking a cow into their awaiting craft. She even found a mother and her adult daughter who had experienced a missing time episode in conjunction with a close encounter with a UFO. In separate hypnosis sessions, with many years in between, both of them recov-

---

1. Moulton Howe, 1989.

ered the same lost memories of being taken aboard the alien craft and witnessing a calf being raised into the ship in a beam of light. They saw the small, gray beings remove the various parts of the calf and then lower the carcass to the ground, once again in the beam of light.

Ultimately, Linda went on to produce two documentaries on the subject of animal mutilations. She started her own production company, wrote two books on the UFO mystery and helped create the Fox Television Network program, "Sightings." Today, she is a much sought after lecturer on the subject of UFOs and she still continues her relentless investigations of animal mutilations. At a Seattle UFO conference in July, 1995, she made it clear that the phenomenon is not subsiding. "Cases of animal mutilations are coming in from all over the world and from every state in the union. The phenomenon continues unabated, and the reports of UFOs and other paranormal phenomena continue to be reported around the mutilation sites. Although the press still likes to connect these acts to satanic cults, there has never been as far as I know, in the many thousands of reported cases, one person identified, much less arrested, in connection with an animal mutilation."

As for her conclusions about the mystery, Linda states in the introduction to her book, *An Alien Harvest*,[2] "The pattern suggests that at least one non-human intelligence is manipulating and harvesting Earth life, that the alien life forms are controlling and using human ignorance to accomplish the harvest, and that the purpose of the harvest is for sustenance and genetic experimentation." Additionally, Linda came to believe that by examining animal tissues, the beings were likely monitoring the level of pollution in the Earth's environment and its effects on the reproductive abilities of various life forms.

After seeing Linda on television that night, I contacted her, ordered her books and videos and scrutinized them carefully for journalistic integrity. What I saw and read affected me profoundly, for I realized that she had succeeded in documenting the paranormal nature of the cattle mutilation phenomenon and in making a good case for its connection to the UFO mystery. I called her and congratulated her on her fine work and asked for her speaking schedule. I wanted very much to meet her and to hear her speak. "Well, why don't you go to a UFO con-

---

2. Moulton Howe, 1989.

31

ference?" she asked. "I'll be speaking at a very good one in Eureka Springs, Arkansas, next April. I think you would get a lot out of it."

"I don't know," I said. "I'm not so sure I would fit in at a UFO conference."

"Sure you would," she said. "You might be pleasantly surprised." And so I agreed to go to my first UFO conference.

Doing the "Paradigm Shift" in the Ozarks

I boarded my flight for Fayetteville, Arkansas, that day in April 1993 with great trepidation. What was I doing? Was I going overboard with this UFO stuff, as my wife kept telling me? What would my clients think if they knew I attended UFO conferences? What would my coworkers and my company think? I liked Linda and believed in her work as a diligent and tenacious reporter, but was it worth risking my reputation to follow her advice? What kind of people would I meet at a UFO conference in the Ozarks of Arkansas? I envisioned hundreds of crystal-stroking, mantra-chanting, astrology freaks, swapping stories about traveling to Venus with their space brothers. Would I be issued a beanie with a propeller on top, shown the secret handshake and be expected to say, "Nanu, Nanu?" What would I possibly have in common with these people? I held a Ph.D. from a fine university and had taught at the college level for ten years. I was a respected citizen of my community. I was sure I was making a big mistake.

As I walked into the crowded lobby of the conference center at the Inn of the Ozarks, I searched frantically for Linda's familiar face, to no avail. Among the hundreds of people in the crowded room were some wearing sweatshirts with faces of gray aliens imprinted on them, confirming my worst expectations, I believed. For a moment I felt very alone and lost. Then I noticed a group of elderly men, conservatively attired in coats and ties, having an animated conversation. Cautiously, I approached them and listened to their conversation. They were discussing the UFO sightings in Gulf Breeze, Florida, a subject I knew something about, having read Ed Walters book, *The Gulf Breeze Sightings*.[3] Soon I was involved in the discussion.

As we made our introductions, I began to realize that many of my concerns may have been ill founded. Two of the men were former Air

---

3. Walters, 1990.

32

Force aviators, retired colonels for God's sake! These were men who had flown more combat hours and participated in more wars than I had and who had also seen UFOs. They had also been investigating UFO cases actively for more than a quarter of a century. One of them had a master's degree in nuclear engineering. As our conversation progressed, my feeling of superiority quickly subsided. I hadn't expected this at all. After a while a tall, lanky rather professorial-looking gentleman walked through the crowd, drawing much attention.

"Who is that?" I asked.

"That's Dr. John Mack," I was told.

"I've never heard of him," I replied, certain that if I had not heard of him, he couldn't be all that important.

"He's a full professor of psychiatry at Harvard University," I was informed.

"Oh?" I responded. "What's he doing here?"

"He is the featured speaker," my new friends told me.

"Well, what's he going to talk about?" I prodded.

"He's going to speak on the reality of the alien abduction phenomenon."

"You're kidding!" I replied, obviously surprised.

"He has been treating abductees at the Cambridge Medical Center at Harvard for the past few years and he's convinced it is real," I was informed.

"Boy," I thought to myself, "I've got a lot to learn." Suddenly, I was feeling quite foolish and humble as I realized how arrogant I had been acting.

"Okay, God. I get the message. You can stop the humbling process now," I thought to myself. But of course He didn't. Over the period of the next few days and in the years ahead, I met NASA scientists, aerospace engineers, numerous college professors, physicists, commercial airline captains, physicians, attorneys and a long list of highly educated and intelligent persons, all extremely concerned about the issue of a seemingly alien presence on Earth. Immediately after the feeling of foolishness subsided, it was replaced with another, much warmer feeling—the feeling of being right at home with my new-found friends. For the first time in my life, I had someone I could talk to openly about my secret passion without having to defend myself or feel embarrassed. It felt good. So good, that I knew a three-day weekend would

33

not be enough time to make up for all the years of silence. Somehow I would have to make new acquaintances back home. There had to be people like these in El Paso, people who had read the same books I had, people who were comfortable with the notion of intelligent civilizations elsewhere in the universe, people who believed that other realities and other dimensions were possible, and people who were past the point of wondering if UFOs were real and were ready to move on to the more pressing questions of where they came from and what they wanted.

Realigning My Paradigm

I had read a number of books on the alien abduction phenomenon, and I felt well versed on the subject, but sitting in an audience of about 600 people and listening to Dr. John Mack, a Pulitzer Prize winning, Harvard psychiatrist, was electrifying for me. Never before had a scientist and a scholar of his magnitude advocated so boldly the reality of UFOs and alien abductions. I was amused as I recalled the fact that the first known abduction case was investigated by another Boston psychiatrist nearly 30 years before. It was Dr. Benjamin Simon, a highly regarded Boston psychiatrist who treated the now famous, mixed-race couple, Betty and Barney Hill. I remember reading the book, *The Interrupted Journey*,[4] and watching incredulously the made-for-TV movie, "The UFO Incident," in the mid-1970s, which told the story of how the Hills had experienced a missing time episode after observing a strange aerial light, while driving on a lonely New Hampshire highway. The case was fascinating because the Hills were such a credible couple and the researchers, including Dr. Simon, had handled the case so scrupulously. Under hypnosis, Betty and Barney, independently remembered having been taken aboard an alien spacecraft and given physical examinations by small, gray humanoids with large, black, almond-shaped eyes.

Although this tale is quite commonplace today, neither the researchers, the Hills nor the psychiatrist had ever heard of such a story before. And for Dr. Simon, who used hypnosis in his practice, this point was critical, for no one could say afterward that it was his personal bias or preconceived ideas that caused the Hills to have those

---

4. Fuller, 1967.

recollections. Yet, today, that is the primary argument being made by the professional UFO debunkers who would have you believe that the alien encounter phenomenon is nonsense.

It is clear from the book that Dr. Simon was extremely uncomfortable with the results of his hypnosis sessions with the Hills. He tried hard to come up with rational explanations for the strange tale they told. But in the end, he simply admitted that it was a mystery. As far as I know, he never handled another abduction case and never sought to pursue the mystery any further.

But Dr. Mack was different. Here he was, in Eureka Springs, Arkansas, lecturing at a UFO conference on the reality of the abduction phenomenon. He had already treated more than 80 abduction cases and was leading a support group for abductees in his home on a weekly basis. He had written articles on the subject for reputable medical journals and had become a vigorous advocate for the reality of the phenomenon. What, I wondered, caused him to get involved in this in the first place? And why had he risked so formidable a reputation for such a cause? I was already in awe of this courageous man, even before he lumbered to the podium, looking very much like Ichabod Crane with his hunched shoulders and protruding Adams apple.

Slowly, he began to tell his tale, seeming a bit uncomfortable by all the attention and possibly recognizing the incongruity of his presence at such a meeting. He told the story of how he had been introduced by a friend to famed abduction researcher, Budd Hopkins. His immediate reaction: "He and his abductees must all be crazy." Yet, on a trip to New York in January 1990, he made time to go to Hopkins' studio/office and hear the man out. "Nothing in my nearly 40 years of familiarity with the field of psychiatry prepared me for what Hopkins had to say. I was impressed with his warmth, sincerity, intelligence, and caring for the people with whom he had been working."

Hopkins, realizing he had a potential ally, casually asked Dr. Mack as he was leaving if he would be willing to accept abduction cases on a referral basis in the Boston area. Without seriously considering the consequences, Mack agreed. Before long, he was scheduling appointments with what would become a long list of persons who believed they were having alien encounters. When Mack met his first abductees, he was impressed immediately by their lack of mental illness. "None of them seemed psychiatrically disturbed, except in a secondary sense, that is they were troubled as a consequence of something that had apparently happened to them. There was nothing to suggest that their stories were delusional, a misinterpretation of dreams, or the product of fantasy. None of them seemed like people who would concoct a strange story for some personal purpose," Mack said.

Later, he wrote the best-selling book, *Abduction: Human Encounters With Aliens*[5] in which he described some of his most profound cases and in which he boldly dealt with some of the more controversial, metaphysical aspects of the phenomenon, such as out-of-body experiences and past-life memories in alien bodies.

Mack stands today as the most prestigious scientist not only to publicly declare the reality of the UFO phenomenon, but also to devote his career to investigating the UFO mystery.

Hospitality at the "Lone Star Bar"

Later that night, after a long day of lectures, it was impossible to go to my room and sleep. There was too much to know, too many amazing people to meet and too many incredible stories to hear. I was invited by a couple of fellow Texans, regulars at the conference, to drop by their room, dubbed the "Lone Star Bar" by the conferees, where many of the regular attendees and speakers were going to congregate. I eagerly accepted. Before long, I was in a crowded, smoke-filled room surrounded by people who had somehow been touched by the UFO phenomenon, as I obviously had been. Among them were several who with trembling voices, tried to tell about their abduction experiences. These were the first abductees I had ever met in person, and I was anxious to hear them tell their stories first hand. Some were aware that they were having experiences, but were too afraid to undergo hypnosis. Others had confronted their demons long ago and spoke more easily about the alien beings they had encountered. One of these, Mary, a slightly overweight blonde in her mid-twenties, had driven from Colorado to attend the conference. At first, she spoke calmly about her missing time experience on a lonely Colorado highway and her efforts to come to terms with the terror she experienced. But when she tried to tell me about the lizard-like creatures she

---

5.   Mack, 1994.

remembered, her voice cracked and tears welled up in her blue eyes. She began to breathe heavily and found it difficult to continue.

"What do these creatures look like?" I asked. I had read about the reptilian-looking entities who sometimes appear in the stories of alien abduction.

Fighting back the tears, and visibly shaking, she said, "I can't talk about them because when I do, I get terrible shooting pains in my legs. They don't want me talking about them." Then she began to quietly sob. I had no idea how to console someone in such a situation, so I simply stood and watched while she worked through the emotion. Taking a deep breath, she eventually looked me in the eyes and raised her right hand. "I remember seeing a greenish, brown hand with scaly skin and long, sharp claws, reaching for me," she said, choking back a sob. "It had four fingers with webbing in between and (moving her index finger) had an extra joint in its fingers that allowed it to flex in a peculiar way." Then, she broke down again and couldn't continue the conversation. I felt bad that I had prodded her to talk about such a painful subject, thereby causing her even more trauma. It was my first opportunity, of what was to be many opportunities over the coming years, to learn from the amazing people we call abductees, those who have been called the "shamans" of the modern age for the secret knowledge of other realities that they possess.

By this time, Linda had arrived and I left the abductees to visit with my mentor. We sat in a quiet corner of the room and had our first chance to talk at length. "Linda," I asked, "What does this all mean? What's going on? What's the bottom line?"

"I can't tell you," she said. "You have to find out for yourself. There's a lot you have to learn."

"But I've read everything I could get my hands on. What is it I don't know?" I asked with agitation in my voice. "Just tell me what your theory is about where they come from and what they're doing. I think I can handle anything you might say."

"I can't," she insisted. "This phenomenon is much deeper and much more complex than most people understand. There are layers upon layers of understanding, and you're just beginning your journey. Let me give you a list of books to read, then, the next time we meet, you'll be better prepared to have this conversation."

I had no alternative but to accept the list she quickly jotted down on a cocktail napkin. There were six books on the list, two of which I had already read. But at the top of the list, was one I knew nothing about. It was *The Holographic Universe*[6] by Michael Talbot and she explained that it was essential reading because it would help me learn about the true nature of reality. I should buy it here at the conference at one of the vendors' tables where all manner of books, video tapes and assorted new age items were for sale. I found the book, bought it and, on the airplane on the way home, I began my studies, determined to reach a higher level of understanding—a level that would allow me to have the meaningful discussion I craved with my new-found mentor.

Back to Reality

On the way home, my mind spun with the incredible things I had learned at the conference. I reviewed my notes on everything from the crop circles in England to the symbols seen aboard spacecraft by the abductees. It had been pointed out that there were some similarities. For example, a symbol found commonly in both phenomena was the equilateral triangle, either inscribed within a circle or with a circle inscribed in it. We were told that in ancient times this symbol represented power and knowledge. Aboard the alien ships, this symbol had been reported as an insignia worn on the tight fitting suits used by the beings. In the crop circles, the symbol appears frequently, sometimes by itself and other times as part of a much more elaborate design.

Another lecturer had spoken about the interconnectedness of everything in the universe that accounted for such things as Extra Sensory Perception (ESP) and something called synchronicity—meaningful coincidences that should be heeded for their deep meaning, rather than discarded as merely chance. As I breezed through Talbot's book, before getting down to serious reading, I noticed that he also discussed this curious concept. According to many, the concept of synchronicity implies that there is no such thing as a coincidence. All things are planned at the subconscious level, in unison with a mass consciousness that permeates the entire universe.

But as the plane landed in El Paso, and thoughts of returning to work and to my normal life began to dominate my mind, such con-

---

6. Talbot, 1991.

cepts as crop circles, power symbols and synchronicity began to seem a bit far fetched. Anyway, how was I going to incorporate all these new ideas into my ordinary life? I still had to deal with my job in the financial services industry, raising three kids and living an ordinary and somewhat humdrum life. By the time I pulled into the driveway of my home, the conference was beginning to fade in memory, my old reality was taking hold of me again. Parking my car in the garage, I noticed my wife's car was missing and concluded correctly that she had taken the kids to the country club for dinner. The side entrance to our house, closest to the garage, leads into our playroom, which is furnished with a big-screen TV and a pool table placed directly in front of the entryway door. As I let myself in, I suddenly found myself frozen in place, staring at the pool table in amazement. The pool table was clear of all the pool balls and cue sticks. In the center of the table was the triangular rack, used to rack the balls before each game. Someone had stood it upright, facing the door. And centered in the rack, balanced neatly in the middle, was the cue ball—a circle inscribed within an equilateral triangle placed precisely in a way that I could not miss it. I stood there, staring at the scene before me in disbelief. Never had I seen the table arranged in that manner. Who could have done this and why?

Later that evening as we were readying for bed, I asked my wife, "Honey, who put the triangle and the cue ball on the pool table in that peculiar way?"

"I did," she replied.

"Why did you do that," I pressed.

"Well, we were leaving to go to dinner and I wanted to leave you a note so you would know where we were."

"But there was no note. The note was in the kitchen," I responded.

"Well, at the last moment, I decided that you would be more likely to find it in the kitchen, so I took the note out from under the cue ball and put it on the kitchen counter," she explained. "What's the big deal, anyway?"

"I don't know, I had just been thinking about circles inscribed in triangles just before I walked into the house."

She thought over my strange reply for a moment and then she said, "Gee, what a strange coincidence."

"Yeah," I said. "It sure is."

CHAPTER 3 RECONCILING
SCIENCE AND
RELIGION

*To those searching for the truth—not the truth of dogma and darkness, but
the truth brought by reason, search, examination and inquiry, discipline is
required. For faith, as well intentioned as it may be, must be built on facts,
not fiction. Faith in fiction is a damnable false hope.*

—Thomas A. Edison

A Search for Spiritual Truth

Early in my transformative journey, it became evident that in order
to incorporate my new-found knowledge into my view of reality, I
would have to review everything I had ever been taught about science
and religion. Somehow I had to account for how my culture could possibly have taught me such an erroneous view of reality. How could science and religion be so wrong about the most important issues facing
humankind? I began to realize that I had never really been comfortable
with the standard explanations for the nature of reality. As a child and
young adult, I rebelled against the teachings of the church, refusing to
accept the dogma taught in Sunday school, questioning every
accepted tenet of the institution. I simply couldn't accept that the minister, or the church in general, had a true understanding of events that
occurred thousands of years ago.

Yet, I quietly embraced a deep spirituality based on an intuitive
belief that Jesus had been a real person, whose teachings were worthy
of serious consideration. I have always felt a close, personal relationship with Jesus and still consider myself a Christian, although not one
who is married to the dogma of a particular church. (Something that

will be obvious to the reader in later chapters.) Perhaps my rebellious nature was the result of my unusual experience with religion at an early age. Coming from a Mexican-American family, whose ties to Mexico are still quite strong, I was brought up in the Catholic Church until about the age of eight. It was then that my father befriended a Presbyterian missionary whose small, one-room mission in Juarez, Mexico, spread the Protestant faith to the poor in that predominately Catholic city.

I still remember those hot, steamy nights sitting in that little, adobe mission, transfixed by the passionate words and dramatic gestures of the devout Reverend Pablo Delgado as he preached the glory of Jesus and his sacrifice on the cross to the crowd of wide-eyed listeners. Certainly they had never before heard the likes of Rev. Delgado's impassioned and terrifying descriptions of the damnation awaiting them should they stray from the Word of God and the path of righteousness. He seemed like such a mysterious man to me at the time. Perhaps it was because he looked like Santa Claus with his stout, five-foot frame and his white, bushy beard, or perhaps it was because his exhortations were so loudly and boldly delivered, in sharp contrast to the priests I was accustomed to. Or maybe it was because even then I realized that what we were doing, attending services at this tiny mission, had an element of the provocative and the dangerous.

Everyone we knew, our friends and our relatives, were all Catholics who lived in a world where non-Catholics were outsiders. My mother, having grown up in that culture, was afraid that people would find out about our family heresy, or rather my father's foolishness. She had no intention of forsaking her religion just because of my father's whims. Making matters worse was the fact that the little mission stood on a busy corner, across the street from a large cathedral. Often, both congregations would arrive at the same time for services, creating a bit of nervousness and tension in the air. At such times, Reverend Delgado would start up a hymn and urge his congregation to sing the praise of the Lord loudly so the Catholics could hear. In this way, the little mission attracted the curious who would stand in the open doorway and listen to the fiery sermons of that little, Santa Claus-like figure with the voice of a lion.

In the end, we all became Presbyterians, even my mother, and a great scandal tore a rift in the Lewels and Cisneros families (my mother's maiden name) that still lingers to this day. We began attending a Bible Presbyterian Church near our home and attending not only the services, but Bible study classes as well. This is where I had a problem. The language of the Bible was difficult for a young boy to understand, and the stories it told were confusing and in many cases, contradictory. First of all, in the Old Testament, God was depicted as a jealous and wrathful being who was personally involved in helping the Jews plan their wars against the Canaanites, yet in the New Testament, God was a kind, loving and merciful entity who forgave people of their sins. Could this possibly be the same God of the Old Testament, I wondered? It didn't seem so to me. In addition, many of the stories in the Bible seemed too fantastic to be true. Could I really accept through blind faith alone that the Red Sea parted for the Israelites, that Jesus walked on water, or that he resurrected from the dead? I wanted to, but I just couldn't. It seemed unfair at the time that I was being pressured into accepting these stories as true on blind faith alone.

I think I knew instinctively that I was simply not ready to deal with the Bible, for in trying to do so, I would have to accept whatever meaning the Bible school teacher attributed to a particular passage. For some reason, I didn't believe that the Bible teacher or the minister really knew what those passages meant. At the time, most of the Bible seemed like a lot of jumbled-up fairy tales made up a long time ago by long-forgotten men. But I did like the stories about Jesus. The stories of love and forgiveness and of sacrifice rang a special chord within me that is hard to explain. It is a chord that still rings loudly, in spite of the unusual conclusions about his life that you will find in a later chapter of this book.

Eventually, as an adult, I would leave the Protestant Church behind me to find my own, independent form of spirituality and, as fate would have it, I fell in love with and married a staunch, Catholic woman and I agreed to raise my children in that church. So for 20 or so years, I have once again found myself dealing with the mysticism, the sacred rituals and statues of which Catholics are so fond and which Protestants are so vehemently against. Only now, Catholics sing hymns too and I make a point of always raising my voice high in singing the Lord's praise, just in case Rev. Delgado is watching.

The Place Between Science and Religion

At the very least, this early exposure to the Bible got me thinking about a lot of things—about what was real and what was not, about scientific discoveries and their impact on religious faith and about how to distinguish between who was telling the truth and who was preaching a distorted view of reality. The Bible, I felt, would have to wait for later—for a time when I would have gained enough general knowledge to put that mystical book into its proper perspective. Looking back now, I can see that those early days in Bible class launched me on a life-long search for answers to many of life's most perplexing questions:

Is there intelligent life elsewhere in the universe? Are there other dimensions and realities? What is the true nature of God? Is there a soul residing in each and every one of us? Is there life after death? Do angels and demons exist? If so, where does humankind fit into the hierarchy of life in the universe?

These are and always have been among the most elusive and important questions facing humankind, yet as we approach the end of the millennium, finding answers to them seems a distant reality. Mainstream science long ago abdicated any responsibility for dealing with spiritual questions and assumed such issues constitute the "unknowable." Most scientists today believe that such issues are best left for theologians and philosophers to ponder and are content to define reality as "only that which can be proven in a laboratory or through the scientific method." Intuition and spirituality have, to a great extent, been systematically eradicated from the scientific process, and scientific thought is today dominated by government grants, ultra-secret military research, corporate self interests and a university system dependent on all these. In short, science long ago decided that the universe was a physical place and that it could only be studied in physical terms. Scientists have agreed to place this unfortunate and arbitrary limitation on their definition of "science." The consensus view of the scientific community gradually reached the conclusion that the world of the nonphysical, if it existed at all, is better left to ministers, priests and rabbis. There was little chance that anything nonphysical could have any consequence for the material world. It has been this egregious error that has caused science, until only recently, to go so far astray from the truth.

44

Theologians, on the other hand, have been happy to leave the material world to scientists, believing the spiritual world to be more meaningful than the crass and ugly world of humanity. However, this was not always the case. At one time, religion and science were thought to be one and the Church stood as sole arbiter of what was real and what was not. It was only when the Church failed to accept and incorporate new scientific findings that it began a long slide into disrepute and eventually ceased to be thought of as a credible source in the discussion on the true nature of reality. For 500 years, ever since Galileo proved that the Earth revolved around the sun, and not the other way around, as the Church had taught, religion's authority and credibility as a source of scientific thought has been in severe decline. The resulting state of "peaceful coexistence" between church and science has resulted in a huge void in human understanding, and has misled modern man into believing that science and spirituality are mutually exclusive aspects of reality. This discreditation of theologians and their willingness to abdicate their right to scientific pursuits has, in turn, resulted in a world where science and technology have supplanted theology as the world's dominant religion, spawning technological wonders in a spiritual void. We are left wondering today whether the inventors of such environmentally devastating technologies as the atomic bomb, chemical and biological weapons, or even agricultural pesticides would have carried out their projects had they been as advanced in spiritual knowledge as they were in technological skills.

Is there really a difference between science and spirituality? If so, who created that difference? Who separated them? Was it God? Or is the separation simply a figment of our imagination, created through hundreds of years of conditioning? For centuries, science has told us that the universe is like a machine, made up of separate parts. All we have to do is examine each part, objectively, methodically and we will eventually understand everything about it. So civilized man has become conditioned to see everything as separate from everything else. In school we study psychology, biology and sociology as completely separate concepts, yet the separation is totally man made, a product of a conditioning process in the Western World. Few people today question the concept of separation, and even fewer would believe that there is a science of spirituality, a scientific approach to learning about the spiritual world. Fewer still would believe that there are spiritual laws as well defined as the physical laws taught to us in science class.

But today, propelled by a grass-roots wave of public support, a small, but growing number of highly credible scientists is leading the way toward finding the answers to these previously "unknowable" questions, and they are beginning to define a new science: the science of spirituality that understands that separation is simply an illusion—an illusion that is bringing humankind to the brink of global disaster. In so doing, they are calling into question the very foundations of modern scientific thought as well as commonly accepted Christian and Judaic theology. But more importantly, they are on the verge of defining new, universal laws that will supplant the current laws of physics and provide us with a code of morality and behavior more powerful than the Ten Commandments. This new way of understanding the universe and the nature of reality sets the stage for science's ability, for the first time, to explain those things we previously believed to be unknowable and possibly for an amazing new chapter in the history and evolution of the human species.

In breaking ranks with the establishment, these daring scholars are declaring the reality of such things as flying saucers, alien abductions, reincarnation, near-death experiences, psychic powers, spiritual healing and much more. They are among a rapidly growing number of people who believe that there are, indeed, ways of knowing the unknowable and that the time has come for mainstream scientists and theologians to take off their blinders and throw off the self-imposed chains they have bound themselves in for so long—the chains of scientific methodology and objectivity on the one hand, and the chains of narrow mindedness and tired dogma on the other.

To traditional scientists and theologians, such heretical concepts threaten to destroy the fabric of the reality they cherish—a comfortable reality they have forged over the last 2,000 years. What's more, many are more than willing to fight to save the paradigm they see being shattered before their very eyes. They accuse the mavericks of being "unscientific" at best or "of being in league with the devil" at worst. Yet, few of the critics have ever spent any time researching the "new science" issues. Moreover, the mavericks are not wild-eyed, new age, LSD-tripping kooks. Many are leaders in their scientific fields who have decided to break ranks with their colleagues to advocate highly controversial views, knowing full well the persecution and ridicule awaiting them. They are the leaders of a movement to change the world's scientific and religious paradigm by forging a bridge between science and spirituality—a bridge that a growing number of people today believe is long overdue.

In the wake of these leaders comes a flotilla of lesser-known practitioners and researchers who have been working quietly, in many cases clandestinely, for years on new science projects and using new science techniques. They have networked through new science organizations and attended new science conferences and workshops, learning from one another and lionizing the big name scientists who have had the courage to take a bold stand—people like physicians Deepak Chopra and Raymond Moody, psychiatrists Brian Weiss and John Mack, astronauts Gordon Cooper, Edgar Mitchell and Brian O'Leary, physicist David Bohm, neurophysiologist Karl Pribram; and many others.

The Awakening of Humankind

Today, in every major American city, and in many smaller ones, a person suffering from every imaginable physical or mental illness can walk into the office of a licensed and credible mental health professional and receive therapy that helps him heal his ailments by achieving a relaxed mental state and remembering past lives. Or, in that same altered state, he may rid himself of unwanted spirits which are believed to attach themselves to the human soul. Throughout this country and in many other countries, well educated and highly credible psychiatrists and psychologists are treating persons who have been traumatized by encounters with non-human entities. Many medical doctors, nurses, chiropractors and massage therapists are using psychic energy to help heal their patients with their hands, without even telling the person what they are doing. In fact, Americans are spending more than $10 billion a year on alternative medicine, including herbs, potions, hypnosis, spiritual healing and meditation, a figure nearly as great as what they spend on hospital care! What's more, these treatments are working!

Scientists today are seriously studying and finding evidence for such things as the power of prayer, life after death, alien abductions, ESP, remote viewing, past-life memories, the existence of other realities, and many other previously taboo subjects. In fact it seems that some hidden power is trying very hard to wake us up and to lead us to a new understanding of Earth's place in the universe and humankind's true place in what appears to be a complex hierarchy of intelligent life all around us. Could it be that humanity is on the verge of developing a new science that incorporates an understanding of spirituality and that will allow us to see clearly, for the first time, the true nature of reality, or possibly many realities? Is it possible that we can now know the unknowable? Are we being led to a new understanding of our true relationship to other intelligences that are also part of God's magnificent creation?

This awakening, which some see as the Revelation of which the Bible speaks, comes at a time when the Earth and its inhabitants are on the brink of a disaster of cataclysmic proportions: human overpopulation is threatening all other species on the planet (and ultimately our own); humanity's failure to accept responsibility as custodians of the Earth's resources has caused worldwide environmental disaster; religious, racial and ethnic intolerance continues to threaten world peace at a time when nuclear and biological weapons are capable of destroying all living things on the Earth; and a lack of understanding or even a total denial of our spiritual nature has doomed much of humankind to the world of the physical, totally separated from God.

It seems a paradox that the global chaos evident today comes at a time that should be humankind's finest hour. After all, have we not proved ourselves superior to all other forms of intelligent life? Have we not advanced far beyond the level of primitive hunter gatherers? Have we not developed a sophisticated science and technology that permits us to live a life of luxury, compared to the life of misery and toil that our ancestors were doomed to live? If so, why then, in an age of routine space voyages, yawn-inspiring heart replacement surgery, a plethora of miracle drugs and instantaneous worldwide communication, is the world in such pitiful shape? Why is it that at what should be our finest hour, we are questioning more than ever before the fundamental premises of modern scientific and religious beliefs?

Reality by Consensus

Is it because neither science nor religion has been honest? Is it possible that both have been corrupted and transformed from what were once honest, intellectual pursuits into lumbering, self-serving bureaucracies that have lost touch with spirituality? According to recent polls, more than half of the American public believes that flying saucers are real, that reincarnation is real, and that angels exist. Thousands of people are seeking professional help for dealing with the trauma of alien encounters, millions are reporting sightings of UFOs all over the world, visions of the Virgin Mary are appearing to people from Georgia to Yugoslavia. Untold millions have had out-of-body experiences (OBEs), witnessed poltergeist activity, had precognitive visions, or have been visited by the spirits of deceased relatives, but have never reported the events to anyone. A national poll, conducted by the Roper Organization on behalf of the Bigelow Foundation and several UFO organizations in 1992, quantified the extent to which Americans have had paranormal experiences. In a report titled "Unusual Personal Experiences,"[1] it was concluded that approximately 3.7 million Americans have had experiences that might be construed to be alien encounters. Furthermore, the study found that a wide range of paranormal experiences are fairly widespread. Eighteen percent (possibly 45 million people if children are included) have "awakened in a state of paralysis with a strange presence in the room." Fifteen percent (37 million) report having seen, "either as a child or as adult, a terrifying figure—which might have been a monster, a witch, a devil, or some other evil figure" in their bedroom. Fourteen percent (35 million people) reported having had an OBE and seven percent (or 17 million Americans) say they have seen a UFO.

These "experiencers" have been called the "shamans" of the technological age, for it is through them that we learn about the multidimensional universe that we live in; it is through their eyes that we can glimpse into realities that for the rest of us are invisible—at least for now. Yet, for generations, our shamans have been effectively silenced, and the silence they have had to endure is like a dark blemish on the history of the human race and one that needs addressing today. We must begin to understand that the spiritual dimensions are constantly trying to reach us, to communicate with us, to guide us and to gain our recognition. But those persons who can best serve as our guides, our leaders in understanding the universe, have been silenced by a combination of fear of the unknown, religious fervor and fanati-

---

1. Roper, 1992.

cism, scientific arrogance and public ignorance. We have heard about the days of the Catholic Inquisition in which the Church, in the name of Jesus, hunted down, tortured and murdered millions of people with psychic abilities or those who had simply experienced paranormal events. It is assumed, today, that witch hunts are a thing of the past. What they don't understand is that we still live under the cloud of the Inquisition—we just don't burn witches anymore. Instead, we merely ridicule them, medicate them or institutionalize them. We slander their credibility and make it impossible for them to hold productive jobs in mainstream society. The fear of the unknown is still with us, and the fires of the Inquisition still smolder in the rhetoric of religious fanatics, in the sermons delivered from pulpits in middle America, and in the arrogant, uncomfortable smirks on the faces of mainstream scientists as they attempt to discredit those who have witnessed paranormal phenomena.

The general public has, for the most part, accepted, albeit with skepticism, what Church leaders and government-sponsored scientists have told them about the nature of reality. In spite of their obvious incompatibility, both views, however, convey a common message: "The experts have everything well in hand. It's OK to go about your daily business, because the true nature of reality, the true nature of God and human origins have long ago been resolved."

The Big Lie

The fact is, nothing could be further from the truth. These issues have not been resolved. No matter what you have been told, no matter what you have read, no matter what you have seen on television, no matter how much esteem you place on our scientific institutions and in your religion, you do not have a clear understanding of these matters if you have relied on traditional and conventional sources of information. You have been deceived, misled and misinformed by institutions that, because of their bureaucratic structures, must arrive at consensus views on every issue with which they deal. In the process, important and often contradictory information is routinely hidden, destroyed or ignored.

Religious Consensus

It is undeniable that religious zealots throughout the ages have routinely destroyed or kept hidden controversial documents that contradicted their own point of view. In their conquest of the civilizations of South America and Mexico, the Spanish conquistadors set about to obliterate, in the name of Jesus, all evidence of the religious beliefs of the Incas, the Mayans and the Aztecs. Thousands upon thousands of precious texts were heaped in piles and burned. Statues and golden idols that could have revealed to us much of the beliefs of these ancient and noble people were either destroyed or melted down to be poured into golden ingots. Such behavior has been common among conquering nations throughout history. But in other cases, crucial information is controlled and hidden from view, particularly from those who might interpret it differently than the powers that be.

The Dead Sea Scrolls, discovered in 1947, are an example of religious zeal obstructing the pursuit of spiritual and historical truth. After being kept hidden from view, even from legitimate scholars, for 45 years, they were finally made public only after frustrated scholars schemed to smuggle them out to the public in the form of photographs. For all those years, the only information dealing with the nature of the documents and the only interpretation of their meaning, came from a carefully selected group of religious scholars whose vested interest it was to protect the consensus view of Judaism and Christianity. Clearly, such documents that shed important light on the very nature of God, belong to all of us, but religious institutions, just as governments, are political bodies and are in the business of making political decisions, and ultimately, much of what we know and believe today about religion is the result of a long tradition of filtering information through the hands of a select few.

Such institutional thinking began long ago. Anyone who looks into the early history of the Bible will quickly learn that the book, which is touted by fundamentalists as being the Holy Word of God, is in fact, a heavily edited compilation of ancient writings by many authors, some anonymous, which have been censored and changed over many centuries by political institutions. In fact the book we call the Holy Bible is the product of numerous committees, working under government mandates, dictated by political objectives and is therefore not considered by historians to be a particularly reliable historical doc-

51

ument. This, however, is not to say that the Bible is worthless, only that it should be understood for what it is. Anyone seeking spiritual truth in earnest must see the Bible as only one of many ancient documents that should be studied.

From the earliest times, great obstacles stood before those who sought spiritual enlightenment through an understanding of the ancient scrolls said to hold the secrets of everlasting life. First there was the problem of language. These ancient documents which had been handed down over thousands of years, suffering the recopying and editing of many unknown hands and the ravages of time, were written in archaic forms of Aramaic (a Semitic language) and Hebrew that at times defied easy translation. In addition to using idioms peculiar to their culture, the meanings of which have been lost forever, the texts lost further meaning when translated first into Greek, then into Latin and finally into English. It wasn't until 1957 that an English version of the Old and New Testaments, translated directly from the original Aramaic texts of the fifth and sixth centuries, was published. This version, known as the Lamsa translation, after its author, Dr. George M. Lamsa[2], included nearly 12,000 differences from the popular and already accepted versions.[3] Furthermore, new methods for interpreting and translating scriptures based on the discovery of previously unknown ancient texts and archeological discoveries, have created a need for constant revisions.

Perhaps even a greater obstacle has been the intolerance for new ideas that could enlighten the masses. It was such intolerance that caused the authors and curators of the ancient scrolls to bury them in secluded caves on the shores of the Dead Sea. Such intolerance persisted into the Christian era and was the cause of massive revisions of Biblical texts during the early years of the Christian movement. In the fourth century, when Christianity was adopted as the official religion of the Roman Empire by Emperor Constantine, it was by official decree that all references to reincarnation were deleted from the New Testament. Prior to that time, the belief in past lives was a tradition handed down throughout the centuries in the Jewish teachings and was a widely held doctrine among early Christians. [4]

---

2. Lamsa, 1985.
3. Leedom, 1993, p. 94.

However, Constantine was concerned that the belief in reincarnation threatened the stability of the empire because people might be less obedient if they thought they could make up for their misdeeds in another life. Thus, for the sake of social and political control, the idea of a single judgment day for all became "sacred" doctrine. Two centuries later, at the Second Council of Constantinople, reincarnation was declared a heresy, punishable by death and consequently, through the persecution, torture and murder of many innocent people, the concept was eradicated by brute force from the Christian faith. However, their efforts to censor the Bible were not entirely successful, due to the fact that Jesus often spoke in parables that required interpretation. For example, when Jesus said, "As ye sow, so shall ye reap," it could be said that he was speaking of farming or it could be that he was subtly stating the law of Karma—the basis of Eastern religions (see Chapter 6). This second, deeper meaning reflects an understanding of ancient Vedic philosophy characterized by a belief in a universe in which everything is interconnected and in which doing harm to others is no different than doing harm to oneself. The law of Karma states that we must atone for our wrongs in future lifetimes, if they are not corrected in the present one. Hints such as these have led some to believe that Jesus actually taught the concept of reincarnation to his disciples as secret knowledge and that such teachings were later expurgated from Christian texts by the Church.

As for the Jewish faith, belief in reincarnation was common until the early 1800s when orthodox Judaism was "modernized" and reincarnation was removed from its avowed beliefs.

To truly understand today's religions, one must recognize that religious doctrines were often molded by those who had little regard for spirituality and who held the intellectual capacity of the common people in total contempt. For example, in 1199, Pope Innocent III, declared that:

> The secret mysteries of the faith ought not to be explained to all men in all places, since they cannot be everywhere understood by all men.[5]

Pope Gregory VII declared:

4. Weiss, 1988, pp. 35-36.
5. Leedom, 1993, p. 91.

Not without reason has it pleased Almighty God that Holy Scripture should be a secret in certain places, lest, it were plainly apparent to all men, perchance it would be little esteemed and be subject to disrespect; or it might be falsely understood by those of mediocre learning and lead to error. [6]

So much did the Church wish to keep the Bible a secret unto itself, that upon the publication of the first English translation by John Wycliffe, a British scholar, Archbishop Arundel wrote the Pope in 1412:

...that wretched and pestilent fellow of damnable memory, the very herald and child of anti-Christ, who crowned his wickedness by translating the Scriptures into the mother tongue....[7]

And an early 15th centuryprovincial council at Oxford declared:

No one shall in the future translate on his own authority any text of Holy Scriptures into the English tongue—nor shall any man read this kind of book, booklet or treatise, now recently composed in the time of the said John Wycliffe or later, or any that shall be composed in the future, in whole or in part, publicly or secretly under penalty of the greater Excommunication.[8]

This, however, did not stop a virtual flood of English translations from being published, beginning in the 15th century, which prompted both the Catholic Church, as well as the newly formed Protestant Church, to struggle throughout the next hundred years to arrive at some agreement. By submitting the Sacred Word to a torturous committee process, a consensus view was finally achieved, culminating with an Authorized Version of Scripture in 1611, commonly known as the King James Version. (King James I of England, who was believed to rule by "divine right," it should be noted, was believed by many to have been a homosexual who murdered his young lovers and who ordered the torture and murder of countless "heretics.") Such a process for arriving at an official version of the Holiest of books, caused one disenchanted writer to pose the following question: "Can a document, tampered with by kings, tyrants, fools and scholars be the 'true' inspired words of God?" [9]

---

6. Leedom, 1993, p. 91.
7. Leedom, 1993, p. 92.
8. Leedom, 1993, p. 92.

The Jesus Seminar

Nowhere in the effort to interpret the Bible has the debate been more rancorous than in the attempt by Bible scholars to agree on the truth behind the story of Jesus as told in the New Testament. The harder they have tried to reach a consensus on how much fact lies in the Gospels of the apostles, the stronger their conviction has become that very little of the Jesus story can be considered historically authentic. In 1993, a group of Bible scholars calling themselves "The Jesus Seminar" published their preliminary conclusions in a book called *The Five Gospels*.[10] Among the few things they could agree on was that most of the Gospels are "inauthentic" and that the picture most people have of Jesus may be radically misguided, and is in fact "an imaginative theological construct (crying out for) liberation from the grip of those whose faith overpowered their memories."[11] These scholars have in recent years attempted to expurgate from the official Church account of Jesus those portions that are suspect as being the creations of religious fanatics, rather than factual accounts. Their ultimate conclusion was that "we can't be sure of anything that Jesus actually said."

Contrary to what is still being taught in Sunday school classes and preached from the pulpits, most New Testament scholars today do not believe that the four main Gospels (Matthew, Mark, Luke and John) were actually written by the Apostles themselves, but rather by their followers, or their followers' followers. Each of these narratives tells the story of Jesus slightly differently—in some cases causing irreconcilable contradictions, as in the confusing chronology of events describing the day of resurrection. Today's, more objective Bible analysts pose a question that most Christians have been unwilling to address: Did faith and church policy—the need to conform to the consensus views of the time—cause the writers to embellish on actual fact? If so, how can we differentiate between those portions that are factual from those which are myth? The obvious answer is that we can't—at least not through traditional investigative means. So unreliable are these texts, in their opinion, that as early as 1926, one of the most respected Protestant scholars, Rudolf Bultmann of the University of Marburg in Ger-

9. Leedom, 1993, p. 120.
10. The Jesus Seminar, 1996.
11. Van Biema, 1996, p. 54.

many, called for a halt to research into the historical Jesus, saying "We can now know almost nothing concerning the life and personality of Jesus."[12] (Although the Jesus seminar raises important questions about the scriptures, it is the author's belief that, in fact, much of the Bible is factual and that it merits our careful attention.)

To be sure, the Bible, far from being the perfect, unblemished word of God, is riddled with contradictions and mistakes. Many worthwhile manuscripts and ideas were deleted because religious institutions found them too controversial or simply contrary to the consensus views of the moment. However, there is still a core of truth in the Bible that can best be understood in light of other ancient texts. Fortunately, many of these still exist and are available to the general public. In addition, now that the Dead Sea Scrolls have been liberated from their "captors," new translations and interpretations have become available for those who search for spiritual truth.

Scientific Consensus

Science, like religion, is full of zealots whose biases predetermine the results of their research and their experiments. Information and data are sometimes altered, or they are simply ignored if they do not agree with the scientist's views. Sometimes the scientist simply arrives at conclusions that are in complete contradiction to the data, particularly if those data are counter to the prevailing views.

In order to maintain the consensus views of their disciplines, scientists in every field simply ignore contradictory evidence and hypotheses that would help them arrive at the truth. For example, anthropologists regularly find evidence that the history of humankind extends much further into the past than previously believed and that our ancestors possessed a high level of scientific and technological knowledge. Yet they ignore it and disavow it.

In 1966, a respected woman archeologist by the name of Virginia Steen-McIntyre and her associates, while working on a U.S. Geological Survey team under the auspices of the National Science Foundation, were asked to date numerous artifacts found at archeological sites in Mexico. Her incredible encounter with the brick wall known as "scientific consensus" is told in a remarkable book titled *The Hidden History*

12. Van Biema, 1996, p. 55.

of the Human Race.[13] What Steen-McIntyre and her team discovered were stone tools exactly like the best work of Cro-Magnon man in European sites. Using four different, but well accepted, dating methods, the team conducted an exhaustive series of tests and concluded that the implements were in the neighborhood of 250,000 years old. Even though the results were quite conclusive, they completely contradicted the accepted view among archaeologists and anthropologists who long ago agreed that Cro-Magnon did not appear until, at the earliest, about 100,000 years ago. To accept Steen-McIntyre's findings would have meant rewriting all the textbooks on human origins and a complete rethinking of the Darwinist point of view. Needless to say, neither of these occurred. What did occur was a concerted effort by the scientific community to discredit the team's work and to vilify the character of its leader. Ultimately, because she stood steadfast by her research and was unwilling to repudiate the validity of her work, Steen-McIntyre was driven out of the academic community and has not been able to find work in her field.

The authors of the book, Michael Cremo and Richard Thompson, uncovered a virtual mountain of archeological evidence suggesting that the mainstream theory of evolution is a sham and that there has been a massive cover-up of such findings by the scientific community. They cite evidence for the existence of modern humans dating back to more than one million years ago.

Ancient Civilizations

If mainstream scientists are unwilling to accept that human origins may be much more ancient than they have been telling us, one can imagine that they would be even more reluctant to consider the possibility that advanced civilizations might have flourished as long ago as 15,000 years and beyond, yet that is precisely what a growing number of maverick scientists are beginning to realize. These amazing beings are believed to be the true builders of the monolithic structures found around the world, including the pyramids of Giza in Egypt, the Sphinx, and numerous megalithic sites of Mexico and Central America. In British journalist Graham Hancock's excellent and courageous exploration of this thesis, *Fingerprints of the Gods,*[14] he examines

---

13. Cremo, 1994, pp. 91-94.

another important case in which controversial, but important scientific evidence for the antiquity of the human race has been ignored and swept under the rug by the scientific community. He relates the case of the late professor Charles Hapgood, who taught the history of science at Keene College in New Hampshire for many years.

Hapgood caught the attention of Albert Einstein in 1953 with his amazing theory of "Earth-crust displacement," a phenomenon in which the Earth's crust becomes loosened from its inner, molten core and suddenly slips, causing massive changes to the Earth's geology and geography. Einstein wrote an enthusiastic forward to Hapgood's book on this theory which accounts for Antarctica's well-known sudden change in climate in ancient times. He believed that the entire continent of Antarctica shifted suddenly from its original position 2,000 miles further north from its present location. If this is so, then Antarctica could well be the fabled lost continent of Atlantis and startling evidence of its existence could lie buried today under two miles of ice.

Furthermore, Hapgood later discovered important evidence that some unknown, but highly advanced civilization created detailed and extremely accurate maps of Antarctica at a time when that continent was not covered by ice at all. At the earliest, such maps must have been drawn 15,000 years ago, at a time when mainstream science tells us human civilization did not exist. The evidence, in the form of old maps dated to the early 1500s (but drawn from much older charts), the authenticity of which is not questioned by scientists, show clearly that the consensus chronology of Earth's history and of the human race is entirely wrong.

Hancock points out that in spite of Einstein's endorsement, Hapgood's evidence was quietly ignored by the scientific community:

...far from being applauded for making a serious new contribution to the debate about the antiquity of human civilization, Hapgood until his death was cold-shouldered by the majority of his professional peers, who couched their discussion of his work in what has accurately been described as "thick and unwarranted sarcasm, selecting trivia and factors not subject to verification as the bases for condemnation, seeking in this way to avoid the basic issues."[15]

14. Hancock, 1995, pp. 9-15.

58

Although Hancock stops short of advancing the idea that the creators of the maps and of the megalithic structures were of extraterrestrial origin, he makes it clear that their highly advanced science is in many ways superior to that of ours. In addition, he acknowledges the fact that references to these advanced beings in the ancient texts of the Egyptian, Mayan, Incan and Sumerian civilizations make it clear that they were regarded as gods, not merely as human beings. It is this understanding, that human origins and human civilization are tied directly to highly advanced, godlike beings who came to Earth in the long-forgotten past that is missing from the scientific attempts to understand the nature of the human experience. Since scientists will not entertain the possibility that the Earth might have been visited by extraterrestrial intelligence, now or in the past, they cannot consider the hypothesis that genetic intervention might account for the amazing jumps in human evolution evident in the fossil record, a subject discussed in a later chapter of this book. We must thus ask ourselves an important question: If science is not willing to consider every possible hypothesis in its search for answers, how can it ever hope to arrive at the truth?

In short it is a big mistake for us to put any more faith in scientists than we do in theologians. Both are subject to the same biases and pressures that consume the institutions they work for. But, in one way, scientists are more dangerous than theologians. At least we know that theologians have a preconceived bias. But scientists go to great lengths to convince us of their objectivity and most people have believed them. This has the effect of placing scientists in the same position the theologians were in years ago as the authorities on the nature of reality. But if scientists were true to the principles of science, they would be completely open-minded. They would give equal weight to all possible hypotheses, no matter how absurd they seemed. They would examine all the evidence and then they would reach the logical conclusions, regardless of how unpopular they were or whether or not they violated the consensus views. Unfortunately, this is simply not the way science is conducted in the world today.

15. Hancock, 1995, p. 9.

Science and Spirituality are for You and Me

Today, science and religion have left us with two untenable choices: either we accept the scientific view that reality consists only of what can be proven in a laboratory, or we accept the dogma and mythology of religious institutions that are still teaching a notion of reality that was formulated thousands of years ago. On the one hand, science tells us there is no God, there are no angels, there is no human soul and there are no other realities. On the other hand, religion, with its emotionally charged rhetoric asks us to accept a sugar-coated and fanciful theology, populated by two- dimensional characters representing the forces of good and evil.

Faced with these choices, we are all forced to live a schizophrenic existence, trying to balance two mutually exclusive ideologies. In most cases, the end result is that people simply give up trying to make sense of it all, or they choose one side over the other and cling to it like a newborn to its mother's breast. Neither solution is likely to lead to a proper understanding of the nature of reality. Those who adopt the scientific view lose all connection to the spiritual world and reject all evidence to the contrary. Those who choose the religious path disavow scientific discoveries that contradict their theology, thereby limiting severely their perspective of reality.

Perhaps what is happening today is that more people are becoming aware that there is another way—a middle road that can be taken. This middle road is the path of the independent mind and is for those who are capable of accepting the truth, regardless of which view is eventually supported.

Independent researchers who wish to test their powers of reason against the prevailing religious and scientific views need only to open their eyes to find a wealth of new science texts, and ancient religious documents, translated into very readable English, available at any good bookstore or library. What he will find, if he looks carefully, is that the origins of our monotheistic, Judaic-Christian beliefs lie in the dim and ancient times when people believed in multiple gods who came to Earth from the heavens to create humankind, to teach them the sciences and to create law and order. He would soon learn that much of the Old Testament consists simply of heavily edited versions of ancient Sumerian and Babylonian stories of the ancient gods, still preserved today in the clay tablets of our ancestors. These tablets tell of a time when science and religion were one and when interaction between humans and higher life forms was taken for granted. They also tell a far different story of human origins than what you and I have been taught by science and religion.

Does this mean that the Bible is worthless as a guide to spirituality? No, in fact the Bible has many truths. But it is incumbent upon the reader to have learned enough to put it into proper perspective, and that is not an easy task. It requires the reader to be acquainted with the ancient writings of the Earth's first-known civilizations as well as the latest discoveries of modern science. Understanding God and spirituality requires that each and every one of us become a theologian and a scientist. We must put blind faith aside and use the intellect that God gave us to think for ourselves. The stakes are too high to leave this to others to do for us. It is time that we reclaimed the fields of science and theology for ourselves, for these are highly personal pursuits. We must stop letting institutions dictate to us what is real and what is not.

If you are still reading this book, there is a good chance that you are an independent thinker, an adventurer, perhaps even a courageous explorer. That is good, for you will need courage to follow me on this journey into forbidden science. You will need the courage to put aside your previously held convictions about science and religion and to consider that the universe may be much more complex and amazing than you have ever dared to dream. Or perhaps you are among the many who are already aware that reality is much more plastic than most people understand. Perhaps you are simply looking for explanations for the experiences you have had. If that is so, then you should be willing to learn the scientific basis for your experiences, even though you feel science is boring or over your head. If so, relax. Your guide is not a scientist nor a theologian by education. He is not a member of any institution which has a vested interest in maintaining the current consensus view of reality. He has no reputation as a scientist or as a theologian to protect. He is not worried about being published in scientific journals, receiving tenure, getting government grants or about what his colleagues will say about him. He is not worried about what his congregation or his church hierarchy thinks of him, for he has no church or congregation. Everything he learned, he learned on his own and by the grace of God, through independent research, by following his intuition and by making it his business to meet the right people, to attend the right conferences and to interview the real experts—the shamans of the scientific age.

CHAPTER 4   DISCOVERING THE NATURE OF REALITY

...There is evidence to suggest that our world and everything in it—from snowflakes to maple trees to falling stars and spinning electrons—are also only ghostly images, projections from a level of reality so beyond our own it is literally beyond both space and time.

—Michael Talbot, The Holographic Universe

Meeting a Mystical Man

Michael Talbot was a man for whom the nature of reality was very important. This was because the reality he lived in and understood was not the same as the one other people knew, nor was it the same as the one described in science class at school.

By the age of three, Michael had vivid memories of past lives, refusing to call his parents "mother" and "father," since he remembered other parents in a former existence. His family was amazed and amused at his habit of asking for strong, black tea and then sitting on the floor in the lotus position, sipping it like a wise, old man. Mysterious entities visited him in his room at night, and he encountered glowing balls of light hovering in his room. At age five, his father and a friend saw a UFO come down in the woods near his house in East Lansing, MI. Soon, a woman with long white hair and a long white gown came out of the woods and stood motionless in a nearby cornfield. Talbot described what happened next during an interview in 1992 on the Public Television program, *Thinking Allowed*. (Talbot died an untimely death at the age of 39 of leukemia, six months after the interview was aired.)

"The whole family got in the car and went to look. My father and his friend became very frightened...[but] when I looked at this being, I thought, 'Oh, it's her, it's the woman in white,' I had always called her the woman in white." It was the same being that had come to his room at the age of three. "My father wanted to get out of the car and go and talk to this being, but my mother said, 'No no no!' And finally, we watched her for about ten minutes and then drove off."

It was after this amazing event that the household began experiencing poltergeist activity—objects materializing out of thin air, flying across the room and strange thumping noises seeming to go up and down the stairs. So common were these experiences that often his family would simply ignore the mysterious events and continue with what they were doing at the time. In addition, Michael experienced psychic phenomena which included precognitive visions and out-of-body experiences (OBE).

Talbot's UFO experiences continued as he grew older. "As an adult, I had a period when I was in college where I was driving with a friend and we saw a UFO. We got out of our car, we were going from East Lansing, Michigan, to Sawgatuk, which I believe was something like a two hour drive.... We watched it for what we thought was about five minutes, and we made no other stops, but when we arrived at our destination, our friends said, 'Where have you been? You're hours late.' This is the first time we had looked at our watches and was the first time that we realized that we had this proverbial missing time." Although later in life he attempted to discover, through the use of hypnosis, what transpired during that episode of missing time, he was not able to recover the lost memories. "But I believe that I had an encounter with non-ordinary reality that, in this instance, we are labeling 'UFO,' but which I think is just the tip of the iceberg of something vaster." [1]

(Ultimately, Michael sought the acquaintance and counsel of famed UFO abductee, Whitley Strieber, author of the books, *Communion*[2] and *Transformation*,[3] in order to gain a better understanding of his own abduction experiences. Strieber devoted a chapter in his book,

---

1. Talbot, 1992.
2. Strieber, 1987.
3. Strieber, 1988.

Breakthrough,[4] to his close relationship with Talbot and to their joint efforts to understand and cope with the strange world of alien encounters.)

Today, Talbot's symptomology would be readily recognized by UFO researchers as that of the "abductee," but in the mid-1970s, when he began a quest to cope with his experiences, little was known about this traumatizing phenomenon, and there were few people to turn to for help. Many in the same situation have turned to religion or to alcohol and drugs to help deal with such otherworldly experiences, but Talbot turned to the world of science. A keen interest in science since early childhood transformed itself into a compulsive search for scientific explanations for his lifetime of paranormal experiences. Ultimately, he devoted much of his life to studying and writing about the cutting edges of science—those areas that stretch science to its limits and leave scientific minds bewildered.

His search for answers began in earnest while he was working on a graphic arts degree at Michigan State University in 1974. In his book, *Mysticism and the New Physics*, he describes the unorthodox way in which he began:

...I employed a technique that I have practiced often and with great success throughout my life. Instead of searching out the answer with the aid of my conscious mind, I began by first relying on my deeper and more intuitive abilities. To do this, I set off aimlessly through the labyrinth of book shelves. As I did so, I did not look at any of the titles but instead waited for a book to "call" me. Several minutes later and without any conscious intervention on my part, I felt a sudden compulsion to stop. Just as abruptly, my hand reached out and grabbed a volume off the shelf, seemingly opening it to a page at random. Only then did I look at the book. I discovered that I had taken down a bound set of *Physics Today* magazines and had opened it to a September 1970 article titled "Quantum Mechanics and Reality."[5]

The article by physicist Bryce S. DeWitt explained that quantum physics (the study of subatomic particles called "quanta" by physicists) discovered that reality is dependent on the human mind and

---

4. Strieber, 1995.
5. Talbot, 1981.

suggested that, at the subatomic level, the universe may be split into any number of parallel universes. The epiphany of that moment was to have profound consequences for the youthful Talbot.

> ...as I hungrily devoured the article, I discovered that quantum physics had come to many of the same conclusions about reality I had arrived at, only working from a completely different direction and based on an entirely different class of phenomena. Words cannot express the joy, even the familiarity, I experienced at encountering the strange and wonderful ideas offered by quantum physics.... [This knowledge] made me realize that others also had recognized that our current picture of reality was, in a sense, the emperor who has no clothes, but launched me on a passionate study of quantum physics....[6]

The Holographic Universe

Early in his research, Talbot began to realize that much of what he had been taught about science had simply been wrong. He learned that there was a well established body of knowledge which proved that the true nature of reality is far different than that described by the traditional scientific view of a "sticks and stones" universe in which time and space are inviolable absolutes. The universe Talbot discovered in his research was far less substantive and much more illusory than mainstream science would have us believe. He began to understand that the universe, instead of being like a machine, was more like a holographic image, and much more like the reality he had known all of his life. Ultimately, he would write three books on the holographic nature of reality as discovered by quantum physics: *Mysticism and the New Physics*,[7] *Beyond the Quantum*[8] and *The Holographic Universe*.[9]

In order to understand the basis for the holographic model of the universe, one must first understand the holographic image. Most people today have seen three-dimensional images called holographs, but few understand how they are created and the implications of their bizarre nature.

---

6. Talbot, 1981, pp. 137-138.
7. Talbot, 1981.
8. Talbot, 1988.
9. Talbot, 1991.

Holographic images that appear mysteriously in three-dimensional space, much like an apparition, are created with the use of a laser beam which is split into two separate light beams. (See Figure 2 on page 67.). One half of the beam is directed at the object to be photographed, through a diffusing lens and then onto the photographic film. The other half is directed to a series of mirrors, through another diffusing lens and onto the same piece of film. The resulting image on the film, unlike a typical photographic negative, bears no resemblance to the object photographed. All that can be seen are a series of overlapping concentric circles, like ripples in a pond caused by falling drops of rain. It is in this wave pattern that

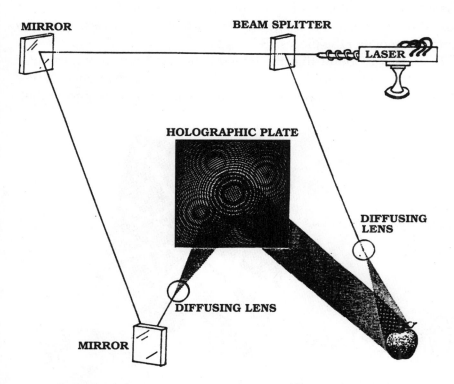

FIGURE 2. *A hologram is produced when a single laser light is split into two separate beams. The first beam is bounced off the object to be photographed, in this case an apple. Then the second beam is allowed to collide with the reflected light of the first, and the resulting interference pattern is recorded on film. ©1990, Michael Talbot. (Reprinted by permission of HarperCollins Publishers, Inc.)*

the image of the object is stored. But where exactly? No matter how hard we look at the pattern of circles, we cannot discern the image of the object. There is only one way to unlock the secret of the interfering wave pattern, and that is by directing a laser beam of the same frequency as the original one used in the recording process, onto the film. When this is done, a perfect, three-dimensional image of the object appears in thin air, on the other side of the film.

The incredible and mystical nature of this discovery earned a Nobel Prize in physics to its discoverer, Hungarian-born engineer, Dennis Gabor, in 1971. But the most incredible aspect of the holographic story is yet to come. For it was found that if you take a pair of scissors and cut the film into any number of pieces of any shape, the entire three-dimensional image can be reproduced by directing a laser beam at any one of the pieces. (See Figure 3.)

Thus, it was found that the image is not stored in any particular place on the photographic film, but rather everywhere at once! Never before had scientists been faced with the dilemma of having to explain

FIGURE 3. *Unlike normal photographs, every portion of a piece of holographic film contains all of the information of the whole. Thus if the holographic plate is broken into fragments, each piece can still be used to reconstruct the entire image. (©1990, Michael Talbot. Reprinted by permission of HarperCollins Publishers, Inc.)*

such an occurrence, and in the late 1940s when the first rudimentary holograms were discovered, it was simply considered one of those strange but inexplicable phenomena of nature to be filed away. Later, this principle came to be known as the principle of "nonlocality"—the condition in which location ceases to be relevant, and in which every portion of a whole is encoded with all the necessary information to replicate the whole. But ever since it was first discovered, scientists have been finding evidence that nonlocality exists throughout the universe and indeed is the basis for understanding the true nature of reality. Nowhere has this been more true than in the study of quantum physics.

Quantum Physics

In brief, here are some of the amazing findings of quantum physics that led to the startling conclusion that the universe is holographic:

Under certain conditions, subatomic particles communicate with each other over vast distances, instantaneously, like twins who feel each other's pain. When this was first verified in laboratories around the world, there was a great debate about its meaning. Physicists were frustrated because they knew that, according to Einstein's theory of relativity, nothing could travel faster than the speed of light, and "instantaneously" meant faster than the speed of light. It was physicist David Bohm who ultimately realized that what they were observing was the holographic principle of nonlocality. The information was not traveling through time and space from one location to another; the subatomic particles simply existed in a dimension that rendered time and space irrelevant and where information existed in all places at the same time. Quantum physics had discovered the world of the paranormal where such things as ESP and other psychic phenomena are routine!

The behavior of electrons is totally unpredictable. Unlike a bullet, a BB, or a ball shot through the air, an electron has no predictable trajectory. An electron shot at a pane of glass might penetrate the glass and continue on its course, or it may simply stop in front of the glass and reverse its course, as if to aggravate the scientists who are used to a predictable universe. Or, the electron may simply vanish in front of the glass, reappear on the other side and then continue. Or it may choose an infinite array of other trajectories to follow.

69

Quanta (subatomic particles) are shape shifters! They can appear in the form of a solid object, a particle, or a wave. Most troublesome for the physicists who discovered this fact was that the particles only appear as solid objects when they are being observed by the scientists! The mere act of looking at them causes them to change their behavior. This led Bohm to conclude that there is a direct connection between the minds of the scientists and the subatomic particles in their experiments. And, he further concluded, since everything is made of subatomic particles, including the brains of all living creatures, everything in the universe must be interconnected at the quantum level. If this is true, then the entire foundation of modern science—the belief in objectivity and scientific methodology—is simply an illusion.

This interconnectedness was also found among quanta in general. When grouped together in great quantities, just like a colony of ants, they cease to behave as individuals and begin to demonstrate a group consciousness. In fact, it soon became apparent that all subatomic particles in the universe are interconnected, forming one, giant, universal consciousness, an intelligence that directs the activity of the universe. To those with a philosophical bent, such a description comes very close to describing another, more ancient concept—the concept of God!

Scientists eventually stopped trying to distinguish between one electron and another because they are all identical. They are all encoded with the same information. Even speaking of them as separate is pointless. It became apparent that, at the quantum level, all points in space and time are the same. Nothing is separate from anything else. Bohm finally concluded that every subatomic particle may be encoded with all the information necessary to replicate the entire universe. Thus was born the holographic universe theory of reality.

Scientific Visionaries

As delighted as Talbot was with his discoveries, he was also greatly disturbed that mainstream science and the general public seemed so little aware of this other way of looking at reality. With the exception of a few courageous and prestigious scientists, most members of the scientific community were simply not willing or able to accept the conclusions and implications of the "new" physics. What's more, the startling implications for the nature of reality were simply not being conveyed to the general public. Most of the discussions about these amazing discoveries were taking place in obscure scientific journals and in highly technical physics textbooks. Very few people had ever heard of the leading proponent of the mystical nature of quantum research. Indeed, even today, the same could be said about the founding father of the holographic universe concept, Dr. David Bohm.

Bohm detailed the fantastic findings of quantum theory in a textbook he authored simply titled, *Quantum Theory*.[10] Formerly of Princeton University, Bohm spent the last years of his life as Emeritus Professor of Theoretical Physics at Birkbeck College, University of London. As a young man, he had been one of Albert Einstein's brightest and ablest protégés. In his classic textbook, Bohm calmly and in a scholarly fashion stated the difference between the "classical" physics and the quantum physics:

Classical concepts are characterized by three assumptions:

1. The world can be analyzed into distinct elements.

2. The state of each element can be described in terms of dynamical variables that are specifiable with arbitrarily high precision.

3. The interrelationship between parts of a system can be described with the aid of exact causal laws that define the changes of the above dynamical variables with time in terms of their initial values. The behavior of the systems as a whole can be regarded as the result of the interaction of all its parts.

It is a characteristic of the classical domain that within it exist objects, phenomena and events that are distinct and well defined and that exhibit reliable and reproducible properties with the aid of which they can be identified and compared.

It is this aspect of the world that is most readily described in terms of our own customary scientific language, in which the ideal is to express every concept in terms of well defined elements with well defined, logical relationships between them.[11]

(Rough translation: The universe is an orderly, predictable place, much like a machine. It can be broken down into its various parts and examined objectively, using scientific methodology and objectivity. By

---

10. Bohm, 1951.
11. Bohm, 1951, p. 264.

observing and labeling the various parts, and by understanding various physical laws, science can ultimately understand how the universe works.)

Bohm then proceeds to explain how the findings in quantum physics have totally discredited the aforementioned understanding of the nature of reality. The quantum properties of matter, on the other hand,

> ...clearly imply the indivisible unity of all interacting systems. Thus we have contradicted assumptions 1 and 2 of the classical theory, since there exists at the quantum level neither well defined elements nor well defined dynamical behavior of these elements. It is not surprising then, that assumption 3 is also not satisfied in the quantum theory, since exact causal laws would be meaningless in a context in which there were no precisely defined variables to which they could apply.[12]

Again, roughly translated, Bohm calmly states that the entire notion of objectivity and scientific method is inoperative at the quantum level! At the quantum level there is no such thing as separation between parts! At the quantum level, all things in the universe are one! In other words, the nature of reality as defined by Newton and Einstein, the reality we all know and love, is simply an illusion!

Needless to say, this paradigm-shattering conclusion, couched in scholarly language and cautiously tucked away in the concluding chapter of a graduate-level physics textbook, if true, changes everything regarding the validity of scientific thought and the consensus view of reality constructed over the past several hundred years! Yet, in the nearly half a century since it was written, scientific and educational institutions have continued, for the most part, as if quantum physics did not even exist. In fact, rather than accept the implications of subatomic laws and incorporate them into their own fields, most scientists continue to simply ignore these findings, preferring to believe that quantum reality applies only to electrons, photons, protons and the myriad of other subatomic particles so far discovered, rather than to human reality. This belief, an effort to cling to the existing paradigm at all costs, conveniently ignores the fact that subatomic particles, the smallest elements known to science, are the basic building blocks of all matter and permeate the entire universe.

---

12. Bohm, 1951, p. 264.

In addition, since Bohm's textbook was published in 1951, his conclusions about the true nature of reality have been substantiated over
and over again, not only in physics laboratories around the world, but
in practically every other field of science as well. Bohm's conclusions,
as well as those of other highly esteemed scientists in diverse fields,
have become the basis for what is known today as the holographic theory of the universe, a concept so elegant and all encompassing that it
opens up an entirely new vista for humankind of a multi-dimensional
universe which operates more like a living consciousness, rather than a
machine as previously believed.

As Michael Talbot put it:

> ...there is evidence to suggest that our world and every-
> thing in it—from snowflakes to maple trees to falling stars and
> spinning electrons—are also only ghostly images, projections
> from a level of reality so beyond our own it is literally beyond
> both space and time.[13]

Talbot gives equal credit for this amazing conclusion to two vision-
ary scientists who dared to go against the mainstream views of their
particular disciplines. The first, David Bohm, the brilliant theoretical
physicist whose acquaintance we have already made, and Dr. Karl Pribram, a neurophysiologist at Stanford University and author of the
classic textbook, *Languages of the Brain*.[14] Amazingly, but perhaps not
coincidentally, they both arrived at the same conclusion independently
while working in completely different scientific disciplines. However,
each man reached his conclusion through a similar process. Both were
dissatisfied with the fact that the standard theories in their fields were
unable to explain the phenomena they were encountering in their
research. When they applied the holographic principle of nonlocality
to their separate fields, each immediately recognized that the holographic model not only explained the mysteries in their own fields, but
also that it suddenly made sense of a wide range of phenomena that
had always been considered outside the realm of scientific understanding. It was at this moment that modern science rediscovered the
paranormal and began to understand that the realm of the mystical
and the spiritual might in fact not be the realm of the "unknowable."

13. Talbot, 1991, p. 1.
14. Pribram, 1977.

Pribram's pioneering work in brain research challenged the conventional view that the brain is organized like a file cabinet, with each memory stored in a cell or a group of cells, in a specific location in the brain. Scientists believed that if you could locate the memory, or "engram," you could erase it and excise it forever. But Pribram recognized that persons who suffered traumatic brain damage as a result of an accident did not forget half of a novel or part of the alphabet or some of their grandkids, but not others. Memory loss in such cases was more general. To test his theory, Pribram trained rats to run through a maze, then he systematically removed portions of the rats' brains, in order to determine in which area of the brain the memory was stored. What he found was that regardless of which section was removed, all the rats continued to be able to run the maze, even though their motor skills had been impaired. He concluded that the memory was not stored in any particular location in the brain, but everywhere at once. The only theory that applied to this finding was the holographic concept of nonlocality. In later experiments on how the brain processes images it receives through the eyes, he also found nonlocality at work. Pribram concludes that the brain operates through a system of interfering wave patterns, similar to those found on a holographic plate, thus, the brain is holographic.

Scientists in nearly every other field who have applied the knowledge that the universe is holographic have begun to realize that such previously elusive phenomena as telepathy, precognition, remote viewing, and even psychokinesis (the power of the mind to move objects) are now understandable, for the model implies that everything in the universe is interconnected, including the human mind, to everything else. In the years since this concept has been put forward, numerous progressive and reputable scientists have begun to apply it to an astonishing variety of previously unexplainable phenomena. Dr. Deepak Chopra, author of the book, *Ageless Body, Timeless Mind*,[15] uses it to explain the power of the mind to heal the body and retard the aging process. Psychologist, Dr. Kenneth Ring, author of *The Omega Project*,[16] uses it to explain the Near-Death Experience. Psychiatrist Stanislav Grof, author of *The Holotropic Mind*,[17] believes it can explain

15. Chopra, 1993.
16. Ring, 1992.

74

unusual phenomena experienced during altered states of consciousness. And physicist David Peat believes that synchronicities are evidence that our minds are intimately connected to the physical world.

Further evidence that all living things are structured on holographic principles came in 1953 when scientists James Watson and Francis Crick discovered the structure of DNA, the substance that transmits genetic information from one generation to the next. Today it is commonly accepted that each cell of every living thing contains the DNA code necessary to replicate the whole. Scientists have already been successful in using the process called "cloning" to create duplicate mice in a laboratory and much attention has been paid in the media to the ethical consequences of the probability that they may someday be able to do the same to humans. So, it should come as no surprise to conclude at this point that DNA is another example of the holographic nature of the universe and that you and I are living, walking, breathing examples of nonlocality, from the bottoms of our feet to the tops of our heads!

The Nature of Consciousness

Perhaps the greatest controversy surrounding the holographic model of reality exists in the debate over the location of consciousness in the brain. Already you will be able to see that the word "location" immediately makes a light bulb go on in your mind, for as we know, location is a tricky business in this amazing universe we live in. Mainstream science believes it has located consciousness within the brain in the area called the frontal lobe, located at the front of the brain, between the eyes. This, of course, coincidentally, is where Eastern mystics tell us our third, all-seeing eye is located, through which we may become aware of other dimensions. However, the nature of consciousness is now being seen by progressive scientific minds as a holograph. In other words, there is a growing body of scientific knowledge that is leading scientists to believe that consciousness is also nonlocal in nature—that it is not located in any particular part of the brain at all, but is everywhere at once.

17. Grof, 1992.

Talbot, whose lifetime of experiences with the paranormal gave him insights into the nature of consciousness, described how he discovered the nonlocal nature of the mind:

> At a young age, I had an out-of-body experience where I left my body and it became quite apparent to me while I was having this experience that I was thinking, but my brain was back in my body, which I could see in my bed. I knew it wasn't just a dream because I floated out over the ground outside my family's house and I saw a book lying on the ground and it was a book by the French, short-story writer, Guillermo Passont, and the next day a neighbor of mine said to me, "by the way, Michael, I lost a library book by Guillermo Passont, have you seen it?" ...It was really the first time I had to confront the difference between my spiritual beliefs that we can survive our bodily death and this deeply held scientific belief of mine that it's the brain that is doing the thinking.... I had a kind of epiphany where I realized that it's not the brain that's doing the thinking.[18]

If the brain is not doing the thinking, then where is it being done? If we don't need the brain to think, then what happens when the brain perishes? Is there some subtle energy field that cannot yet be measured or detected by science that simply attaches itself to all living things, giving them intelligence and animation, but which simply goes on its merry way when that living thing decays and dies? Is there any scientific evidence for the existence of such energy fields? The answer to these last two questions, is a resounding *yes!*

Such fields are called "morphogenic fields" and were first proposed in 1981 by biologist Rupert Sheldrake in his book, *A New Science of Life.*[19] Sheldrake offended and enraged mainstream science by suggesting that chance alone did not account for the development and organization of matter into the wide variety of plants and animals in the world. He proposed that an additional causal principle was necessary that did not rely on chance. That principle he called "formative causation" but he might as well have called it "universal intelligence." And he further stated that this intelligence operates through what he called "morphogenic fields," which he believed did not themselves

---

18. Talbot, 1992.
19. Sheldrake, 1981.

76

consist of energy or matter, but which exist in a dimension unaffected by time and space. In layman's terms, what Sheldrake was proposing was that intelligences from other dimensions are responsible for the organization of matter into plants and animals in our reality!

To illustrate how a morphogenic field works, we need only to examine carefully the example of the highly organized societies of the social insect—the ants, bees and termites. Biologists who have studied insect colonies have been mystified at the ability of the creatures to maintain highly organized societies, in which they utilize division of labor to construct intricate and architecturally-sound structures, housing sometimes millions of individuals. Among the more impressive structures of the insect world are the termite mounds of Africa, which, though they take on a variety of forms, all represent engineering marvels. Each one is constructed in such a way that it becomes a cooling tower, using intricate venting systems to air condition the interior so that the inside temperature remains within one degree of 30° C and carbon dioxide concentration is fixed at less than 3%. This not only keeps the insects perfectly comfortable in the blistering African heat, but also creates a perfect environment for growing the delicate fungus on which they exist. The architecture of the mound construction is elaborate and is accomplished by hundreds of thousands of individuals in a society that has no schools for architects or engineers, much less for soldiers and nursery attendants. How do they do it?

The common answer to this question is that they do it through instinct. But whose instinct? Is every worker conscious of the overall plan? No one believes this. Then who is in charge? Where are the blueprints? Perhaps these questions were answered many years ago, when French naturalist, Eugene Marais, in his book, *The Soul of the White Ant,*[20] concluded that the organization of the social insect is due to "a separate soul situated outside the individual termite." Marais reached this remarkable and holographic-like conclusion during years of observing ants and termites in the wilds of Africa. In one experiment, he dug a trench through the middle of a termite mound and then placed a large steel plate in the center, effectively dividing the mound in two, so that the insects on one side had no contact with the ones on the other. When he eventually removed the plate, he found that it had

---

20. Marais, 1971.

made no difference to the termites at all. The termites on either side had repaired the damage and when the plate was removed, both sides matched perfectly! "We cannot escape the ultimate conclusion," Marais said, "that somehow there exists a preconceived plan which the termites merely execute."[21]

In more recent times, many reputable scientists have begun to realize that the concept of a nonlocal, morphogenic field may also account for the experiences reported by thousands upon thousands of persons who claim to have had OBEs and NDEs. Led by Dr. Raymond Moody, author of *Life After Life*,[22] these researchers have documented volumes of cases which seem to indicate that human consciousness is not attached to the body at all and that it continues to think and reason independently of the body, even after the body is declared clinically dead.

Dr. Moody's many years as a practicing physician put him in a position to hear first-hand accounts of patients who had similar, mystical experiences while being officially dead. He was impressed with the emotional impact that the experience made on the patient and with the consistency of the details reported by people of all ages and from all over the world. Perhaps what impressed him the most were the cases in which the person experienced his spirit traveling to other Earthly locations, such as a waiting room where bereaved relatives were waiting during an operation. In such cases, the person was able to remember specific details of conversations that took place while he or she was on the operating-room table. Over the years, other scientists, such as Dr. Melvin Morse and Dr. Kenneth Ring have continued researching such cases and correlating the data, so that today there exists an impressive accumulation of evidence favoring the conclusion that consciousness exists in a timeless dimension, separate from the body, and continues to exist after death.

Another physician who, as a result of his professional practice, learned about the nonlocal nature of the human spirit was Dr. Brian Weiss, author of *Many Lives, Many Masters*.[23] Weiss was a mainstream psychiatrist who had reached the highest levels of respectability and

---

21. Watson, 1987, pp. 123-127.
22. Moody, 1976.
23. Weiss, 1988.

credibility within his profession. He graduated Phi Beta Kappa, magna cum laude from Columbia University in 1966 and subsequently completed medical school at Yale University School of Medicine. Ten years later he was serving as Chief of Psychiatry at Mt. Sinai Hospital in Miami and had published 37 scientific papers and book chapters in his field. His commitment to mainstream science and to traditional psychiatric methods and theories ran deep as did his concern for his reputation and his credibility. As he states in the introduction to his book, "Years of disciplined study had trained my mind to think as a scientist and physician, molding me along the narrow paths of conservatism in my profession. I distrusted anything that could not be proved by traditional scientific methods."

But then, he met a woman who came to him for therapy to overcome mental disorders. For eighteen months he tried using conventional psychotherapy to no avail. Finally, he resorted to hypnosis to help her recall childhood memories. But, in a series of trance states, his patient spontaneously recalled "past-life" memories that proved to be the cause of her symptoms. She also acted as a conduit or "channel" for information from highly evolved "spirit entities," who proceeded to reveal many of the secrets of life and death to him. In short order, the woman's symptoms disappeared and her therapy ceased, but Weiss was left with a shattered paradigm. "Nothing in my background had prepared me for this. I was absolutely amazed when these events unfolded."[24]

Weiss's transformative experience caused him to reevaluate everything he had ever been taught about the nature of science, reality and religion. Ultimately, he decided to actively pursue past-life therapy with his patients, due to the fact that the healing experience he had witnessed was so much more effective than anything he had ever seen before. But his activism proved costly. Upon the publication of his book, the hospital failed to renew his contract, proving once again that the mainstream scientific community punishes those who stray outside the carefully defined consensus views of reality to which it subscribes.

---

24. Weiss, 1988, p. 10.

The Nature of Time and Space

As early as the late 1920s, Albert Einstein was beginning to understand that time and space were not absolutes, but rather, were based on the concept of relativity. Together with his colleague, Nathan Rosen, he predicted that different points in the universe might be interconnected by timeless tunnels. These timeless tunnels, they theorized, were places in space that ripped through the fabric of reality known to humans and created passageways to other, unknown parts of the universe, other dimensions or even other universes that might exist parallel to ours. Today, it is commonly accepted by mainstream science that such timeless places exist. We know them by the name "black holes." Together, they constructed a simple diagram (See Figure 4.), called an Einstein-Rosen bridge to illustrate how a space traveler might conceivably use a timeless tunnel to traverse the universe or travel to another universe, instantaneously, by bypassing normal reality.[25]

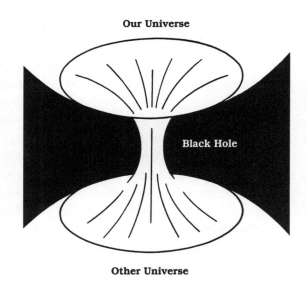

Our Universe

Black Hole

Other Universe

FIGURE 4. *How an Einstein-Rosen bridge might constitute a passage between our universe and a parallel one. (Time Travel, John Macvey, Scarborough House. Reprinted by permission of the publisher.)*

It is important here to point out that a belief in black holes is basically a belief in another, timeless dimension, for the center of a black hole is a place where time and space do not exist. This is precisely the kind of reality described by mystics, near-death experiencers, out-of-body experiencers and UFO abductees. Yet, few mainstream scientists are willing to connect Einstein's proposal to other mystical phenomena.

However, today theoretical physicists are seriously examining the possibility that this dimension might be used for space travel. In the 1980s, scientists at the California Institute of Technology seriously proposed that space may actually be riddled with miniature black holes, called "wormholes," that might be used for interstellar space travel. Using the concept first espoused by Einstein and Rosen, they concluded that if all points in space are connected at the quantum level, it should be possible to travel through a wormhole, instantaneously, to other locations in the universe. Contrary to what mainstream scientists say about the stars being too distant for humans to reach, they argue that the concept of nonlocality neatly negates the need to travel through space and time. Instead, there should be short cuts to anywhere in the universe, and it is just a matter of finding out how to use them.

Theoretical physicists are seriously examining the possibilities that space and time might simply be folded into themselves by means of localized, artificially created energy fields that essentially manufacture wormholes that can be directed to any location in the universe. Indeed, that seems to be exactly what one of Dr. John Mack's abductee patients seemed to be describing when, under hypnosis, he remembered being aboard an alien spacecraft. As reported in his book, *Abduction*, Dr. Mack asks his patient, "How do they get from one place to another?" The answer he gets from the alien beings: "Energy like folds into itself, inverts into the folds inside itself.... You can move one at a time or you can move vast numbers of people." [26] This rather awkward explanation sounds very much how a lay person would try to describe the complex concept of nonlocality as it applies to the manipulation of time/space.

25. Macvey, 1990, p. 45.
26. Mack, 1995, p. 224.

There is no doubt that quantum science and technology, based on the concept of nonlocality and the knowledge that the universe is holographic, is the science of our future. But is it possible that it is also the science of someone else's past? Most scientists today, even mainstream conservatives, will agree that the universe must be full of intelligent life and that there must be many civilizations more advanced than our own existing, even in our own galaxy. The argument scientists use to dissuade us that ETs have ever been here is that they are too far away from us to have ever traveled to our region of space. But in light of our understanding of the true nature of reality, that, we can now see, is a feeble and cowardly out. In truth, given the vastness of the universe, it is only logical to assume that highly advanced civilizations long ago discovered the interconnectedness of the universe, the holographic nature of reality, the nonlocal nature of the human soul and the secrets of time/space manipulation. Such entities have traveled the universe (and possibly through parallel universes) using quantum/spiritual technology for perhaps millions of years. Their relationship with the human race is an intimate one, even though few of us have the spiritual and scientific maturity to realize that truth. In ancient times, these beings were called "gods." In Judaeo-Christian theology, they are called "angels" or "demons." Today, we call them "aliens."

Section Two:

Toward A New Reality

CHAPTER 5 # CONSCIOUSNESS UNLEASHED

I found that my experiences shook me to the core of my being...all of the belief facade that structured my view of the world collapsed.... I had to reformulate my understanding of God and all religion.

—*Dr. Courtney Brown, associate professor of political science at Emory University, upon remote viewing extraterrestrials*

Surfing God's Internet

At the time of his death, Michael Talbot was working on a new book about the practical applications of the holographic universe concept. Although the work was incomplete and, hence, never published, it no doubt would have addressed the issue of remote viewing, for it is the controversy surrounding the nature of consciousness that lies at the heart of the holographic universe and of the UFO phenomenon.

For those who understand the holographic nature of the universe and are aware that consciousness is non-local, as is the entire universe, it should come as no surprise that the human mind has the capacity to focus its attention on and receive information from any given point in time/space, far beyond the reach of the five physical senses. In fact, such a conclusion is only logical, given what is known about the nature of reality as described by quantum physics. For most of us, this ability lies latent, possibly as a result of centuries of conditioning, and is apparent only occasionally in flashes of insight or through our dreams. In such cases, where we receive premonitions from unknown sources about significant events that are about to happen or have just occurred in some remote location, we tend to discount it as a mere coincidence or to describe it as "mere intuition." But there is nothing trivial about intuition, for it is the tip of a giant iceberg, being held down by our unwillingness to recognize it and nurture it.

It is this possibility, and its astonishing implications that caused the Soviet Union and eventually the U.S. intelligence community to begin serious experimentation into ESP more than a quarter of a century ago. It should also come as no great surprise to the reader to learn not only that these experiments were successful in providing intelligence agencies with an amazing array of useful information, but also that a scientific method or technique was discovered which can be used to train anyone to develop their latent psychic abilities. (It should be noted here that official Pentagon spokespersons have attempted to minimize the value of the project, even though those directly involved with it speak of its resounding success.)

Furthermore, there are those connected with this ultra-secret project who have spoken publicly about the unexpected discoveries and amazing implications of the program—the realization that Earth is being visited by extraterrestrials and that the human species may eventually have to develop its psychic abilities if it wishes to survive.

Scientific Remote Viewing

Much of what we know today about the military use of psychics and the development of a technique known as "scientific remote viewing" (SRV) became public in 1995 when a Congressional report, released as part of a CIA housecleaning effort, detailed a more than 20-year history of top secret experimentation with psychic and paranormal phenomena. Originally, it was the CIA that demonstrated an interest in the use of psychics to "remote view" intelligence targets with the hope that a psychic weapon could be developed to impair or kill America's enemies anywhere in the world. It was felt that if the Russians were doing it, then America could not be left behind. The race was on to develop the ultimate weapon: the Shaman Spy—a warrior who could infiltrate behind enemy lines, steal the enemy's secrets and, if necessary, kill—all from the comfort of his Langley, Virginia, office.

However, it was U.S. Army Intelligence, not the CIA, that ultimately carried out much of the research into psychic powers. When the Army realized that it had stumbled onto something important, it began providing remote viewing services to other agencies such as

Naval Intelligence, the Defense Intelligence Agency (DIA), the CIA and the National Security Agency (NSA). For years, the program, under the top secret code name, "Grill Frame," trained military officers and non-commissioned officers using techniques developed in the private sector at Princeton University's Princeton Engineering Anomalies Research (PEAR) laboratory and at the Remote Viewing Lab at SRI International (formerly the Stanford Research Institute), under the directorship of physicist Dr. Hal Puthoff. According to Sgt. Mel Riley, one of the first chosen for the program, among those recruited were those military personnel with known psychic abilities as well as some who had reported near-death experiences or UFO encounters.[1]

Spending more than $20 million over a 25-year period, the project used remote viewers to spy on Russian nuclear submarines, nuclear facilities, and missile silos, as well as to assist with strategic missions such as the Iranian hostage crisis and the effort to locate Libyan leader Muammar Qadhafi during the U.S. bombing of that country.

But, eventually, the program became a liability for the intelligence community, in part, according to Dr. Courtney Brown, author of *Cosmic Voyage*,[2] due to resistance from higher levels of command "aimed at preventing a focus on particular unwanted targets, such as UFOs." It seems that in the course of their remote viewing, the viewers became aware of an ET presence on this Earth and began, on their own, gathering data and information about ET activities under the guise of "advanced training." This training was conducted by Army major Ed Dames, who had become the protege of the chief psychic of the project, a New York artist by the name of Ingo Swann who was the first to develop a protocol or discipline for teaching others to remote view. His book, *Everybody's Guide to Natural ESP*,[3] was published in 1991.

Dames, in a TV documentary for the Discovery Channel's "Sky Watch" series, titled "Psi Files: The Real X Files," aired in August 1995, revealed for the first time just how far the program had gone. "I was mostly interested in such things as (remote viewing) the Arc of the Covenant and UFO activity," he said. His ex-wife, Christine, was also interviewed about the personal difficulties that the project created for

---

1. Schnabel, 1995.
2. Brown, 1996.
3. Swann, 1991.

the viewer's families who at times could not understand the personality changes undergone by the project members. "He became more and more obsessed with it (the program). He wanted to make a dent in the world and to change humankind.... He was mostly interested in the extraterrestrials, the ETs."[4]

Dames explained that after a while, viewing military targets for the intelligence community became boring and trite. He, and other members of the project realized that there were more important and exciting uses for their abilities. They realized that they could view anything they wished at any time in the past or future, but this was not what the military wanted.

Some of the military commanders objected to this activity, some on religious grounds, reports Dr. Brown. "The resistance extended beyond the military. Indeed, I was told of one instance in which a very high-ranking civilian political appointee serving directly under the Secretary of Defense began to object strenuously during a top secret briefing on the subject of UFOs when the matters of alien technology and psychic information were raised. The official asserted that this information was not supposed to be known by any humans until we died and learned it from heavenly sources." [5]

In addition, higher ups began getting nervous in the early 1980s when the program, then under the direction of Major General Edward Stubblebine, began experimenting with such things as psychokinesis, often having group spoon bending sessions (which according to a witness, resulted in the successful bending of metal utensils using only the power of the mind), and hiring tarot card readers, channelers and clairvoyants to give "readings" to Congressmen and top officials. Major Dames reported that "This was too much to bear for professional military officers." After the Oliver North scandal, Dames reports, the Pentagon began reviewing operations that could be potentially embarrassing, so they began to scale back the project and eventually shut it down. In 1995, the remnants of the program were transferred to the CIA, which terminated the project officially. But, unofficially, Dames reports, he and other viewers started their own private companies and have continued working for the intelligence

---

4. Schnabel, 1995.
5. Brown, p. 12.

community through a contractual arrangement. As former CIA chief Admiral Stansfield Turner said in the Discovery Channel documentary, "If I were still in charge, I would want to use every source of information available."

Interestingly, General Stubblebine, who earned the nickname, "spoon bender," for his involvement in the project, retired to Maine in 1985. His wife, a psychiatrist, claims to be a UFO abductee.

Incident at Cheyenne Mountain

That remote viewers had become aware of the UFO presence first became public information in 1990 when New York Times reporter and Pulitzer Prize nominee, Howard Blum published his book, *Out There: The Government's Secret Quest for Extraterrestrials*, an expose' about a U.S. government cover-up of UFO information. Blum reported that he had uncovered evidence that intelligence agencies, in the course of using psychics to locate and track Russian nuclear submarines, (a fact that has now been verified) discovered that mysterious, saucer-shaped objects were "seen" by the viewers (independently of one another) hovering above the subs.

Blum's book begins with an account of a UFO incident that occurred in 1986 deep within the bowels of Cheyenne Mountain outside of Colorado Springs at the NORAD facility known as the US Space Surveillance Center, where U.S., Soviet, Chinese and other nation's satellites and space junk are tracked around the clock and where a vigil is kept for signs of incoming enemy missiles. The incident triggered an immediate security alert and an eventual investigation into the UFO phenomenon.

On a cold December evening of that year, the sophisticated electronic monitoring system that tracks objects as far away as 15,000 miles in space, was tripped in the sky above Lake Kickapoo, Texas. But although NORAD personnel monitor more than 7000 known space objects, and it is nearly impossible for any country on Earth to sneak a new object into Earth orbit, they were not able to identify or categorize what appeared on their screens that night. Blum reports:

> It wasn't just that the bogey first targeted by the Lake Kickapoo transmitter didn't fit into any of the usual categories, there was also the problem of its orbital characteristics—they didn't resemble any known operational pattern.... The object

was going through a series of complex maneuvers and rapid changes of inclination at speeds and altitudes that were— impossible.[6]

But just as suddenly as the strange object had appeared on NORAD screens, it disappeared and all efforts to pick up its track were to no avail. A world-wide network of high-tech detection equipment was activated to find the object, but it was gone. The only evidence of its existence was the computer printouts generated that night. Ultimately, a classified report stating that an Unidentified Flying Object had penetrated US airspace and performed maneuvers that seemed technologically impossible was sent to the Pentagon and eventually, a brief report made its way to then President Ronald Reagan as part of the President's Daily Brief.

President Reagan looked up from the page and, without a trace of humor, announced that he, too, had once seen a UFO. He had been riding in a plane during his campaign for the governorship of California, and there, right outside his window, was a flying saucer. "We should follow up on this," the President said thoughtfully. Still, when no one in the room did any more than nod sagaciously, he let the matter drop.[7]

However, when the report made its way to the Pentagon's office of the Defense Intelligence Agency's Directorate for Management Operations, an obscure Army Colonel, who himself had once had a UFO experience, decided to try an experiment. He decided to take the coordinates and the time information to the top secret, remote viewers within the DIA, known as Project *Aquarius*, to see what could be learned.

Armed with the precise information needed for the remote viewing experiment, Colonel Harold E. Phillips of the DIA instructed the remote viewers to scan for anything unusual at that location during the time of the incident, 48 hours previously, and to draw what they saw. Each viewer was placed in a separate isolation chamber before given the instructions. At the conclusion of the experiment, all three submitted their sketches. "They were all crude, largely geometric pencil drawings. Each was obviously the work of a different artist, but all

---

6. Blum, 1990, p. 30.
7. Blum, 1990, p. 32.

were quite similar. They were all rounded, wingless aircraft." With this evidence, Blum reports, "the DIA was persuaded the time had come to convene a top-secret working group to investigate the possibility that extraterrestrials were making contact with this planet...."

Interestingly, the DIA's entry into remote viewing started only the year before as the result of another incident involving UFOs. The initial meeting that started Project *Aquarius* was conducted right next door to the White House in the old Executive Office Building in the fall of 1985 in the office of George Keyworth, President Reagan's Science Adviser. The meeting, as reported by Blum, was conducted by two scientists from the Stanford Research Institute (SRI). It consisted of a demonstration in which a psychic was asked to focus his attention on specific longitudinal and latitudinal information and asking him to see what was there. The answer to the first part of the test, which was correct, was a mansion. As it turns out, it belonged to Mikhail Gorbachev.

The next phase of the demonstration was conducted by a Naval Commander, presumably from the Office of Naval Intelligence. He showed the psychic a group of about six photographs of Russian and American submarines, some armed with nuclear warheads, and asked the viewer to give him the whereabouts of each of the subs by stating the specific coordinates of each site. The Commander had in his briefcase a list of the current actual locations of each craft.

The viewer then went into a trance, "his head gently bobbing up and down." Then he began announcing the locations of the ships: off the coast of South Carolina, off the northern coast of Iceland, etc. But when he got to the photograph of a Soviet delta class submarine, he stumbled, "his face suddenly became twisted with the surprised look of someone who had just encountered a small, but unexpected trouble in his path.... His trance broke...and he was clearly uncomfortable. No, one of the witnesses decided: he was scared. 'What is it?' he was asked. The viewer explained that he had seen something else at the same coordinates, which were off the coast of Nova Scotia. It was hovering above the submarine." The scientist asked the viewer to draw what he saw. Blum reports that it was the drawing of a "wingless aircraft. To many in the room the drawing was quite familiar. 'A rocket?' the scientist prodded. Then finally he blurted out, what was on the minds of nearly everyone in the room: 'You're not going to tell me it's a flying saucer.' 'Yes,' said the viewer, 'that's it exactly.'"[8]

Viewing the ETs

One of the inevitable results of the declassification of the remote viewing project and the release of the capabilities of SRV to the general public was that civilians would eventually begin to make use of SRV for non-military projects. (No doubt to the chagrin of the Pentagon.) According to former project members, this has already begun to occur in the form of corporate spying and data gathering. Former military remote viewers are now for hire by anyone willing to pay for their services and formal training in out-of-body states may be obtained for a fee from the Monroe Institute in Virginia.

One who has availed himself of these courses and services is Dr. Courtney Brown, an associate professor of political science at Emory University in Atlanta, Georgia, who specializes in nonlinear mathematical modeling of social phenomena. He has held the Charles Grove Haines Professorship at UCLA and was a Hewlett Fellow at the Carter Presidential Center. He is the author of three books on political and social issues and enjoys a fine reputation as a scholar and as a social scientist. His interest in remote viewing as a means of studying extraterrestrial societies came when he met one of the military remote viewer trainers at a conference and ultimately convinced him to be his mentor. Subsequently, Brown received the same training given to military remote viewers and, using his training, set out to investigate alien civilizations.

However, since his book's publication, some former members of the military remote viewing community have claimed that Brown went too far and violated the strict protocol of the military project by conducting portions of his research alone, without the guidance of a trained monitor. Some feel that remote viewing performed in this manner is simply not reliable. On the other hand, it could be argued that Pentagon insiders are seeking to discredit Brown because his book strikes too close to the truth. In any case, if the general public is ever to know what the military remote viewers found when they viewed UFOs, Brown's book, *Cosmic Voyage*, may be as close as they can get. Perhaps Dames or others will eventually publish their own findings, or better yet, other independent scientists may attempt to replicate Brown's work, thereby validating or repudiating his findings. This, by

8. Blum, 1990, pp. 33-38.

the way, is what Brown invites others to do. He claims that, when the discipline of SRV is followed strictly, the results are nearly 100% accurate and can be authenticated by anyone who is likewise trained:

> I am not asking anyone to believe what I write in this book.... As with all scientific investigations, this one is independently replicable by anyone trained in the protocols of SRV. Thus, other researchers can corroborate everything that I report here.[9]

One thing is sure—Dr. Brown, even though he was proficient at transcendental meditation before his training began and was open to the idea that extraterrestrial civilizations existed, was in no way prepared for what he would encounter as a remote viewer. He was not prepared to be transformed so completely and so quickly. He was not prepared to have his reality shattered and his world turned upside down:

> I found that my experiences shook me to the core of my being. In only two years, all of the belief facade that structured my view of the world collapsed. I learned that we were not alone in the universe, and that nonphysical beings shared this dimensional reality with me. I learned that ET civilizations rose and fell in my own planetary neighborhood, and that some traveled through time with the ease with which I walk across the street. I had to reformulate my understanding of God and all religion. It is impossible to relate to you how much I had to adapt and grow in order to confront the realities that were opening to me.[10]

What caused Brown's sudden and complete transformation was the absolute certain knowledge that extraterrestrials not only exist in the universe, but they are already here and have been interacting with human society for a very long time:

> ...[this book] describes the history of two alien worlds that died, and how the civilization of each survived beyond its home world's death to arrive here, on Earth. These survivors have needs, desperate needs. But as it turns out, so do we humans, and this galactic tryst is leading to a future in which three races share a common destiny. The great link connecting

---

9. Brown, 1996, p. 19.
10. Brown, 1996, p. 250.

the three races is that all three home worlds either already experienced, or will soon experience, planet-wide ecological disasters of spectacular proportions. Indeed, it is from these other two races that humans will learn much regarding how others have survived on planets of dust.[11]

Brown claims that he and other remote viewers have discovered many extraterrestrial societies as well as an entirely distinct realm which he calls "subspace," populated by spirit beings, including humans and ETs who no longer exist in the physical dimension. (Additionally, he claims that those trained in SRV not only can view these beings, but also can communicate with them.) But because of the particularly important role they play in the development of Earth's civilization, he chose to focus on two of these races. One of these ET civilizations is that of the "Greys" who are well known to UFO researchers and abductees. Another is an ancient civilization that "flourished on Mars during the time that dinosaurs roamed the Earth." These Martians live in underground bases on Mars and to a limited extent, here on Earth

The Martians

While remote viewing Mars, specifically those enigmatic structures in the Cydonia region of the planet's surface that look like pyramids and a sphinx, remote viewers discovered an underground civilization that has existed there for millions of years. According to Brown, this race of extraterrestrials thrived millions of years ago, but nearly became extinct when a large asteroid, passing through Mar's atmosphere, did irreparable damage. Gradually, the planet's atmosphere was sucked out into space and the planet's surface became uninhabitable. It was then that the Greys came to the rescue. They "stored" the Martians to preserve their genetic material, and they genetically altered them to aid in their survival. The Martians were recently "reactivated" and installed in underground facilities both on Mars and on Earth. But the genetic alterations were not perfect, and the species is in dire straights. They desperately need genetic help if they are going to survive. Additionally, their technology, although more advanced than

---

11. Brown, 1996, p. 1.

94

human technology, does not give them many options. Their only place of refuge is Earth.

Brown describes them as similar to humans, but "like they are a different race." They are light skinned beings with humanoid faces. They have no hair and their eyes are larger than humans.[12]

The Greys

Brown's viewing of the Greys led him to conclude that they are also in need of genetic help. When asked by his monitor to focus on their sense of purpose, Brown responded, "Survival is primary, and evolution. It [the Grey society] is one collective organism, and survival is paramount.... I get the sense they need to get out of their physical bodies.... There is near panic...the Greys are working with humans and others for a collective escape. It's like getting...off a sinking ship." His sense was that the Greys have reached an evolutionary dead end and must change if they are going to progress. They have lost their emotions and their individuality. "They are preparing to leave the collective identity and become linked individuals instead.... They need help. They are stuck."

Brown discovered that the genetic engineering program that involves the creation of a new hybrid species is an effort on their part to evolve away from what they have become. "It is easy to see how the activities (abductions) and intentions of the Greys could be misunderstood as hostile from a human perspective...they may do things to us that we do not understand or like, but they are not evil—of this I am now certain...they need us, spiritually as well as physically. And lest we judge too quickly, we may need them for our own evolutionary survival just as dearly." He has also seen the Grey's involvement in a program to help the human race survive. He saw a distant planet, with two suns that is being made ready for human occupation. "They are getting a class M planet ready while waiting for humans to self destruct." When asked by his monitor to see what else is being transplanted, Brown responded: "Genetic material is dominant. They need as wide a selection as possible of genetic material to ensure the survivability of a better, more advanced gene pool.

Monitor: Cue in on the needed genetic changes.

---

12. Brown, 1996, pp. 63-75.

CB: There needs to be a better connection between spirit and body. The current genes downplay this...new or modified genes are needed for growth and survival....

Brown's understanding is that the Greys are working on a project to create a new breed of humans that does not have our "current destructive tendencies, which are driving the global population in the direction of planetary-wide ecological and climatic disasters.... It seems some humans will be 'space lifted' to a safe haven" in the near future.

Nonphysical Entities

Perhaps the most controversial aspects of Brown's book are those dealing with his viewing of nonphysical entities, "subspace" life forms, the spirits of the deceased and the spirits of famous people such as Buddha and Jesus Christ. Perhaps it is in these areas that Brown and his mentor had a parting of ways. In any case, Brown's research complements quite nicely the work of many UFO researchers who have found themselves confronted with data dealing with such things as past-life memories, out-of-body experiences and discarnate entities.

Brown claims that the military remote viewers also discovered and investigated certain nonphysical targets, one of which they learned about from a controversial book, long known in UFO circles, called *The Urantia Book*. This work is a voluminous tome of channeled information purporting to tell the true story of human origins and describing the complex hierarchy of extraterrestrial and nonphysical life forms inhabiting the universe. The book describes a particular type of subspace (nonphysical) beings known as the "Midwayers" who are assigned to Earth to assist in matters dealing with human evolutionary potential. These highly advanced beings, who work with souls, are not extraterrestrial because they are permanently based here on Earth, coexisting alongside humankind in a nonphysical dimension.

Brown also tells of making contact with a nonphysical group of beings known as the Galactic Federation which serves as a kind of political body or "United Nations" of many species in the galaxy. This organization, headed by Buddha, works toward the betterment of all species, aiding them in spiritual and physical evolution.

When asked by his monitor to remote view Jesus, Brown at first was shown a scene in which a new science building was under construction at his home campus of Emory University. The facility's purpose was to house a project that would study environmental problems. He was shown that the scientists would not be able to solve the world's ecological disasters with physical science. Then he began to perceive a being. He perceived Jesus as a light being, "somewhat transluscent…his hair seems to be made of light…this being seems to be telling me that the situation [for the human race] has been set up so that no physical solution can remedy the problem. The idea is to force humans out of their physical entrapment, and thereby save the race…. I then asked if humans should view the Greys and Martians with compassion. The answer was 'Yes.' This is the idea of helping others. Without this, no one goes forward. There must be no limits to the human desire to help…. Prejudice—racial, species or otherwise—simply cannot co-exist with the higher evolutionary forms."[13]

Future of the Human Race

Like other UFO researchers and abductees, some remote viewers have begun to realize that at the core of the UFO phenomenon lie the issues of spirituality, human evolution and survival. They discovered that the ecological problems faced by the human race are far greater than scientists today are willing to admit. In fact, it may be too late for humankind to reverse the effects of the environmental pollution that has already taken place. As a result, a concerted effort is being made by both extraterrestrials and nonphysical entities to awaken the human race to its spiritual connections and to attempt to preserve the genetic material of planet Earth for use at a future time.

"I am being told," Brown said, "that there will be a movement off the planet in the future for humans…. Earth humans are violent and troublesome currently…. Humans need to undergo some sort of change before extending far off the planet…there will definitely be a planetary disaster, or perhaps I should say, disasters. There will be political chaos, turbulence, an unraveling of the current political order…consciousness must become the focal concern of humans in order for us to proceed. Widespread enhancement in human understanding of consciousness is a necessary precursor to human participation in galactic life."

---

13. Brown, 1996, pp. 121-128.

It must be made clear here that this is not an endorsement of Dr. Brown's research *per se*—his research will have to stand the test of time. It is quite possible, as some claim, that his work is tainted by a lack of strict adherence to rigid scientific methodology. If so, future researchers will either support or deny the claims made by Brown and a new understanding will be gained. However, much of what Brown claims to have received through remote viewing makes sense and complements the information coming from abduction research and, therefore, bears consideration.

As the reader will see in later chapters, his depressing forecast for the human race and his description of ET activities are consistent with information being received by the abductees. But whereas Brown's research gives us the big picture, perhaps varnished by his own perceptions and beliefs, abduction research gives us insight, from many viewpoints, into the complexity of the activity and interaction taking place between humans and a variety of alien species, some of which have not yet been mentioned by remote viewers. It may be that future remote viewers will arrive at different conclusions or be given contradictory information, but at this point, Dr. Brown's contribution to our understanding of the UFO phenomenon appears to be a breakthrough not only in UFO research, but for the entire future of the human race.

CHAPTER 6

THE SCIENCE OF THE SPIRIT

As the human race moves into adolescence and adulthood, it can no longer afford to guide its affairs via those simple myths. Our human ancestors thought long and hard on who and what they were and came up with the best explanations they could make. The frightening thing is that we—almost at the end of the 20th century—are still hanging on to the those explanations, which date back to our Stone Age. I think we need a more fruitful way to analyze these questions. We need exciting philosophical thought.

—Gene Roddenberry, creator of "Star Trek"

Who or What is God?

Science today, and quantum physics in particular, has reached the edge of a bottomless chasm, beyond which lies the realm of the mystical, the spiritual—the "unknowable." In order to progress beyond this point, humankind must first learn that science and spirituality are not separate fields of study, but, in fact, are one in the same. When this is understood, we will see clearly that the next frontier of science is not in outer space, nor is it to be found at the end of a microscope. Science's uncharted New World, waiting to be explored, is the vastness of the world within ourselves—the mystical dimension of the human spirit and of the hierarchy of higher life forms that exist at levels beyond our current understanding, but to whom we are intimately connected.

If science can help us understand the true nature of God, it is through the bizarre new world, discovered by physicists as they probed deeper and deeper into the reality they understood, only to find that, like Alice in Wonderland, they had passed through the looking glass and entered the world of the Mad Hatter and the talking tea pot. Knowing that the universe and everything in it is all "one" at a more basic level of reality reveals to us clues about the true nature of

God, which we can now see is like a vast intelligence or consciousness that exists in a timeless and spaceless dimension, but whose thoughts are capable of organizing matter that manifests itself in the dimension of the physical world. This understanding is far different from the one taught in the Judeo/Christian world, where we have been led to believe that God is a being, pictured in religious mythology as an old, wise man with a long, white beard who looks down upon us and decides who is to be rewarded and who is to be punished.

When we see God from a scientific perspective, without the emotional baggage that comes with the religious teachings of our childhood, we can begin to deal with this difficult concept intellectually, rather than emotionally. We can understand that this prime creative force of the universe is too vast to think of as an individual, a father-like figure, residing in the clouds above and occasionally taking human form to walk among his children. We can begin to understand that the personification of God as an individual does not give credit to the vastness of our universe, but is an oversimplification used by humans to conceptualize the unfathomable. The personification of the gods is a tradition as ancient as the history of humankind, as we can easily deduce through the study of Sumerian, Egyptian and other ancient religions. But the personification of the Judeo-Christian God evolved during a time when it was believed that the universe revolved around the Earth and that, as a result, humankind was the center of God's attention. After all, it was reasoned, if the Earth was the center of the universe, humanity must be extraordinarily important—so important that the heavenly Father must have taken special interest in our creation and our welfare. Over the centuries this father image, promoted by Western religions for the purpose of simplifying the concept of God for the illiterate masses, was humanized and took on the characteristics of a concerned parent, sometimes showing wrath and seeking vengeance, other times showing love and mercy. But never could it be explained with any great satisfaction how such a perfect and omnipotent God could have possibly erred so horribly when he made, in his own image, the miserable, sinful creature known as man.

Today, we know not only that the Earth is not the center of the universe, but that it isn't even near the center of even its own galaxy! Like the country bumpkin who went to the city for the first time and realized how big the world really was, humankind has slowly come to the realization that we exist on a lonely speck of sand which revolves around an average-sized star on the outskirts of an unexceptional galaxy, which is one of approximately 50 billion galaxies in the known universe. Today we know that among the billions of galaxies, there are many which are much larger and much more spectacular than our own, and we are beginning to suspect that the universe itself may simply be one of an infinite number of universes in a creation so vast that it humbles even the greatest of egos. But whereas our scientific understanding of our lowly place in the universe has served to mature and humble even the greatest of our scientific thinkers over the last 500 years, our notion of God seems to be frozen in some kind of spiritual adolescence. Western religions continue to preach the notion of a heavenly father-like figure who punishes our sins and condemns us to hell or welcomes us to heaven if we have been good.

Understanding the Negative Forces

Quantum physics has shown us that the true nature of this creative force we call God is one of balance. Every electron, photon, proton, quark, etc., in the universe has been found to be made up of both a positive and a negative charge. Physicist Richard Morris, in his book on quantum physics, The Edges of Science,[1] explains that all matter is electrically neutral: "There are as many negatively charged particles in the universe as particles with positive forces."[2]

These two parts are so intimately connected that physicists, long ago, stopped referring to "positive electrons" and "negative electrons," because it was simply easier to use the term "electron," assuming everyone understood the positive and negative characteristics of each particle. In fact, when physicists have attempted to separate the positive and negative charges of quanta, they have failed. In such cases, scientists find that when they pull the particle apart, they end up with two identical particles (like twins), each having both positive and negative charges. (See Figure 5 on page 102.)

Morris describes the discovery of this mysterious force (we can now recognize as an example of nonlocality) during an experiment involving those particles known as quarks:

---

1. Morris, 1990.
2. Morris, 1990, p. 21.

The reason that free quarks are not seen seems to be that the attractive force between quarks is very weak when the quarks are close together, but that it rapidly becomes very strong when the quarks are pulled apart.... [This force] behaves in a manner very unlike that of such familiar forces as magnetism or gravity.[3]

He compares such a force to a spring which exerts no force while it is at rest, but exerts considerable force when it is pulled apart. However, unlike a spring which would eventually break into two separate pieces, "...if the spring behaved like a pair of quarks in every respect...you would find yourself holding a pair of springs, each of them like the original one that you had been attempting to pull apart."[4]

What this implies is that the balance between positive and negative is an essential ingredient at all levels of reality, and without it, the universe would simply not exist. It is easy to see at the quantum level that the Creator gave equal importance to the positive and the negative forces it created. In fact, so equally weighted are the two that they create a paradox, in that positive and negative become one in the same. They are simply two faces of the same coin. If we look, we will find other examples of the paradoxical nature of the universe. For

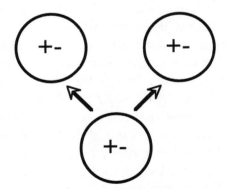

FIGURE 5. *Subatomic particles each have a positive and a negative charge. When scientists have succeeded in dividing them, the result has been two identical particles (like twins), each with its own positive and negative charges. This is another example of nonlocality.*

3. Morris, 1990, p. 16.
4. Morris, 1990, pp. 15-16.

example, light and darkness are both equal and totally bound together. Both are essential for life to exist and, without one, we could not recognize or appreciate the other. In other words, God is neutral, for he created a universe that loves both the negative and the positive forces equally! It is this balance between opposing forces that produces a dynamic and ever-evolving universe. Opposing forces are dynamic in that from their interaction emerges change. Evolution requires environmental change so that adaptation may occur. Male and female (opposites) must join together and interact for new life to be born. Even great cataclysms, like the one that destroyed the dinosaurs, helped the evolutionary process by creating conditions in which mammals, and ultimately humans, could flourish.

It is time for humankind to grow up and stop believing in Santa Claus. It is time for us to adopt a more mature understanding of the creative force of the universe and to realize that negativity is part of God's creation, and as such deserves our love and respect as well. Negativity should be understood and respected, not feared, as we have been taught by the churches of the world. If we look at an electron and see that it has both a positive and a negative charge, we do not think of the negative charge as being evil because we are viewing it from a perspective of great distance. The negative charge seems too small to be a threat to us. When we see a wolf pounce on a bunny and devour it, we may be disturbed by the cruelty of nature, but as adults, we understand that the wolf is merely trying to survive and is not really evil. If while studying science, we discover that most of the living things on this Earth were killed during the time of mass extinction that eradicated the dinosaur, we marvel at nature's power, but we don't condemn God for his cruelty. This is because we have the perspective of many hundreds of millions of years between us and those events. Yet, if an earthquake in China, or a hurricane in Florida or a drought in Africa takes hundreds, maybe thousands, of human lives, many question the existence of a heavenly father. It is harder to keep our perspective in events that strike closer to home. And if a car accident or cancer or a brutal murder takes a loved one from us, our faith in God is often shattered and we begin to deny the existence of God. Many who maintain their faith in such a situation wonder what they did to deserve such a punishment from a wrathful heavenly Father.

Eastern Philosophy and the Law of Karma

In the Judaeo/Christian view of the nature of God, negativity is feared rather than accepted as a natural force that keeps the universe in balance. In Western religions, the negative forces of the universe are personified (simplified) by an entity known as Satan, who, we are taught, should be feared and loathed. Satan is believed to have domain over a place called "hell" where bad people go when they die. This place is so bad that no sane person would ever wish to go there, for there is no escape. It is by teaching people to fear the devil, to fear hell and even to fear God that churches and governments of earlier times sought to control the masses and thereby create an orderly society. (I must interject here that it doesn't appear to have worked very well!) This, together with the adoption in Western culture of a mechanistic view of life in which all life forms are reduced to soulless, biological machines, has resulted in societies in which many people have lost their connection to the spiritual world. Many who would like to deny the mechanistic view simply refuse to accept a view of God that requires them to live in a state of constant fear and guilt.

On the other hand, Eastern religions and philosophy teach a much different view—one that is amazingly similar to the lessons we learn from quantum physics. This view, founded in Vedic philosophy, teaches a soul-based model of reality characterized by a "oneness" of all matter, in which everything in the universe is interconnected like a richly woven tapestry of life or a vast ocean where every wave, eddy or ripple eventually is felt throughout the entire sea. In such a universe, where nothing is separate, what an individual does to others or to the world around him, comes back to him eventually, either in his present life or in one of his many succeeding lifetimes. This is known as the concept of Karma. In such a universe, doing harm to others or to nature is the same as doing harm to oneself, and there is ultimately a price to pay. On the other hand, acts of love, mercy and kindness ripple through the fabric of reality until they, in turn, are felt by the originator of the act. Eastern philosophy realizes that the physical world is but an illusion, called "Maya," and it is said that what we call reality is simply God's dream. This is merely another way of saying that matter is organized in this dimension by an intelligent force from another dimension, as is stated in the scientific concept we previously learned about called "formative causation" by Sheldrake. Sheldrake's discovery gives credence to the many gifted shamans of the East who describe the Earth as a school for souls. They see the Earthly plane as a place where eternal, spiritual beings (you and me) incarnate into the flesh for brief periods in order to gain spiritual growth, as part of a long process of spiritual evolution. This process of incarnation, death, processing what was learned, planning the next life (with the aid of higher life forms) and rebirth continues until the soul has learned the lesson of life and is ready to progress beyond the physical world. And what is the lesson of life? It is love. Unconditional love of all of God's creation—the same kind of love it takes for God to create, love and respect both the positive and negative forces of the universe equally. Such love is hard to come by, for it is the nature of the physical being to see the world around him as being separate from himself and to lose the perspective of the Creator. It is the nature of the physical being to indulge in unnecessary fear of the negative forces and to cling to and worship the positive.

According to Eastern philosophy, each time the soul incarnates into the flesh, it loses its memories of previous lives and of who it really is. But there is an important purpose for this. If life is to be an effective school, and if we are to have an opportunity to exercise free will and learn from our experiences, those memories must remain hidden. If we remembered why we came to Earth, then the opportunity to benefit from our mistakes would be lost. In this view of reality, the term "immortality" means arriving at a level of achievement at which the soul, no longer needing to incarnate, is free to remain in the non-physical dimension and retain all his previous memories. Such a soul, should it choose to reincarnate again, would retain his memories and would appear to the rest of us as a remarkable, God-like being. In Eastern teachings, there have been numerous such Masters throughout the centuries sent to teach humankind and help to set him on the proper course.

This way of understanding spirituality allows us to put good and evil into proper perspective—and perspective is everything in dealing with this difficult concept. Negative events, rather than being punishment from God for our sins, are simply opportunities to learn and to gain spiritual growth. Instead of being condemned to hell for our mistakes upon our death, higher beings help us to see where we went wrong and help us to continue on the correct path of spiritual evolution. (To be sure, there are also higher beings whose main goal is to lead us in the wrong direction! But, according to spiritual law, even they must be treated with love and mercy.)

A Scientist Discovers Spiritual Laws

Those who do negative things to their fellow humans or to other living things, including the Earth, must continue the process of reincarnation, placing themselves in lifetimes and developing scenarios in which they can atone for their wrongdoing and thereby gain spiritual growth. For example, Dr. Brian Weiss, in his book about past-life regression therapy, *Through Time, Into Healing*, describes a case in which a man with a shriveled arm came to him for counseling, unrelated to the condition of his arm. Under hypnosis, the man remembered that in a past life he had been a pick-pocket and that he had chosen to have a shriveled arm in this life, as a means of atonement. Although not all of his clients' past-life memories deal with the issue of atonement, Dr. Weiss has detected a pattern in which spiritual growth is attained through a series of life experiences.

Early on in his work, Weiss began to understand that he was learning about spiritual laws. In his very first case of past-life regression, one of his patients, while in a hypnotic trance, was able to remember the times between lives in which she, with the aid of spiritual beings she called the "Masters," reviewed the mistakes and successes of her past life and made plans for her next. These beings eventually communicated directly to Weiss and informed him that the purpose of his patient's visits to him was for his spiritual enlightenment. During the course of exploring past lives with his patient, she recalled a past death in which her soul was taken up into a beautiful light. "Suddenly she spoke, but not in the slow whisper she had always used previously. Her voice was now husky and loud, without hesitation." The voice began explaining the rules of spiritual evolution:

> Our task is to learn, to become God-like through knowledge…. By knowledge we approach God, and then we can rest. Then we come back to help others.[5]

5. Weiss, 1988, p. 46.

After the masters revealed to him, through his patient, information about himself and confidential information about his family, Weiss was stunned. "This unsophisticated laboratory technician was a conduit for transcendental knowledge. And if she could reveal these truths, what else was there? I needed to know more."[6] Gradually, the lessons became more advanced:

> There are seven planes in all...each one consisting of many levels.... On [one] you are allowed to see your life that has just passed.... We have debts that must be paid.... You progress by paying your debts.... With each life that you go through and you did not fulfill these debts, the next one will be harder...you choose what life you will have.[7]

Weiss was stunned by such revelations, coming from a Christian woman who had no belief in Eastern philosophy or in reincarnation. He became convinced that the information he was receiving was from a higher spiritual level, rather than from her subconscious mind:

> I was acquiring a systematic body of spiritual knowledge. This knowledge spoke of love and hope, faith and charity. It examined virtues and vices, debts owed to others and to one's self. It included past lifetimes and spiritual planes between lives. And it talked of the soul's progress through harmony and balance, love and wisdom, progress toward a mystical and ecstatic connection with God. There was much practical advice along the way: the value of patience and of waiting; the wisdom in the balance of nature; the eradication of fears, especially the fear of death; the need for learning about trust and forgiveness; the importance of learning not to judge others...and perhaps most of all, the unshakable knowledge that we are immortal. We are beyond life and death, beyond space and beyond time. We are the gods, and they are us.[8]

This way of understanding God, so different from the Western way of thinking, removes the emphasis that Western religions have placed on fear of the negative forces (Satan) and the fear that one's failings in life (sin) will condemn him to hell for eternity. This idea that we have but one chance to make it to heaven fails to account for the dis-

---

6. Weiss, 1988, p. 56.
7. Weiss, 1988, pp. 171-173.
8. Weiss, 1988, p. 173.

parity that occurs when one person dies as a child while another has 90 years to make mistakes or do good deeds. It also does not account for the unfairness that life deals out to some who are unlucky enough to be born into an existence of dire poverty, ignorance and brutality, while others are born into loving, kind and religious families. The unreasonableness of this view is what makes atheists out of many who refuse to accept a God that created such an unfair world.

The Eastern concept explains the fairness of God and makes it immeasurably easier to understand how we should react to events in our lives that we perceive to be negative. For example, when we suffer the loss of a loved one, a great financial setback or a horrible illness, instead of questioning the existence of God or wondering why we are being punished, we can ask ourselves what the event is meant to teach us. We can understand that such events are not accidents, but rather that they were planned on a higher plane to teach us important lessons that we failed to learn in previous lives. Viewing negative events as opportunities for spiritual growth allows us to realize that there is a positive side to every negative event. In fact, it illustrates the essential nature of God and his magnificent universe—that positive and negative are the same thing; they are simply opposite sides of the same coin. However, it takes an advanced soul to view the physical world from God's perspective. It isn't easy, yet it is what we came here to Earth to accomplish and it is what we must try to do.

In short, the science of spirituality, like the Eastern philosophies of old, teaches us that negativity, rather than being evil, is merely the other side of positive, and is necessary in a balanced universe. In this view of reality, life is fair, and the woes of humankind are not due to the fact that God has forsaken his children. It is just the way things work in a universe where God is neutral.

More Lessons From Beyond

If we can accept that quantum physicists and traditional psychiatrists are finding evidence of other realities that do not fall within the physical laws of science we are familiar with, it should come as no surprise that the same is occurring daily among the relatively small number of researchers who are seriously studying the enigma of the Unidentified Flying Object (UFO). These men and women fight a daily battle to prevent themselves from being drawn into the looking glass to a world where scientific objectivity serves no useful purpose. One such researcher is Raymond Fowler, a well-respected and meticulous researcher who has written numerous books on the UFO phenomenon and who has chronicled one of the best documented and enigmatic abduction cases—the story of Betty Andreasson Luca.

Betty's story of a lifelong relationship with non-human entities called "The Watchers," whom she perceives as angels, was first revealed in Fowler's book, *The Andreasson Affair*, first published in 1979.[9] Since then, he has written three more books on this case, including *The Watchers*[10] and *The Watchers II*.[11] Betty and her husband, Bob, who has also had abduction experiences, have interacted with the typical small, gray beings we are all familiar with, as well as with human-looking, tall blondes who have identified themselves as the "Elders" and who are in charge of the Greys. In his book, *The Watchers*, published in 1990, Fowler records a hypnosis session in which Betty remembers an abduction that took place in 1973 from her home in Ashburnham, Massachusetts. Here, she remembers having asked the beings who they are:

> He says that…they are the caretakers of nature and natural forms—the Watchers. They love mankind. They love the planet Earth…and they have been caring for it and man since man's beginning. They watch the spirit in all things…. Man is destroying much of nature…. He's saying that they have collected the seed of man, male and female… And that they have been collecting…every species and every gender of plant for hundreds of years…. They love the planet Earth and they have been caring for it and man since man's beginning.[12]

The Watchers explain to Betty that they exist in a timeless dimension where past, present and future are all one. They demonstrate this by taking her on numerous journeys outside of her body into their dimension. She is made to understand that "man is not made of just flesh and blood."[13] They further explain that their technology, one that combines science and spirit, permits them to coexist with humans, to whom they are genetically related. They have conducted a long-term

9. Fowler, 1994.
10. Fowler, 1990.
11. Fowler, 1995.
12. Fowler, 1990, p. 202.
13. Fowler, 1990, p. 345.

THE SCIENCE OF THE SPIRIT

program of genetic manipulation to prolong and improve life on this planet, which has included the use of human surrogate mothers for the production of hybrid offspring. This program has been accelerated in recent years, they said, because the human race is going to become sterile. Environmental disaster on a global scale will lead to the death of life on this planet. As a result, they are taking steps to preserve Earth's life forms for existence elsewhere in the universe.

In his most recent book, *The Watchers II*, Fowler reports on an equally amazing hypnosis session in which Betty's husband, Bob, recalls a similar conversation with an alien entity who explained certain spiritual laws:

> You see, the body...is the shell.... The real you is the light person inside...the light force, the part that does not die, the part that goes on and on.... That's the real you.... That part...advances through stages. Our existence here...is only one step of many in a long, learning process. This process, the human mind is unable to comprehend. It is a never-ending process. We are all constantly being monitored. Nothing that you do in your life escapes them. It's just like...a recorder.... All is recorded from the time you are born until the time you die.... How you react, what you do.... Even your innermost thoughts, feelings and emotions.... This process determines how rapidly you will advance and what your next step...will be, what hardship you must undergo to deepen your understanding.

"Are you saying that, at some level, life is fair?" asks the hypnotherapist incredulously. Bob's answer, as learned from the aliens:

> Life is wonderfully fair. Those of us in this plane just don't understand it. When you see a small child that becomes ill and dies, people weep.... They grieve for themselves. The child does not need to be here any longer. The child has already advanced, much as you would skip a grade in school.... People that are sick or injured...their faith is being tested. The reactions are recorded. This determines whether or not they need more teaching.

Bob is then asked about evil.

> Without evil to overcome, the righteous could not advance and triumph. It's all part of the system.... There must be suffering, because without these things, there is no advancement.

"Are you saying that evil is positive?" Bob is asked.

Evil on an Earthly plane is the negative aspect. Evil on the larger plane is part of the overall plan that gives us all a chance to advance and rise above it.... Everything in nature...has a plus and a minus, a light and dark, a negative and positive, a good and bad. It must be, for without some content of evil, there can be no good. There can be no growth.... The creator gave us choice. We cannot use that choice unless we have two choices to make. Evil or good.[14]

The obvious consistency between Dr. Weiss' patient, Raymond Fowler's investigation into UFOs and the findings of quantum physics regarding the nature of subatomic particles is rather startling. Yet, such consistency would be natural if both persons, under hypnosis, were indeed accessing higher knowledge from other dimensions. These two examples could simply be dismissed as the result of powerful imaginations or the delusions of the mentally ill, except for the fact that similar information is being obtained from thousands of well-documented cases all over the United States and in various other countries where such work is being done. In addition, hundreds of highly trained and esteemed psychiatrists and psychologists have gone on record stating firmly that the witnesses are not mentally ill, nor are they prone to fantasy or fabrication.

Defining a New Reality

Perhaps we can now begin to summarize the findings of those intrepid researchers who have dared to venture beyond the boundaries of "acceptable" science into the world of "new" science. In doing so, we can begin to build a foundation of knowledge by which we may learn truth about how the universe is structured and about how we should perceive our role within it.

The universe and everything in it is part of a vast, living intelligence—the prime creative force that we could call "God." Everything in the universe, including ourselves, is manifested by intelligences from a timeless and spaceless dimension. This means that we are, in fact, nonphysical, immortal beings, temporarily occupying physical bodies.

---

14. Fowler, 1995, pp. 342-347.

Because everything in the universe is interconnected, any action we take affects the entire universe, like a ripple in a pond, and will eventually affect us. Therefore, unconditional love, mercy, respect and forgiveness are the only actions that make sense.

The interconnectedness of the universe allows us as individuals to access the knowledge available to our true selves (our higher consciousness) and to other intelligences in the universe.

The universe was created in balance between equal forces of positive and negative. This means that the universe is a paradox in which positive and negative are the same and God is a neutral force that places equal value on both.

Those things that we perceive as evil are simply manifestations of the negative side of the universe and should be understood and respected, rather than feared. The negative forces simply give us an opportunity to react in a positive, loving way. If we do so, we progress in our spiritual evolution.

The universe and everything in it is constantly evolving. As spiritual beings, we are able to manifest into the physical dimension numerous times in order to learn the lesson of unconditional love, and, thus, progress in our spiritual journey.

We are assisted on this journey by other, higher intelligences who are part of a complex hierarchy of intelligences. These beings have existed since time immemorial and utilize a technology that combines science and spirituality to create and evolve physical life forms throughout the universe.

Please note that all of these amazing conclusions come not from reading the Bible (although you will find them there if you look hard enough), nor do they come from studying the religions of the world. These scientific/spiritual truths have emerged through the efforts of researchers who have tried to understand the true nature of reality by engaging in open-minded, intellectually-driven studies. Together, these findings form a reasonably good foundation for a new way of seeing reality that could lead humankind away from the brink of extinction. This new paradigm could be called the science of spirituality.

New Science Experiment

It is time now for you the reader to take a bold step. There is a simple way for you test this new scientific/spiritual knowledge. You can now put it to the test. By carrying out the following experiment, you can learn for yourself if you are a spiritual being who is connected to the rest of the universe by a higher consciousness that exists in a timeless and spaceless dimension.

Step 1. Get into a meditative state (preferably in quiet isolation) and recite the following prayer. (Note: it makes no difference what your religion is or even if you consider yourself an atheist. Remember, this is a scientific experiment.):

> Dear God (you may use "higher consciousness" or "Prime Creator" if you so choose) I ask you to help me to learn about the true nature of the universe by showing me examples that I cannot deny and by bringing to me learning opportunities in the form of people to talk to, events to attend, books to read and TV shows to watch. I promise that I will accept the truths that you reveal to me, regardless of how they may contradict my previously-held beliefs and I promise to take advantage of the opportunities you provide for me. *Amen*

Step 2. Now that you have read the prayer above and made a firm commitment to carry out your part of the bargain, the experiment can begin. In fact, it begins *now*! In step 2 you must play the role of the researcher by keeping a journal of events that occur in your life that fulfill the terms of the agreement. Give particular attention to synchronicities, those amazing but meaningful coincidences that you might normally ignore as being the result of mere chance. Be sure to include in your journal any unusually powerful dreams that seem relevant to your study. Our higher consciousness and other, higher intelligences are constantly trying to send us messages through our dreams. Be sure to write these down as soon as you wake up so you don't forget them! (Note: A word of warning for skeptics. Even if you did not recite the prayer in earnest, your higher consciousness may still insist on providing you with the above-mentioned experiences. You may wish to carry out the instructions in step 3 anyway.)

Step 3. Keep the journal for 90 days. At the end of this period, make a photocopy of the journal and send it to me along with your comments and observations to the address you will find in the back of this book. The results will be analyzed and compiled in a study to be published at a later date. Be sure to indicate whether or not you wish your name to be withheld, but please include a return address and phone number so you can be part of any follow-up study that may be necessary.

Good luck with your research!

CHAPTER 7

ALIEN SALSA

"Oh no! I don't want to see that. I don't want to see that.... They've got little things there. They look like little babies, but they're strange looking. They got them lined up...in long tubes.... They want me to know that this is what they are doing, that it's really important to them."

—Rita Perregrino under hypnosis remembering the hybrid babies she was shown when she was 13 years old.

Abductions on the Border

As I flew home from the Ozark UFO conference I began to realize that there was still a great deal to learn about the mystery of the Unidentified Flying Object and I resolved to launch my own investigation into UFO sightings and possible abductions right in my own hometown. As the plane winged westward, the Earth below changed from verdant green, then gradually to a pale yellow and finally to the familiar brown of the vast desert from which rise the jagged peaks of the rocky mountains. The muddy waters of the Rio Grande flowed like a brown ribbon Southward, providing nourishment for the more than one million desert dwellers in the area, and serving as the dividing line between the twin cities of Juarez, Mexico, and its American neighbor, El Paso. The traffic below flowed smoothly over the international bridges linking the sister cities, as well as on Interstate 10, which parallels the river on its route through town. Everything looked normal. Business as usual. Was it possible that aliens were abducting people all the way out here in this remote desert oasis? Would I really be able to find people in my own hometown that were having alien encounters? How would I find them?

Even before the plane landed, a plan was formulating in my mind that I believed might work. At the conference, I had been introduced to Walt Andrus, a conservatively dressed, elderly gentleman whom I was told was an engineer who had retired from Motorola. In 1969 he had organized a regional network of investigators to begin monitoring and investigating UFO sightings. That organization eventually grew into the largest, international association of UFO investigators in the world, a 5000 plus member group known as the Mutual UFO Network, which boasts more than 500 scientific consultants from every field of science, most of whom hold M.D.'s or Ph.D.'s. MUFON played a key role in many of the famous UFO investigations, including the Roswell incident, the Gulf Breeze, Florida, case in which hundreds of respectable citizens had seen, photographed and videotaped unidentifiable flying craft over a period of several years; and the Travis Walton case, in which a forest worker was abducted by a UFO for five days in Arizona. In this last case, six witnesses to the event took and passed lie detector tests and the story was turned into a Hollywood movie called *Fire in the Sky*. (It should be noted here that the motion picture totally misrepresented the events that Walton remembered experiencing aboard the craft, in order to make the movie more exciting.)

I also liked the fact that the organization had a reputation for questioning cases that its experts believed to be hoaxes, such as that of the well-known Swiss contactee Billy Meier, whose close-up photos and home movies of flying saucers gained world-wide attention. (It should be noted that many UFO investigators are extremely skeptical of contactee cases and have an automatic prejudice against them. However, much of the data which is currently coming from abduction research, particularly those cases in which the Tall Blondes appear, bear close resemblance to the contactee cases of the 1950s.)

MUFON has also played an important role in investigating the so-called "alien autopsy" film promoted by a British music and film producer as a possibly authentic government document. MUFON, although continuing to investigate, has made it clear that the film, in all likelihood, is a hoax. Even though I had not reached a strong conclusion on either of these cases, it was important to me that any organization I belonged to could never be accused by serious UFO critics of being made up of fanatical believers or of being a cult. (The more comical and fanatical debunkers, like the famous professional skeptic, Phil

Klass, will always use these accusations against anyone who expresses even the slightest interest in the subject.) The only way I could get involved is through an organization that leaned over backward to be objective and scientific. That, I soon learned, was what MUFON was all about.

After the introductions had been made, Walt made me an offer similar to the one that Dr. Hynek had made me nearly 20 years before. "Why don't you help organize the El Paso chapter of MUFON?" he asked. "You mean El Paso has a chapter?" I responded.

"Well, we have a few members there, but they haven't been meeting. Maybe you could get the ball rolling. You know, get them together and start investigating cases in your area. Here, take my card. Call me when you get home and I'll give you the names of our members in the El Paso area."

"Thanks, "I said. "I'll think it over."

At the time, the idea seemed far fetched. How, I thought, could I, an esteemed businessman with a reputation to uphold, get involved with a UFO organization in my hometown? The idea seemed too risky. Yet, as I returned home, the idea began to seem like a possibility. After all, MUFON was made up of many reputable scientists. Even Dr. Mack of Harvard University served on its board of directors. Certainly I had no more to lose than they. Each of them must have faced a similar dilemma when they decided to join the organization and, in each case, they were able to cross the line. I realized then that if I was going to learn any more, I would also have to cross the line and stand up for what I believed. It would take people like me all over the world to stand up and be counted if the truth about the UFO was ever going to be revealed.

So, within a few days of my return to El Paso, I made that fateful call, beginning a series of events and investigations that would astound and astonish me and ultimately lead me to conclude that the answer to the UFO mystery was not as simple as that of an alien invasion, as many researchers believed.

The El Paso MUFON Chapter

Within a few weeks, the El Paso MUFON chapter began to grow, and to bring in speakers that attracted audiences in excess of 400 at the local community college and at the university. The well-publicized

117

speakers attracted all sorts of interesting people. Among those who showed up and became involved in our group were military personnel from Ft. Bliss, the home of U.S. Army Air Defense, and from Holloman Air Force Base in New Mexico, as well as from the ultra-secret White Sands Missile Range nearby. It also attracted physicians, psychiatrists, psychologists, nurses, lawyers, engineers, housewives, schoolteachers, college professors and, interestingly enough, abductees. The latter came with their diaries and their sketches of alien beings or with copies of the letters they had drafted, but never sent to abduction researchers. They came with their stories of missing time, their fears that their children were also involved and their concern for total confidentiality and anonymity. Often they came with tears in their eyes and with cracking voices, describing the nights of sleepless terror and their fears of going insane. Over and over again, the same patterns, or symptomology, were presented to us—a pattern so familiar to abduction researchers throughout the country.

The Abduction Research Team

Soon, we assembled a team to work with the abduction cases that were coming to us. A psychiatrist, Dr. Roberta Fennig, who had accompanied her architect husband to hear one of our speakers, volunteered to examine abductees for free. She knew nothing about UFOs and had never encountered an abduction case. She was eager to learn even though she expressed her fear about what her peers in the psychiatric community might think. Later, when she realized that the abduction phenomenon could simply not be explained away by conventional psychological theories, she became State Section Director of the El Paso Chapter and a dedicated abduction researcher, volunteering much of her valuable time to counsel traumatized abductees.

A native of Chicago with a nursing degree from Loyola University, she spent ten years as a psychiatric nurse, mostly at Loyola Medical Center. Later, she received her Doctorate of Osteopathic Medicine at the Chicago College of Osteopathic Medicine and she completed her psychiatric residency at the Texas Tech University's Health Science Center in El Paso. Fennig admits that before becoming involved with abduction research, she was a bit arrogant. "Before, my eyes were totally closed to the possibility of other realities. I had heard about the possibility of alien abductions, but I didn't believe it. I hadn't read

UFO books, but I had seen the TV movie, *Intruders*, in about 1988. My response was, "I'll believe it when I see it." After the Walt Andrus lecture, when I volunteered to examine abduction claims, I felt sure I would be able to tell if someone was lying, hallucinating or fantasizing. I thought I had seen it all.

But, she soon found out she hadn't seen it all. "My first case was a black woman who had come to Andrus's presentation carrying her sketches of the gray alien beings she remembered seeing while fully conscious. I was determined to be very scientific and to treat her the same way I would any other patient. But, as I interviewed her, I realized that she didn't demonstrate any of the psychoses I would have expected. Instead, she exhibited extremely high anxiety, expressing a lot of emotion, fearfulness, confusion and stress. She told me about a time when she was in her bedroom, wide awake, and she saw this gray being float across the room to her and touch her on the hand. That was all she remembered until the next morning when she woke up in her nightgown, lying on top of her bed, which had been fully made. It seems that her husband had made the bed on his way out that morning, believing that she had awakened early and left. She had no dissociation or other problems with memory loss that would account for the period of missing time."

"Still, I could not accept the reality of the abduction phenomenon until after I had interviewed about 15 such cases and sat in on numerous hypnosis sessions," said Fennig.

Together, with the aid of local hypnotherapists, Dr. Romeo Di Benedetto and Mary Azar, we formed a team that began offering free counseling for anyone who believed he was having alien encounters. When the service grew large enough, Dr. Fennig started a support group for abductees, meeting monthly to share their fears and concerns and to gain comfort in the knowledge that they were not alone. Within six months of my return to El Paso, we had identified more than two dozen cases of abduction and many more potential cases that refused investigation and assistance. Many of these were people who were paranoid about anyone ever finding out their deep, dark secret. They were people whose standing in the community prevented them from revealing to anyone the bizarre, paranormal events that had followed them throughout their lives. Many of these were visibly traumatized and were simply too fearful to even speak of their experiences in more than a few short bursts at a time. Others had figured out what was happening to them by reading books such as *Communion* and *Missing Time*. They served as their own therapists by dealing with their experiences alone, in the privacy of their own homes, watching TV shows and reading books that detailed the experiences of others like themselves.

Dealing With Hypnosis

As part of my training as chief abduction investigator for the group, I decided I had to learn more about hypnosis, a subject that had always fascinated me, but of which I knew little. It was obvious to me that hypnosis played a central role in the investigation of abduction cases and that its use was one of the most criticized aspects of such research. Professional debunkers, and the uninformed public alike, argued that the hypnotists themselves were responsible for the abduction phenomenon by leading their highly-suggestible clients to believe they were taken by little gray humanoids into an awaiting spacecraft, for the purpose of genetic research. Although I knew that such a hypothesis was absurd, based on the large number of cases treated by many different hypnotherapists and on the fact that many abductees did not even need hypnosis to remember what happened to them, I felt I needed to know more about how hypnosis worked. In fact, in every credible abduction case I know about, the individuals have had conscious memories of a wide variety of paranormal events throughout their lives. More often than not, the phenomenon has also affected the lives of their family members as well. Hypnosis in abduction cases is merely used to break through the amnesia surrounding "missing time" events. These events quite often included several people who experience "shared amnesia" for a specific period of time ranging from about half an hour to several hours, and might have occurred many years ago or the previous week, in which case, the conscious memories are still quite vivid. This concept of shared amnesia is not even discussed, much less explained, in psychology books, yet it is something that occurs regularly in abduction investigations. Often the conscious memories include having seen the alien beings and their spacecraft, thereby nullifying the argument that the hypnotist is responsible for leading the witness.

Nevertheless, I felt that to be an effective investigator, I must understand how hypnosis works. I had to feel absolutely sure that the hypnotherapist was doing his job correctly and professionally. Most importantly, I had to be sure that the therapist was not in any way leading the witness or putting subtle ideas in his or her head. It was for this reason that I sought out a course on hypnosis and enrolled as one of a dozen students. The course, taught by a local hypnotherapist whose advertisements promised to help people stop smoking or over-eating, was held in his strip shopping center office, near a residential area of town. Sitting in folding chairs under the fluorescent lights of the windowless, nondescript room, we were taught the current theories about how the brain works on two levels—the conscious and the subconscious. The conscious mind is the part of the mind that is aware of being in contact with physical reality through the use of the five senses. It gathers and sorts information, tests probabilities and then makes decisions. The conscious mind also presents information to the subconscious mind for storage in the memory banks and has the ability to call forth memories from the subconscious when necessary. It is believed that much of the work of the conscious mind is done in the left hemisphere of the brain.

On the other hand, the subconscious mind functions much like a robot, carrying out the instructions of the conscious mind without question, and controlling such automatic functions as respiration, eye blinking and the rhythm of the heart, even while we are asleep or unconscious. Our textbook, *The Wizard Within,* by A.M. Krasner, explained the subconscious mind in this way:

> Your subconscious mind consists of associated sense
> impressions and memories of all your past.... [It controls]
> every bodily move, every thought and every emotion.... Sub-
> conscious communication [to all parts of the body] goes on all
> day and night, whether you are awake or asleep.... It is always
> active. Not only are the memories of your every experience,
> both good and bad, stored in your subconscious mind, but also
> therein are the memories of the emotion and the environment
> that accompanied the experience.... It responds only from the
> information stored within its memory, retrieving that informa-
> tion very much as you would pull up a letter from a file cabi-
> net.... The relaxed state of hypnosis provides easier access to
> your subconscious mind.[1]

121

This discussion focused on my primary interest—memory retrieval and memory storage. It reflected the common view among psychologists that the subconscious mind, acting something like a video camera, records all aspects of events experienced by a person. When those memories are triggered, they emerge into consciousness with the full force of all the original emotion and sensory perception of the original event. Hypnosis, then, is simply a state of mind in which the conscious mind relaxes enough for the subconscious mind to take over, allowing the hypnotherapist to make suggestions which bypass the conscious mind. Although this sounds suspiciously like mind control, I found that individuals are not easily swayed to believe or to remember something that is not true. (In fact, as the reader will see later in this chapter, hypnotherapists often test their subjects with misleading suggestions in order to determine if the person is remembering or if he is fabricating. With regard to the abduction phenomenon, such tests almost invariably show that the subject cannot be lead away from his or her true memories.) If we wish to correlate this to the teachings of Eastern philosophy, we might say that in the hypnotic state, the person's "higher consciousness" is in charge, giving the individual access to that timeless and spaceless dimension that connects him to the rest of the universe.

The subconscious is also in charge of storing all of our memories, even those we may not want to remember, going all the way to birth, and some would argue, even beyond. The ability of the conscious mind to access those memories, however, is quite often blocked by the subconscious, which protects the conscious mind by not allowing it to remember those things that are too traumatic. This important gate keeping function is the most important aspect of the use of hypnosis in dealing with trauma. For example, in abduction research it has been found that not even the most clever hypnotherapist is able to open the gate to an abduction memory until the person has consciously made the decision that he is ready to deal with the information. If the individual is too fearful or is only mildly curious about the process of hypnosis, the process will simply not work. In a way, subjects self-hypnotize themselves through their willingness to confront the issues at hand.

---

1. Krasner, pp. 76-79

Alien Mind Control

There is another, more disturbing aspect to abduction cases that researchers have discovered. The gate to the hidden memories can also be controlled by outside agents—the beings themselves. In case after case, researchers have been stymied in their efforts to gain access to certain hidden memories by memory blocks apparently put in place by these higher beings. "I'm not allowed to know that now," an abductee will say under hypnosis. "They won't let me remember that. The time is not right yet." At times, efforts to break through the barrier result in excruciating pain for the abductee or he will simply come out of the trance. In some cases, the person believes that "something terrible will happen" if he tells what he knows.

It sometimes seems that abduction memories are like time-release capsules in the minds of the experiencers and that different aspects of their life-long experiences are made available to them only when the time is right.

The aliens also have a way of taking control of a hypnosis session. For example, hypnotherapists are taught ways to make the recovery of the memories less traumatic for the experiencer. One such way is to suggest to the subject that he will be able to watch what happened during the abduction as if it were a movie being played on a screen. He is told that he can slow down the action or speed it up or even play it backwards if he chooses, thereby gaining control over a situation where he, in real life, had no control at all. However, in one of our local cases, the beings, apparently not happy with the use of this technique, jumped right off the screen, jolting the subject almost out of his chair. They told him, while still in trance, that they did not like the technique, because it did not allow him to feel the fear and anxiety he would feel if he were allowed to relive it. The knowledge that the beings could control the hypnosis and communicate directly with the subject and also with the therapists, left all of them in a state of awe and quite shaken. In another case, one in which I did the hypnosis, something similar occurred. Hypnotists have a commonly used technique to help a subject reach a hypnotic state. This is to suggest that the subject imagine a beautiful place (often a beach) where he or she would feel completely safe. The hypnotherapist may spend ten to twenty minutes helping the subject to imagine every aspect of this imaginary place, until the person feels extremely relaxed. But on one occasion, the beings simply showed up on the beach, demonstrating to the subject that there was no place she could truly be safe from them! In this case, the woman had recently become tired of pursuing her search for the truth of her experiences and had been thinking of ceasing to speak out publicly. They explained to her that if she chose not to carry out her mission in life of speaking out publicly, she would not be permitted to remember any more about her abduction experiences. Needless to say, this came as quite a shock to her as well as to me and our psychiatrist, Dr. Fennig.

This aspect of the subconscious mind, however, was not taught or discussed in a hypnosis class dedicated to helping someone stop smoking. In fact, the instructor, when told of my interest in abduction research and my experience as an observer during abductee regression sessions, reacted with cool interest. It was not anything he had ever had to deal with in his practice, nor did he take the issue of UFOs seriously. Yet, coincidentally, within a few weeks of my completion of the course, he phoned me in a highly excited state to tell me about a woman who had come to see him for weight loss therapy. He subsequently wrote me a letter explaining what happened:

> I was recently working with a new patient and had a spontaneous regression to a traumatic event [in this lifetime] involving aliens. This was one of those bizarre happenstance events that leaves one questioning consensus reality. She had been visited in her bedroom, on numerous occasions in her earlier years, and usually had an out-of-body [experience] and watched the aliens perform various experiments with her. In her adult years she noticed several scars on her body, but could not recall how she got them. In her sessions with me, what she described seeing matched the general area where she now has scars. I mentioned MUFON to her, but she is too unstable for an encounter group. I am the first person that she ever shared this with and it will have to be her choice. But it sure changed my concept about the whole alien concept.[2]

Experiences such as these serve as further evidence that the hypnotist is not responsible for the memories of alien abductions, for the therapist often has little knowledge of the phenomenon and doesn't

---

2. Private letter, 1996.

124

even believe that it is real. This case is similar to what happened to Dr. Benjamin Simon in the Betty and Barney Hill case, with Dr. Brian Weiss, with Dr. John Mack and with countless other mental health professionals who have encountered paradigm-shifting phenomena in the privacy of their own offices.

Fortunately for our team, several of us had the opportunity to further our learning by attending workshops and conferences on alien abduction research, conducted by Dr. Mack and other experts such as John Carpenter and Yvonne Smith. Carpenter is a psychiatric social worker in Springfield, Missouri, who serves as MUFON's director of abduction research and who has treated well over a hundred cases of alien abduction since the late 1980s. Smith is a hypnotherapist from Los Angeles who runs project CERO (Close Encounter Research Organization) and who counsels numerous experiencers, including many celebrities, in southern California. Eventually, we had the opportunity to watch, first hand, as John Carpenter, one of the most experienced hypnotherapists in the abduction field, performed hypnosis on one of our own cases, during his lecture visit to the University of Texas at El Paso in September of 1994.

The "Maria" Case

Shortly after returning from the Ozark conference, I learned that there was already an active, but rather secretive, UFO study group meeting regularly in El Paso. Using the name Project Sigma, the group of about 20 or so individuals met monthly to view videos, conduct investigations and discuss the alien encounters of several of the members. Attendance at the meetings, which were held in the members' homes, was strictly by invitation and being invited once was no guarantee of a future welcome. In short, the group was gripped by paranoia—a fear of being ridiculed and of being infiltrated by government agents. The idea of opening their meetings up to the general public was abhorrent to them and, even though some of them were MUFON members, they didn't even trust that organization totally, believing that it had already been compromised by government operatives. Although I knew I could not be associated with such a group, I gladly accepted an invitation to attend one of their meetings and talk about my interest in activating the El Paso Chapter of MUFON. It was there that I first met an obviously traumatized and highly anxious Mexican-

American woman whose memories of strange, paranormal phenomena had haunted her since she was a child. Although she eventually went public, using her real name of Rita Perregrino, we at first referred to her as the "Maria" case in order to protect her identity. (See Figure 10 on page 185.)

Rita is a 48-year-old mother of one. She worked as a job counselor in the public schools before she left El Paso to live in North Carolina. Her dark skin and dark hair serve as evidence of her Mexican-Indian heritage, yet today, her primary language is English and like many Mexican Americans, she struggles with the language of her childhood and of her parents. Rita's story is both incredible and typical at the same time. When one listens to the audio tapes of her hypnosis sessions, as she recalls visits to other worlds and of being taught wondrous things by her strange, alien tutors, one's imagination and credulity is stretched to the limit. Yet her experiences parallel those of hundreds, perhaps thousands, of others who bear the same scoop marks on their legs, who have had the same missing time experiences and who have been gripped by the same mind-shattering terror that characterizes abductees wherever they are found. The fact that Rita is a Mexican American and that some of her experiences took place within a short distance of the Mexican border in a predominantly lower class, Spanish-speaking "barrio" (neighborhood) and that her primary language was Spanish in her youth make her case unusual. When I met her on the night of the Sigma meeting, her voice cracked and her breathing quickened as she struggled to relate her earliest abduction memories to the Sigma group:

In 1955, when I was eight years old, a group of us kids were out playing in back of our apartment building which was located near Beall Elementary School in south-central El Paso. It was summertime and we got to stay up late. I had the feeling that there was something strange happening, like someone was watching us. Finally, somebody looked up and there was this big, round thing just hanging in the air over a nearby tree. Everybody saw it and nobody knew what it was. It was almost right over us, but we hadn't noticed it because it was black and quiet. At first we just ignored it, but then, I remember everyone running to get their parents to come and look. The next thing I remember is that I was in my mother's arms in our apartment and everyone was very upset because they had been out searching for me for more than two hours. They had even called the police. Then they noticed that I had a wound on my right ankle. It was an oval hole that went clear to the bone, but it wasn't bleeding and it didn't hurt. I have no idea how I got it, but I know it happened during the time I was missing. At the time, I did not realize that I had been missing and I didn't know where I had been. My parents didn't take me to the doctor because the wound healed very quickly and there was no infection.[3]

I asked to see the scar and Rita showed everyone a dark, oval mark just above her right ankle on the outside of her leg. It looked somewhat like a cigarette burn, but it was slightly indented. At this point, another group member came forward to show the similar scar he bore from childhood, located also on his ankle. He also had suffered a lifetime of terrifying alien-related experiences. As far as abduction cases go, Rita's was no more amazing than the rest, but what was unusual was Rita's courage. As terrified as she was, she seemed determined to get to the bottom of the phenomenon that had dominated her life, causing her to live in fear of the night and (as it turns out) severely affecting her ability to have meaningful relationships with men. Rita's story serves as a beacon of light to all abductees, for it is a story of a trembling, frightened and lonely woman who was able to make the transition to becoming a radiant, self-assured public speaker on the subject of her alien experiences.

For a long time after I first met her, Rita's fears got the better of her. She became a member of MUFON, rarely missing a meeting, but she was terrified at the prospect of undergoing hypnosis and would often have to leave the room during presentations that showed drawings of beings with the large, black almond-shaped eyes that haunted her dreams. All this began to change when John Carpenter came to El Paso at the invitation of MUFON to lecture at the university. Rita had been building up her courage for a long time and finally decided there would be no better opportunity for her than to be hypnotized by one of the foremost experts in the field. So, between lecturing at the University, giving a workshop for mental-health professionals and speaking to the MUFON group, he graciously consented to conduct Rita's

3. Private files, 1996.

hypnosis session. Rita agreed to allow Dr. Fennig, myself and another local psychiatrist to be present at the session.

John Carpenter is one of the easiest people to get to know and to like that I have ever met. His mild, unassuming character, void of any false sense of self importance, gives him the perfect personality to serve as a counselor. His calm, reassuring way quickly gives confidence to the subject that everything will be all right and that the subject will always be in control of the situation, able to wake up at any time if he or she so wishes. Such reassurance makes it much easier for the subject to achieve a state of maximum relaxation. After reviewing Rita's conscious memories about the event, John began to put Rita in a relaxed state by suggesting that she visualize a beautiful place where she could feel completely safe. Soon he had Rita in a very relaxed state and he began to gently take her back to that fateful summer night when she and her friends were playing outside so many years before. Below are excerpts from that two-hour hypnosis session:

John Carpenter (JC): Do you remember that particular night?

Rita (RP): Yeah…we used to like to sing songs. And we got in a circle and we'd hold hands.

JC: How does this night get interrupted?

RP: It feels funny…. I feel it. I don't know if the other kids do, but they're starting to look strange.

JC: …Just describe what you see.

RP: …We're going back and forth and singing. But then I can't sing anymore. Everybody's kind of just stopped…. We're just standing there, looking at each other. We don't know why…but finally…it's as if whatever was there let us go and we started looking around…finally somebody looked up and there was this thing.

(Note: Rita's subconscious memory differs from her original recollection. Under hypnosis she realizes there was a mysterious period where the whole group experienced paralysis. This happened before anyone noticed the object.)

RP: …Everybody starts running everywhere and looking up and pointing up.

(Note: Carpenter, suspecting that the period of paralysis might be important, takes her back to that point in time.)

JC: Do you feel…any particular sensation?

RP: It was like a tingling thing.
JC: ...Were [you] wearing shoes?
RP: No.
JC: Can you feel the ground?
RP: Yeah...[it's] sandy.
JC: ...Does anything ever change?
RP: I feel as if I'm being taken away.
JC: Did someone come up behind you?
RP: *[disregarding the leading question]* I don't know how it happened. It's as if I can see the kids below me, where I was...I don't know how this can happen. *[becoming very nervous]*
JC: Describe what you see. It's okay, you're safe.
RP: I, I don't want to look...there's kind of this light. There's stuff. There's things.

(Note: At this point, Rita begins to sob quietly and John has to calm her down. He tells her she can look at what's happening as if it is on a movie screen. After she calms down, she proceeds.)

RP: I can see the craft...[there are] narrow hallways.... I don't know why they want me here.... I don't understand.
JC: Did you ever catch a glimpse of what they look like?
RP: I don't want to look.... There's a table.

(Note: Here, John takes the opportunity to use a technique he has devised for testing a subject's suggestibility. He deliberately attempts to lead the subject away from the commonly reported aspects of the phenomenon. If the person is easily swayed, it supports the notion that abduction stories are the products of leading questions offered by the hypnotist. If not, it shows that the subconscious mind cannot be swayed from the facts it believes to be true.)

JC: It's on four legs, isn't it? *[This is a logical assumption, yet abductees invariably describe the examining table as being molded to the floor on a kind of pedestal.]*
RP: All I can see is the top. I don't know. They put me there. They're doing stuff. *[Rita begins crying and showing a great deal of stress as she relives the experience of an eight-year-old child being given a gynecological exam by hideous, alien-looking beings. Carpenter once again calms her.]*
JC: Do you know what frightened you?

RP: They're all over me, they're doing stuff and I don't know what they're doing. I don't want them to hurt me.... They're telling me things.

(Once again, Carpenter tries to lead Rita in the wrong direction.)

JC: Do they tell you in a loud voice?

RP: They're just thoughts. *[Again, Rita passes the test. Her response is identical to other abductees who report consistently that all communication with the beings is telepathic.]*

JC: What do they say?

RP: I ask them why they look so different. "Why do you look like that?" They ask me why I look like [I do]. I tell them I don't know, it's just who or what we look like.

JC: What do they want?

RP: They say they just kind of want to watch.... They have to know how things are going. *[This statement is consistent with what Betty Andreasson was told. The beings watch and monitor life forms on Earth. Thus, the name The Watchers.]*

(Later in the session)

RP: We saw each other again. We know each other. They, they taught me things.

JC: Do you remember what they taught you?

RP: Not to be afraid. They taught me that there's other life, that there's other places. And that even if we don't all look the same, we can all want to do the same thing. I don't understand. I asked them, "Where are you from? Where do you live? Where's your home?" They told me they could tell me, but I wouldn't understand. They told me I would be different because they had done things to me.

JC: How would you be different?

RP: They said that I could help them. I told them I don't want to be different. I just want to be alone. I told them it's just too scary.... [They said] I would forget and later on, I could start remembering everything. I didn't want to remember what they looked like.... They were just too ugly, too ugly, too ugly.

JC: What one thing makes them really ugly?

RP: *[Here, Rita refers to the reptilian appearance of some of the beings.]* Their skin is funny…. I don't think I've ever touched a frog, but I think that's what it would feel like.

(Later in the session)

RP: They did something to my head…. I don't know what it was. They were around my head.

JC: How old were you at that point?

RP: Thirteen or fourteen…. They said they'd come back and they did. *[Rita begins to cry again.]* I almost forgot about them.

JC: Where are you with them this time?

RP: We're going somewhere…. There seems to be movement. They said not to be afraid…. They just want to take me for a ride…. It's nice. They're showing me things.

JC: What do you see?

RP: Oh no! I don't want to see that. *[Rita cries]* I don't want to see that…they've got little things there. They look like little babies, but they're strange looking…. They got them lined up…in long tubes…. They want me to know that this is what they are doing, that it's really important to them.

JC: Do the babies look like our babies?

RP: I don't want—they're hooked up to a machine…. They're like in glass, glass capsules, and they tell me that's what they're doing because it's important for them, and they tried to take good care of them, and it's too ugly.

JC: Are there lots of babies?

RP: Hundreds. It's kind of like growing plants…because they're hooked up and they get everything they need…. They're supposed to be individuals, persons, but they all look the same! *[Rita cries]*

JC: Do they look as ugly as the big ones or do they look different?

RP: There are other things there…. There are the ones we know as the Greys, and they kind of take care of things. And then there's other things, the ones I don't want to look at, they look like bugs or things, they're just so ugly.

JC: Does it look like a bug you've seen on Earth?

RP: Yeah, those praying mantis things…. This is tall and big and, and he's moving around…. They all kind of work together. *[Here, Rita reports seeing another type that is commonly reported by abductees.]*

JC: The praying mantis ones, are they different from the scary ones?

RP: [They're] easier to look at. The other ones are just too ugly.

JC: So there's another type, that's not the little gray ones and not the praying mantis ones that are scary to look at?

RP: They're the ones…that were doing the stuff [the medical procedures]…. They have big heads.

JC: Do they have hair?

RP: Funny skin…they look black or dark…there isn't a nose. It's all big head, big eyes, and there's something about the eyes…they just eat you up with their eyes…. It's as if your whole mind goes into their eyes.

(Later in the session)

RP: They say things that scare me.

JC: What are some of those things…?

RP: They can make people, or they can make anything they want. They can put things together, from different things. *[This is a reference to their mastery of genetic engineering.]* …That scares me 'cause I'm thinking maybe they'll make something out of me, too. Make me into something else.

(Carpenter, suspecting that Rita might have been used as a surrogate mother in the hybrid breeding program, asks a vague question designed to steer her in that direction.)

JC: Well, they never took anything from you, did they?

RP: They've been doing it already *[cries]*…and I didn't even know. *[alluding to removing hybrid fetuses from her body]* But they said it's for a good reason.

(Note: In later hypnosis sessions, Rita recalls being shown her own hybrid child and a room full of hybrid children.)

This first hypnosis session, although feared and dreaded by Rita, had a profound healing effect on her that was the beginning of a remarkable transformation to which many of us in the El Paso chapter were witness. On the Monday following the session, Rita called me at my office bubbling with excitement. "I feel as if there is a new sun in the sky just for me," she said. "Yesterday I went back to the old neighborhood and walked around for the first time since I was little. I've always avoided that place, but after the hypnosis I felt the need to go back and face the reality of what happened that night. I feel like a new person, and I've never slept so well in my life!" Rita also told me of another need she felt, the need to go to a hospital nursery and look at the babies. This was remarkable in view of the fact that Rita had always had a fear of babies. I'm sure that most traditional psychiatrists would have had a difficult, if not impossible, time trying to figure out how a woman with a grown child could have had a fear of babies almost all of her life. "I've never liked to hold babies or be around them. This caused me problems even with my own child until she was more grown up," Rita explained. "But now I know why I have always been afraid. It's because of the non-human babies in the tubes that I saw when I was little. Now I realize that there is no need to fear human babies."

Strange phobias such as this are commonplace among abductees. Many I have interviewed have expressed a fear of dolls, which researchers now know is caused by the same trauma that Rita experienced. John Carpenter, after working with well over one hundred cases nationwide, has cataloged numerous fears that are peculiar to the abduction phenomenon. These include, but are not limited to the following: fear of a particular place or street, fear of looking up when outdoors, fear of falling up (how do you develop a fear like that?), fear of big black eyes (such as shark's eyes, horse's eyes or even people wearing sunglasses), fear of doctors offices, fear of dentists, fear of operating rooms, etc.

Numerous other similarities can be found between Rita's experiences and those of the many hundreds of cases which have been well documented and researched around the world:

1. Evaluation by a competent psychiatrist concluding there is no sign of mental illness.

2. Physical evidence in the form of a scar (scoop mark) on her leg for which she had no conscious memory of an injury.

3. A missing-time experience that can be verified by numerous witnesses.

4. A close encounter with a UFO by numerous witnesses.

5. Mysterious paralysis and tingling feeling prior to being abducted.

6. Being levitated into the craft.

7. Being placed on a table.

8. Enduring painful gynecological procedures.

9. Seeing a variety of beings, specifically small, gray beings with large, almond-shaped, black eyes; praying mantis types and some with reptilian features. (In later sessions, Rita was able to look directly at the "ugly" ones with frog-like skin and see that they were reptilian in appearance.)

10. Being taught many things by the beings and being shown glass tubes or tanks where non-human fetuses were being grown like plants.

11. Memories of having known the beings for a very long time.

12. Displaying strong emotions and trauma as the memories are recovered.

13. Exhibiting great relief from stress and stress-related symptoms, such as sleep disorder after uncovering the memories during hypnosis.

In short, Rita's case confirms the research done by Budd Hopkins, Dr. John Mack, John Carpenter, Yvonne Smith and other researchers regarding the nature of the abduction phenomenon. In fact, in many ways, Rita's case is quite ordinary when it is viewed in light of the existing research on the subject.

CHAPTER 8

SURROUNDED BY ABDUCTEES

> *"Although researchers had assumed that the abduction syndrome was a rare phenomenon, the survey showed that the experiences known to be associated with UFO abductions are surprisingly prevalent in the American population.... We believe that one out of every fifty adult Americans may have had UFO abduction experiences."*
>
> *—Conclusion based on the analysis of the data from three major surveys conducted by the Roper Organization in 1992.*

The Roper Survey

Learning that there already existed a support group (of sorts) for abductees in El Paso came as a mild surprise to me. I had reasoned that since the abduction phenomenon appears to be worldwide (well-documented cases coming from as far away as Australia), that there should be cases even in the remote corner of West Texas that I call home. Meeting Rita and the other experiencers who came to the investigating team for help confirmed my suspicions in that regard, but what I was in no way prepared for was to find abductees among my friends and neighbors, some of whom I had known for more than 15 years. Up until then, the abduction phenomenon was something I could view as a fascinating research project in which I, the objective reporter, tested my theories by interviewing and investigating people to whom I had no relationship, other than professional. The first time that I realized this was not the case I was left stunned and amazed. For the first time, I began to realize that professional researchers may be severely underestimating the numbers of people who have had alien encounters.

The best attempt made thus far to estimate the number of abductees in the U.S. was made in 1992 by the Roper Organization with funding from the Bigelow Foundation. The study, called "Unusual Personal Experiences," is the analysis of the data from three national surveys in which 6000 adult Americans were asked a series of 11 questions pertaining to the types of experiences most often reported in abduction research, such as seeing a UFO, experiencing missing time, finding mysterious scars on one's body, etc. A team of abduction researchers including Dr. Mack, Budd Hopkins, John Carpenter and others teamed up to determine the best questions to ask and to analyze the data collected by Roper. The report, which was sent to nearly 100,000 mental health professionals, concludes that "hundreds of thousands, if not millions, of American men, women and children may have experienced UFO abductions...." The report urged mental health practitioners to learn to recognize the symptoms of the phenomenon and to deal with them appropriately. "They need to be open to the possibility that something exists or is happening to their clients which, in our traditional Western framework, cannot or should not be."

The report finally concluded that, based on the results of the survey, two percent of the adult population of America, or nearly 4 million persons, may have had abduction experiences. This, of course, does not include children, who were not surveyed. As we know, however, the abduction experience begins in early childhood, and cases of children as young as two and three years old are not uncommon. If persons under the age of 18 were included, the number of potential experiencers would be far greater. However, my own experiences have led me to the conclusion that the true number could be significantly larger. It is possible—I believe *probable*—that all of us have acquaintances, neighbors or business associates who have had this experience. The only reason that you don't know about it is because of the stigma placed upon such people by a society that denies the paranormal and fears those who report paranormal events. Those persons having alien encounters are not likely to share the information with anyone who they perceive as unapproachable. The last thing they desire is to be laughed at, ridiculed or even avoided by their friends and peers. This, unfortunately, is all too often the reaction they receive when they attempt to confide in someone they felt they could trust. This reaction is often reported even among the abductee's own family members.

As a result, I would never have found out that several of my friends have had these experiences if I had not finally revealed to those around me that I was involved in UFO research—something I was loath to do out of fear of how they would react.

"The Assessment"

My "coming out" occurred in April 1994 when the MUFON chapter invited Robert Dean to come to El Paso to speak at the El Paso Community College's "Emerging Renaissance Lecture Series," directed by a sociology professor, Dr. Romeo Di Benedetto. It fell on my shoulders to introduce Dean to an audience of 400 or so interested El Pasoans. Dean is a charismatic and inspiring speaker who lectures on the history and theological implications of the UFO phenomenon. Much of what he knows about the subject he claims to have learned while serving as a command sergeant major on the staff of General Lyman Lemnitzer at NATO Supreme Headquarters in Paris in the early 1960s. (That he actually served in that capacity has been well verified.) In his position of high authority, Dean had access to the highest level of classified documents and, in fact, was responsible for maintaining the security of the vaults in which they were stored. (This no doubt would have been the case for a person in his position.) Dean's story becomes controversial when he tells about seeing a document which was classified at a level above top secret and which, he says, changed his life. The document, simply titled, "The Assessment" was a lengthy, detailed report of an investigation conducted for the North American Treaty Organization (NATO) on the subject of UFOs. The investigation was undertaken, according to Dean, because of high level concerns about the many instances in which formations of unidentified objects were tracked on radar and seen visually, crossing the airspace of NATO countries at a time when Cold War paranoia could easily have triggered a nuclear war.

That such sightings actually occurred was verified in writing by one of the original Mercury astronauts, Col. L. Gordon Cooper (USAF Ret.), who witnessed such an event in 1951. In a letter written to the Ambassador to the United Nations from Grenada in 1978, Cooper discusses his belief that UFOs are extraterrestrial vehicles from other planets, recommends that the U.N. undertake a "top level, coordinated program to scientifically collect and analyze data from all over the

Earth...and to determine how best to interface with these visitors." He adds that "I did have occasion in 1951 to have two days of observation of many flights of them, of different sizes, flying in fighter formation, generally from east to west over Europe. They were at a higher altitude than we could reach with our jet fighters of that time." On May 7, 1996, Cooper was interviewed on the UPN Network program, *Paranormal Borderline*, and he added another bombshell to his previous testimony. It seems that six years after his European sightings, while he was assigned to the Flight Test Engineering Division at Edwards Air Force Base in California, a flying saucer landed in broad daylight on the test range while one of his film crews filmed the event! The aging astronaut calmly described what happened next. "They picked up their cameras and walked toward it and as they approached, it lifted off, retracted its landing gear and took off.... We processed the film and forwarded it to Washington and that's the last we heard of it." Before the film left the base, Cooper was able to view two of the reels and describes the object as a "double inverted lenticular saucer...with a metallic-looking surface." It seems reasonable to conclude that such credible testimony could easily have swayed NATO leaders to undertake a thorough study of the situation. According to Dean, the study was indeed conducted and the final product, called "The Assessment," was a super-secret bombshell that would have rocked the world had it been made public, for it not only concluded that UFOs were real, but it included photographic evidence of captured flying saucers and of alien bodies. The report, he says, included a chapter on the theological implications of the phenomenon and concluded that the Earth had been visited for a very long time, at least several hundred years, by a variety of nonhuman entities, including some that were described as reptilian, with vertical pupils and lizard-like skin.

Such conclusions, made by the military top command of NATO, would have been far too explosive to release to the general public in 1963 and could account for the fact that the governments of the world today remain unwilling to deal with the subject openly. To do so would unleash a fire storm of religious criticism and debate that could have widespread political and social ramifications, the likes of which no politician would be anxious to confront. As long as political concerns remain the determining factor in such decisions, documents such as "The Assessment," will be left to gather dust in dark vaults, along with other potentially troublesome papers on much more mundane subjects.

A Chain of Events

The series of events that led me to conclude that alien abductions might be more widespread than commonly believed began two days before Bob Dean was scheduled to speak. The day before, the El Paso *Herald Post* carried a front page article bearing Dean's photograph and detailing the explosive nature of his presentation. Although I had been partially responsible for his coming to El Paso and I had provided the media with a press release regarding the event, very few people, and none of my friends and colleagues, even knew that I had a passing interest in UFOs. Like most people, I assumed that those around me would laugh and scoff at my interest, so I never brought the subject up. This day, I was enjoying the company of three old friends at a popular restaurant where we had met for a drink at the end of the day. These were men I had known for many years—highly regarded businessmen who had reached high levels of professional accomplishment and income, who were active in the community and lived ordinary lives, raising families in upper-class suburban neighborhoods and attending church regularly. They were all highly successful and productive individuals that anyone would regard as stable and sane.

One man in the group, whom I will call Bob, had with him a copy of the afternoon paper and after we had settled in and ordered a drink, he held the paper up, pointing to the article about Robert Dean, and said, "Have you all seen this? This is going to be really interesting." He proceeded to tell us about the nature of the presentation and how he was planning to attend. "Why don't you guys go to this?" he asked.

With that, the conversation turned to UFOs, and I was amazed as my friends began conversing about the very topic I had always avoided around them. "Well, I believe in UFOs," one said. "Me too," said the other. "There's got to be something to them because so many people have seen them," he continued. Finally, after I was certain that my comments would not be scoffed at, I ventured into the conversation. "Well, I saw something very strange when I was an Army pilot," I reported. Seeing that they were eager for my story, I related to them my seeing a strange orange ball in the night sky over Alabama many years before. They listened in rapt attention and accepted my story without ridicule or laughter, much to my relief. Then Bob spoke up again. "That's nothing, wait until you hear my story."

"What happened to you?" I immediately asked.

"Well, about ten years ago, I was driving through New Mexico on the way to Albuquerque with a friend. It was late at night, around 1:00 A.M. and we were about an hour away from Albuquerque when suddenly a very bright, white light came out of nowhere and engulfed the car in light. We couldn't see what it was because it was right above us. Suddenly, all the instruments on the dash started going crazy and then the engine died and the car lost all electrical power."

"What happened then?" I asked.

He paused to think for a moment and then said, "Well, the car just started up by itself. We drove into town and had it checked at a gas station, but there was nothing wrong with it."

Suspecting that there was more to the story, and being familiar with the abduction scenario, I asked "What time was it when you got to Albuquerque? Were you on time?" Suddenly, Bob's face went white and his eyes widened as if he had just had a profound revelation. His hands went up to hold his head and he shook it gently as if trying to digest his thoughts. Finally, he said "No, we weren't on time. The sun was coming up and it should have been around 2 A.M. My friend and I both checked our watches and commented on how strange it was, but after that we never talked about the incident again. I never connected that to the light we saw on the highway."

"So how much time was missing?" I asked.

"About three hours or so," he calculated.

Although Bob was visibly shaken, I decided I had to pursue the matter further. Our other two friends were sitting in stunned silence. "Bob, I need to ask you one more question. Do you have any scars or marks on your body that you can't account for?"

Once again, Bob was visibly shaken. Confused and a little scared, he answered "Yeah, yeah I do. Just two weeks ago my wife asked me how I got them and I told her I didn't know."

"Where are they?" I pressed.

"Right here," he said as he bent down to pull up the right leg of his suit pants. All three of us immediately leaned over to look. There, just above his right ankle, on the back of his leg, was not one, but two, dark, scoop marks just like the many others I had seen before. We all sat and stared at one another in amazement, until one of my friends finally broke the silence. "How do you know so much about this stuff?" he demanded. All attention was focused on me.

"Well," I began, "I know a lot about UFOs, it's been kind of a hobby of mine for a long time." Then I told them about my role as an abduction investigator and how I would be introducing Bob Dean at the lecture on Saturday night. As I spoke, I could see the expressions of amazement and bewilderment cross their faces. "What in the hell is going on here?" they seemed to be asking themselves. Then Bob spoke. "I think we need to talk." "Yes," I agreed. "We have a lot to talk about."

The epiphany of that moment lingered in the air for a long time as we all suddenly realized that the world of UFOs had just reached out and grasped us all in a way that we could not deny. Whatever was going on was big, so big that we were all involved, and "all," we began to realize, was not just those of us seated at the table, but all humanity—the entire human race.

Coping with the Impossible

Later, when Bob and I had a chance to talk in private, he was still in a state of shock and bewilderment. He had never made a conscious connection between his scars, the missing time experience and the light in the sky and making those connections was like having a light bulb turn on in his head. For the first time he could see a pattern emerge that included numerous other strange experiences and vivid, life-like dreams that had haunted him throughout life. But at that moment, what perplexed him most was the manner in which this revelation had come to him. How could it be, he wondered, that one of his close friends, someone he had known for many years, could coincidentally also be an investigator of alien abductions? He could not imagine another situation in which he would have been willing to confide his story to a UFO researcher, or anyone else for that matter. Yet, here he was, presented with the opportunity to have his story heard by one of the few people in El Paso who would understand and be able to help. The coincidence was impressive for both of us.

Bob is not the type of person who would ever have joined MUFON. Attend a lecture maybe, but join the organization, never. He is also not the type of person who would likely seek psychological help. In his position as a highly-paid executive with a fairly high profile in the community, he could simply not risk being associated with UFOs, much less being thought of as an abductee. Furthermore, he is a highly self-sufficient, well-balanced individual and, like most men, he is reluctant to ask anyone for help of any kind.

Until that day, he would never have classified himself as abductee and, in fact, would never have told his story to us if he had understood its significance. Because he had never thought of himself as an "abductee," he was struggling to adjust his self image. Clearly, the thought of what might have happened to him and his friend during those several hours of missing time struck terror into his very soul.

"Bob," I said, "why don't you consider meeting with Dr. Fennig and discussing your case. It's possible that hypnosis would do you some good."

Bob's eyes widened at the thought of giving up control of his mind to another. "I know it sounds scary," I continued, "but there's really nothing to it. It's just a way to relax your mind so you can remember what happened. You won't lose control. Even while you're hypnotized, you will be in control. You can wake up any time you want to."

"But I don't need help," he argued. "My life is great; I don't have any problems."

"Well, aren't you just a little bit curious about what happened and what it all means?" I countered.

"I am curious, but I'm afraid it would change my life and I don't want my life to change. Right now I can just push it out of my mind. I can just not think about it and I can go on living a normal life. Why should I rock the boat?"

I had to admit that what he was saying made sense. There was no use in trying to help someone who didn't want to be helped. Yet, I knew that when the person's time to remember has come, the beings become hard to ignore. Sometimes, it seemed to me, the beings used fear tactics to scare the person into dealing with them. It's as if they are frustrated with humanity's ability to ignore and deny the paranormal. Subtle hints just don't work. I remembered one case in which a friend told me about an experience that another one of our friends had gone through recently. It seems that while he was brushing his teeth, the plastic cup that was sitting on the sink suddenly flew across the room, hit the wall and dropped to the floor. I had the opportunity to speak discuss it with him about a month after the incident. "Hey, tell me about the cup that flew across the room," I said excitedly. "Oh, that. That was nothing. It must have just been the wind."

Already he had rationalized the incident and put it out of his mind, another example of how we go out of our way to ignore those rips in the fabric of reality that they encounter throughout their lives. "Oh, that? That was just a coincidence," could be the motto of civilized man.

So the beings are forced to resort to extreme measures just to get our attention. And nothing works quite so well as fear. Somehow they will find a way to nudge the person and force him to make room in his life for them.

In another case, an acquaintance confided in me his strange and terrifying experiences since childhood that included bizarre dreams of aliens and awakening with scars on his body. This 35-year-old professional, who I will call "Jack," phoned me one day to ask if I would meet him for lunch. When I arrived at the restaurant, I found him hunched in a back corner, looking rather tense. "What's up?" I asked.

"I want to show you something," he said as he unbuttoned the top buttons of his dress shirt and moved his tie to one side. "Feel right here," he demanded, pointing to a spot on his chest. Placing my finger on his chest, I could feel a hard, cyst-like object that could be rolled slightly to either side, just under his skin.

"What is it?" I inquired.

"I don't know, I guess it's a cyst."

"When did you first notice it?"

"This morning."

"You mean it just appeared there suddenly, overnight?" I asked incredulously.

"Yeah, that's right. I'm on my way to have the doctor look at it."

"That's a good idea. Let me know what he says."

Jack's doctor, who also happens to be a close family friend, looked at the lump and recommended that he return in two weeks to have it removed, an operation that he would take care of in his office. But, less than a week later, Jack called me again. "Can you meet me for lunch?" he pleaded, obviously distressed. "Sure Jack, I'll meet you right away."

Again, he began unbuttoning his shirt. "Look at this!" he said pointing once again to the area of the cyst. As I examined the area, I was surprised to see a scar about an inch and a half long, a perfectly straight line of a cut that had healed some time ago. "Was that scar there the last time I showed you the cyst?"

"No, definitely not." I answered. "Did you already have it taken out? I thought your appointment wasn't until next week?"

"I'm not sure," he said haltingly.

"What do you mean you're not sure? Surely you would know, wouldn't you?"

"I called my doctor this morning when I found the scar and I asked him if he had already operated on me, but he said my appointment is next Wednesday. So I rushed over there to show him the scar. After I showed it to him, he had to check his records to make sure I hadn't been in to have the surgery. I hadn't. Then he accused me of going to another doctor."

"What did you tell him?"

"I told him I hadn't. And besides, that thing is still in there."

I pressed my finger against his skin and sure enough, I could still feel the lump. We sat and stared at one another for a long moment, as the realization of what was happening sank in. Finally, he broke the silence. "What do you think it means?" he asked.

"Well, it could be that they don't want you ignoring them. Maybe they're trying to tell you something." Jack's eyes widened as he contemplated my analysis.

"Maybe you're right."

Over the next few weeks Jack's anxiety level had increased and he was having trouble sleeping. "I'm ready," he said one day. "Set up an appointment for me next week. I'll do the hypnosis; I just can't go on this way."

"By the way," I asked "what ever happened with the cyst?"

"Oh, I had it removed and it was just a cyst."

But months later, when he was telling his story to another of our friends, he showed us the scar once more. I could still see the mysterious scar he had shown me before, but there was no other scar indicating that his doctor had performed the surgery. In addition, the object was still there, under the skin.

"I thought you said your doctor removed that thing," I asked incredulously.

"I thought he did."

144

"Well, there should be two scars now, not one. And the object should be gone."

Jack's face registered his confusion. "Well, I remember being on a table with a big white light in front of my eyes. I was sure I had it taken out."

We all three looked at each other with big eyes. It seemed clear that Jack's efforts to have the object removed had met with failure and that his memories were extremely confused. Changing the subject, I asked if his 12-year-old son, who had also been having abduction-type symptoms, would allow me to interview him.

"You know," he continued, "last week we rented the movie, *Fire in the Sky*, about that guy that gets abducted."

"Yes, I know the one."

"Well, the whole family was sitting in front of the TV watching the movie. There's this part in the movie where the forest workers are out in the woods and they see a UFO. A light shines down from above and hits the guy who gets abducted."

"Yeah, I remember that."

"Well, when my son saw that, he jumped up from the couch and bolted out of the room. We asked him to stay, but he just kept right on going. He was shaken up."

"I would sure like to talk to him. Do you think he would meet with me?" I asked.

"He doesn't want to have anything to do with it. He won't talk about it. Period."

Efforts to get Bob and Jack to attend the support group meetings failed. Both seemed determined to push the beings out of their lives and to ignore their communications in spite of a constant high level of anxiety. For Jack, whose night visitations continued, the effort took real determination. He was determined to stay in control of his life. But they just wouldn't go away. In the course of the ensuing year, more scars appeared and then mysteriously disappeared. Then, when family members were passing through town, the subject of UFOs came up. In the course of a discussion late into the night, he learned that both his brother and sister had both missing time experiences and alien encounters. "If they'll do hypnosis first, then I'll do it," was Jack's attitude. "I'll believe it when I see it," I said.

Eventually, Jack's brother, who is a physician living in another city, met with researcher John Carpenter to undergo hypnosis and to learn about a missing time experience he had in the late 1960s as he was driving alone near Pecos, Texas. Under hypnosis, he remembered a surgical procedure in which a bright, white light was shone into his face. Two months later, in June 1996, Jack underwent hypnosis with Dr. Roberta Fennig. He remembered that in the early morning hours of the day he found the object under his skin, he was levitated out of bed and up through the ceiling toward a large, black donut-shaped object that hovered directly over his house. That was as far as he could go in the experience, but it was enough to confirm for him the other-worldly aspect of his strange scar. His sister is still struggling to cope with a traumatic missing-time experience which she had in California recently. Even without the aid of hypnosis, she remembers the strange, antlike creatures that took her up a ramp into some kind of strange vehicle and performed surgery on her. The case is still being investigated.

Other Revelations

Within a month of finding out about Bob's and Jack's experiences, my wife and I were at a dinner party made up of five couples, some of whom were long-time friends. We were in the middle of dinner, when Sandy, who happened to be seated next to me, turned and spoke to me softly. "I understand that you are interested in UFOs." "Yes, I am," I answered.

"Well, I think I need to come and talk to you."

"What about?" I asked innocently.

"Well, I have always had these strange experiences and I think it has to do with aliens."

"What kind of experiences?"

"Well, for example, I'll be at home during the day all alone and one moment it will be 10 in the morning and the very next instant it will be 1 o'clock in the afternoon. I can never figure out where the time went. Then another time I saw a ball of light about the size of a basketball come floating down the hall toward me. Then I don't remember anything. It was suddenly hours later and the ball was gone."

"What else?" I asked.

"Well, there are the strange scars I find on my body in the mornings. There's no way I could get them in bed!"

I was about to ask her another question, when her husband overheard our conversation and interrupted us with a stern look, as if to say, "Don't you dare talk about that!"

Sandy, embarrassed and not wanting to get into an argument, let the subject drop. But I was impressed by the emotion in her voice and the seriousness with which she told her story. I was pretty sure Sandy was an abductee. But again, social pressures made it difficult for her to deal with it. It was clear that her husband did not want her talking to anyone about her experiences and it was likely that he, like Bob, was concerned about his position in the business community.

It was several weeks before I had the opportunity to talk to Sandy again. I had hoped that she would call me, but she hadn't. I didn't feel it would be appropriate to initiate such contact, but I had given her husband some video tapes on the abduction phenomenon and on UFOs to watch. Although he accepted them, he made it clear that he did not believe in alien abductions. "Well, do you believe in UFOs?" I asked. "Yes, I can accept that there are UFOs, but I don't accept that there are little buglike creatures abducting people."

We ran into Sandy and her husband at a large party and when the opportunity came, I asked her how she was doing. "I'm fine. I'm handling it. Thank you for the video tapes. We watched them together and they helped. But I just don't feel the need to go any further with it."

"Okay," I said, "But if you change your mind, I want you to know that we have a highly professional team with a lot of experience ready to help. We also have a support group where you can go and meet other people who have had these experiences."

"Thanks, but I'm fine."

Although Sandy and her husband have attended some of the lectures MUFON has sponsored, their secret is closely guarded and not discussed often. Such is the life of most abductees.

On another occasion, the wife of another acquaintance stopped me in the mall. "I need to talk to you," she said. "Sure, what is it?"

"Well, I've heard that you are interested in UFOs. Is that right?"

"Yes, that's right. In fact, I investigate cases of alien abduction."

"Well," she said, "I'm having those same experiences. You know, the strange dreams of aliens and UFOs and then waking up with scars on my body."

"How long has this been going on?" I asked.

"A long time."

"What does your husband say about it?

"He's paranoid. He doesn't want me to tell anyone. He's afraid people will find out and think I'm crazy or weird."

"That's interesting, because I've talked to him about UFOs and he is very interested in the subject. In fact, that's all he wants to talk about."

"Yes, but he doesn't want people to know about my experiences. Maybe it's too scary. I've got to go. You can't tell him I told you all this. He would kill me."

"Okay, I promise. But please call me if you need help."

"Yes, I will."

And she was gone.

On the month following Bob Dean's lecture, May of 1994, we celebrated Mother's Day by having a large family gathering at an Italian restaurant. A 30-year-old, single woman who is a friend of the family approached me. "Hey, do I ever have a story to tell you."

"What is it, Toni?" I asked.

"Well, you know that I never believed in UFOs, but now I do! I know you believe in them, so I know you'll be interested in what happened to me and my boyfriend the other night."

"What happened?"

"Well, we'd gone to the late movie at the mall and we got out about 11:30. We got in the car and pulled out of the parking lot, heading toward the mountain. At that time of night that road is empty and dark. Suddenly, out of nowhere, came this object and it stayed right above the car. We could see it clearly, it was huge and it had different colored lights, green, yellow and red that were rotating around it."

"What happened next?" I urged.

She stopped to think for a moment, then she continued. "It just took off. It shot off faster than anything I've ever seen. And here's the weird part. It flew right into the mountain. When it hit the mountain, we could see like sparks fly in all directions, then it was gone. We both

148

had goose bumps all over us when it was over. We drove around for a long time talking about it. We didn't feel like going straight home."

"What time did you get home?" I probed.

"I don't know."

"Why don't you know?"

"We just weren't keeping track of the time. I have no idea what time it was when he dropped me off at my house."

"Well, how did you feel after it was gone?"

"We were both very upset. I've never seen my boyfriend so scared. He won't even talk about it any more, it upsets him too much."

"What's so upsetting and scary about seeing a UFO?" I asked.

"Well, it was so close. It was right above the car. It was real."

"You know, oftentimes when people have these experiences, they find that if they think a little, they can remember other strange experiences. Have you had any other strange experiences?"

A look of surprise crossed her face and then she answered. "Yes, I have, but I don't think they have anything to do with this."

"Tell me about them."

"Well, it's kind of hard to talk about," she said, nervously. "It has to do with things that happen to me in the night, in my room."

"What kinds of things?"

"I think I'm being visited by the devil or a demon."

"Why do you think that?"

"Well, sometimes I wake up in the middle of the night and I can't move. I'm just paralyzed. I can tell there is someone nearby, but I can't see anyone. It says horrible things to me. I can't even repeat them. Also, I have terrible nightmares that seem real. Sometimes I'm flying through the air. Ever since I was a child, I've felt I was being watched or monitored."

"Do you have any scars or marks on your body that you can't account for when they happened?"

"Well, there is one—on my knee. I've had it since I was little and I always wondered how I got it. In fact, I remember playing with my friends and we would find little pebbles to put in it because it was so deep that the pebbles wouldn't fall out."

"Will you show me?"

"Sure," she said as she rolled up her pant leg. There, on the front of her knee was a round scoop scar, still bearing a marked indentation.

149

"What does it mean?" she asked.

"Well, it is similar to many scars I have seen on people who have had close encounters with UFOs. I think you should consider coming to one of our meetings and learning more about this."

"Yeah, maybe I will."

Over the following months, Toni and her mother attended several lectures on the subject of UFOs and alien abductions and watched video tapes that I loaned them. But the idea of hypnosis has simply been too scary for her to deal with. On several occasions, she scheduled appointments and then, at the last minute, she canceled them. To this day, she is not totally convinced that she is an abductee. She still believes she is possessed by evil spirits—demons. To cope with her terror, she joined a Bible study and prayer group and is searching for spirituality. Every once in a while she calls me to tell me about a new experience and to let me know she is still thinking about hypnosis.

And so it continues. My involvement with MUFON was like a stone dropped into a great pond and the ripples keep spreading into ever-widening circles. People are still taking me aside to tell me their experiences and then swearing me to secrecy. They, in turn, often realize that others near them are involved as well—a brother, a sister, a son, a daughter, or possibly a spouse. Recently, my wife and I were at a large party which was being given as a benefit for a local charity. It dawned on me that there were four people in the room who had reported alien encounters to me and then asked me to keep their secret. They mingled in the crowd, exchanging pleasantries and standing near each other in the food buffet, but never imagining their common bond. If only they could sit down together and tell each other about their experiences, and learn from one another. How much better off they would be. Yet none knew of the others, and I was not at liberty to tell. Such is the life of many who have experienced alien encounters in a society that makes discussion of such things taboo. They live with their fears hidden in the darkest recesses of their minds, trying desperately to keep them at bay and praying fervently that their worst suspicions aren't true—that those vivid nightmares they keep having might not be nightmares at all, but all-too-real visits by beings from beyond the imagination.

CHAPTER 9

ABDUCTEES: SHAMANS OF THE MODERN AGE

"We recycle souls."

—The visitors' response to Whitley Strieber when asked who they were.

Contactees v. Abductees

Gradually, over the past 40 or so years, ufologists became aware that there were actually intelligent beings aboard the flying saucers they were studying and that these mysterious beings were actually interacting with humans and with other life forms on Earth in complex ways. As improbable as it may seem today, acceptance of extraterrestrials, even by ufologists, took a long time. It was only during the last 20 years or so that researchers began to take seriously the idea that alien life forms were actually a reality. Before that time, the study of UFOs consisted primarily of the examination and analysis of photographic evidence and soil samples. Witnesses were interrogated regarding the height, width and shape of the object they observed, the direction of travel, the time of day, etc., and weather reports were obtained, as well as statements from local air traffic controllers and military officials. It seemed as if researchers were content with studying the spacecraft and had only minimal interest in their occupants. In those rare cases where sightings of alien beings were taken seriously, as in the now-famous Socorro, New Mexico, case in which policeman Lonnie Zamora described seeing two small aliens, such detail was duly noted and put in the file. Follow-up questions regarding such things as paranormal phenomena, telepathic communication, previous missing time experiences, etc. were not standard procedures in traditional investigations. Ufologists, just like everyone else, found it easier to cope with the idea that flying saucers would occasionally land and that ETs might get out to collect a soil sample (or to perhaps "kick the tires,") than with the possibility that they were actually making contact with humans.

Early reports of alien contact in the U.S. and in other parts of the world came in the 1950s when people like George Adamski, Daniel Fry and numerous others received national attention with their sensational stories of being invited aboard flying saucers by their "space brothers" who had given them rides to Venus and other improbable locations and who had imparted to them great wisdom. The space brothers were reported to be beautiful, blonde, blue-eyed, human-like beings who were here to save humankind from the dangers of nuclear radiation. People who made such claims, known as "contactees," were not taken seriously by neither the public at large nor by serious researchers of the UFO phenomenon, who sought desperately to distance themselves from the "kooks" who made ufology look foolish. The incredible claims and photographs of flying discs produced by the contactees were grist for the mill of the tabloid press, but an anathema to serious researchers who believed them to be the product of hoaxes or of the mentally disturbed.

Making matters even more difficult and embarrassing for serious ufologists is the fact that groups of devoted followers frequently spring up around contactees, who may be seen by their devotees as "mini messiahs" who possess secret spiritual knowledge.

A case in point is the ongoing story of Eduard "Billy" Meier, the one-armed Swiss contactee who sells copies of his UFO photos, films and spiritual teachings gained through his reported contact with beautiful, blonde-haired, blue-eyed, human-looking Pleiadians, among others. Among the many strange twists and turns to this controversial case is *The Talmud of Jmmanuel*,[1] a translation from Aramaic through German to English of material that Meier says involves the true teachings of Jmmanuel, the man known more commonly as Jesus. Meier

---

1. Meier, 1990.

still refuses to identify the Greek home of the assassinated Lebanese priest, Isa Rashid, with whom he is said to have found the document, presumedly in order to protect Rashid's family from harm. Although Meier claims that the original, Aramaic text was destroyed, many of his followers and some researchers continue to believe that the document is genuine. The document, which is analyzed by Dr. James Deardorff in his book *Celestial Teachings,*[2] is similar to the Gospel of Matthew, but includes numerous heretical elements. Among these are the revelations that ETs and their ships account for the major events in Jesus' life, such as the virgin birth, the star of Bethlehem and his ascension into heaven. Additionally, it states that Jesus' belief in and teachings about reincarnation, rather than physical resurrection, was the central purpose of his role on Earth. Rather than being resurrected, Jesus is said to have survived the crucifixion and to have continued his ministry for several decades. Many surviving traditions trace Jesus's presence and movements from Anatolia across to northern India and Kashmir.[3] According to the *Talmud of Jmmanuel*, Jesus had children and eventually died a normal death and was buried in Srinagar, Kashmir. Deardorff finds several hundred points of textual criticism that indicate that the Gospel of Matthew was based upon the Talmud of Jmmanuel rather than vice versa.

For obvious reasons, however, ufologists who struggle to gain scientific credibility and good reputations within a predominantly Christian society have been highly skeptical of these claims and have sought to discredit Meier and other contactees, even though, as we shall see in the next chapter, cases of spiritual teachings, beautiful blondes and references to ET involvement in Earth's religions continue to crop up in many abduction-type cases.

By the mid 1960s, a few ufologists became aware of alien contact cases that were far different than those of the contactees. These were cases in which average persons were apparently kidnapped for short periods of time and used for bizarre medical experiments. These were the cases of alien abduction. Unlike the contactees who claimed to interact with ETs in full states of consciousness and who went out of their way to gain public attention, the abductees had little conscious

2. Deardorff, 1989.
3. Deardorff, 1994.

memories of their experiences aboard the spacecraft, and they shunned public attention. Moreover, many of the experiencers were obviously traumatized and in states of near emotional breakdown as a result of something that happened to them. And many cases included multiple witnesses who had shared the unbelievable experiences.

The First Abduction Investigation

Betty and Barney Hill, a middle-aged, mixed-race, New England couple, sought the aid of a psychiatrist in the early 1960s due to severe anxiety and nightmares they suffered as a result of a UFO sighting they shared in upper New Hampshire one September night in 1961. Their well-known case serves today as the model for abduction investigations due to the thoroughness with which it was performed and because the "classic" nature of their circumstances have emerged time and again in hundreds of cases around the world.

As Betty and Barney were driving on a lonely Hew Hampshire road late at night, they noticed a strange looking star in the sky that seemed to be moving. The star soon grew closer and the Hills stopped to get a better look, assuming it to be an aircraft of some kind. Their last conscious memories before the abduction were of seeing the spacecraft up close, hovering just above tree top level, seeing a row of lighted windows and seeing "people" standing inside. Under hypnosis, they each recalled driving to a secluded area on a side road, while in some sort of trance, where the car engine died and several small, gray beings with large black, almond-shaped eyes led them from the car to the awaiting craft. Once inside, they were separated, stripped and placed on examination tables where they were thoroughly examined. Part of the examination included the insertion of a long needle through Betty's abdomen (presumably to remove ova) and, it was revealed in later years, the taking of a sperm sample from Barney.

In their efforts to understand what happened to them, the Hills wrote a letter to Major Donald Keyhoe, author of the book, *The Flying Saucer Conspiracy*[4] in which he claimed that the Air Force was attempting to discredit all UFO sightings and thereby stifle scientific inquiry. Keyhoe, an Annapolis graduate and a Marine Corps Major, had been instrumental in organizing the National Investigations Committee on

---

4. Keyhoe, 1955.

Aerial Phenomenon (NICAP), a highly regarded group of scientists and military officers dedicated to the serious investigation of the UFO phenomenon. The case was referred to Walter Webb, a lecturer on the staff of the Hayden Planetarium in Boston and a scientific adviser to NICAP who had investigated some of the more significant cases in the New England area. His reaction to the referral was noted in John G. Fuller's 1967 book, *The Interrupted Journey:*[5]

> Webb's first reaction…was reluctance. It was plain that this case involved a report of the movement of beings on the craft, and Webb was skeptical of this type of sighting. There had been in the past a rash of this sort of thing from highly irresponsible people, none of whom had provided any type of rational documentation, and who insisted on talking about such incidents in the most exaggerated terms. Webb was determined not to become associated with any such irresponsible case.[6]

But although his intentions were to debunk the case, after meeting the Hills and interrogating them for most of a day, he found himself extremely impressed by the sincerity, high literacy and anxiety displayed by the Hills. His doubts about a hoax and about the mental competency of the witnesses had been dispelled:

> I had read of such cases before, but this is the first time I had come in contact with apparently reliable witnesses who claimed to have seen UFO occupants. Of course, we have to be very careful about such cases. Very careful. I was impressed that the Hills underplayed the dramatic aspects of the case. They were not trying to sensationalize. They did not seek publicity. They wanted me to keep this just to myself, confidential with NICAP. Barney's complete resistance to the idea of UFOs was most convincing…. Mr. Hill had been a complete UFO skeptic before the sighting. In fact the experience so jolted his reason and sensibilities that his mind evidently could not make the adjustment…. A mental block occurred when he mentioned the "leader" [of the beings] peering out the window [of the craft] at him. Mr. Hill believes he saw something he doesn't want to remember.[7]

5. Fuller, 1967.
6. Fuller, 1967, p. 51.
7. Fuller, 1967, p. 54.

Thus began the first scientific investigation into the alien abduction phenomenon, an investigation that would eventually include two more, highly regarded scientists, a former Air Force intelligence officer and Dr. Benjamin Simon, a Boston psychiatrist of impeccable credentials. The ultimate conclusion on the part of the investigators was that the Hills had experienced something that could not be explained through traditional scientific rationales. The case included indisputable elements that precluded a simple psychological explanation. First, a period of shared amnesia for a brief period of time with no obvious cause, such as trauma to the head or exposure to toxic or mind-altering substances. Second, shared traumatic stress and nightmares associated with the missing-time episode. Third, shared conscious recollections of the spacecraft and the occupants and fourth, physical evidence in the form of markings on the car and on the body of Barney Hill (a mysterious circle of warts in the groin area). In addition, both Betty and Barney would undergo many hours of hypnosis in which they separately recalled the events that occurred aboard the ship. The stories they told, from their own points of view, were identical and complemented each other in practically every detail. The investigators could find no evidence of hoaxing, of collaboration or of mental illness. They could only conclude that the Hills were telling the truth and that the Hills' chilling story about what occurred aboard the craft had to be true, or at least that they believed it to be true.

For psychiatrist Benjamin Simon, the case presented an awesome challenge to everything he had ever been taught about mental illness, the human experience, the workings of the human brain and reality itself. Nowhere in his medical books could he find explanations for or even examples of such things as "shared amnesia" of this type and "shared dreams" that resulted in "shared trauma." In addition, the correlation of the witnesses' memories, both conscious and under hypnosis, was so accurate that only through convoluted reasoning could he, or anyone else, arrive at a conclusion that the Hills had not experienced anything but a real event. Yet, ever mindful of his status as a reputable member of the psychiatric profession, Simon was extremely cautious in his public comments about the case and failed to even address the issue of the above mentioned anomalies. He clearly wished to separate himself from any conclusions regarding the reality of their experiences, in spite of the strong evidence to the contrary. In his introduction to Fuller's book, he ducked the issue by insinuating that the whole affair might somehow be associated with fantasies. He also admits having "editorial rights" over Mr. Fuller's work.

The Hidden Epidemic

Little did the investigators in the Hill case know, but a virtual epidemic of abduction cases would flood ufology in the years following the publication of Fuller's book and the made-for-TV movie. Literally thousands of persons cautiously began to come forward to reveal their stories to the few researchers willing to listen. In 1977, Coral and Jim Lorenzen, the founders of the Aerial Phenomenon Research Organization (APRO), published the first book on the abduction phenomenon, titled, *Abducted*.[8] Still, the UFO research community and the public at large remained unconvinced. And then, in the 1980s, beginning with the publication of Budd Hopkins' *Missing Time*, the head gates to a great reservoir of experiences were suddenly cast open. Hopkins' well researched investigation documented 19 abduction cases he had investigated during a six-year period, beginning in 1976. Then, almost simultaneously in 1987, two additional books created a sensation. Hopkin's second book, *Intruders*,[9] detailing for the first time startling information about the alien "hybridization" program, was released on the heels of Whitley Strieber's intensely dramatic personal account of his alien encounters. His book, *Communion*,[10] stayed on the *New York Times* Best Seller list for ten months in the non-fiction category, sold over ten million copies worldwide and caused a sensation in the UFO research community. Never before had a well known person (in this case a best-selling novelist) come forward to admit publicly that he was an abductee. His book and the made-for-TV movie, *Intruders*, based on Hopkins' book,[11] unleashed a torrent of letters to ufologists and UFO organizations from people around the world who claimed to have had similar experiences. These events served to thrust the abduction phenomenon squarely to the forefront of public consciousness and catapult UFO research out of the realm of the physical sciences and into the much more tenuous areas of psychology and the paranormal.

8. Lorenzen, 1977.
9. Hopkins, 1987.
10. Strieber, 1987.
11. Hopkins, 1987.

In the ensuing years, it has become obvious that the Hills' story, rather than being an isolated and unusual case, is merely one of perhaps millions of cases, and, in fact, is to a great extent a fairly typical example of the abduction scenario as uncovered by respectable researchers in every part of the U.S. Indeed, at this point, there is no reason to believe that the same scenario is not being carried out all over the world. Similar cases have been discovered in Mexico, Canada, England, Australia, Germany, Israel and many other countries.

Abduction Research

Even the most conservative UFO researchers and UFO organizations began taking the phenomenon seriously by the early 1970s. Soon after being organized in 1969, the Mutual UFO Network (MUFON) began receiving information on abduction cases and began including abduction researchers among its membership. One of its early members was Dr. Leo Sprinkle, then an assistant professor of psychology at the University of Wyoming, who was one of the first to take the phenomenon and its accompanying paranormal aspects seriously. By 1975, abduction researcher Budd Hopkins, whose research first exposed the alien hybrid engineering program, became a MUFON member and before long, abduction researchers such as John Carpenter, a psychiatric social worker from Springfield, Missouri, and Dr. John Mack of Harvard, came to sit on the MUFON board of directors. In 1981, the annual MUFON symposium, conducted at the Massachusetts Institute of Technology (MIT), featured Dr. J. Allen Hynek as keynote speaker, as well as two abduction researchers who delivered papers on the growing abduction phenomenon. Budd Hopkins delivered a paper titled, "UFO Abductions, The Invisible Epidemic," and psychologist Dr. Aphrodite Claymore spoke on "Missing Time: A Psychologist Examines the UFO Evidence."

Over the last 15 years, abduction researchers have conducted investigations in every major city in the U.S., and today abductees can receive assistance in the form of counseling and support groups in practically every state.

However, no single organization or researcher has access to all the abduction research that has been, and continues to be, conducted throughout the world. Independent researchers proliferate, standardized procedures are lacking, reporting procedures are cumbersome and, in some cases, professional jealousies prevent researchers from sharing their data. As a result, generalizations about the nature of the phenomenon, the purpose for the abductions, the types of beings involved, their origins and the relationships between the various types of beings are difficult to make. The most systematic effort thus far to answer such questions involves a massive study launched in 1992 by MUFON, called the Abduction Transcription Project, directed by Dan Wright. Funded in part by the Fund for UFO Research, the project collects transcripts of audiotaped interviews and hypnosis sessions with experiencers, provided by well known and respected researchers from different parts of the country. The verbatim transcripts are entered into a sophisticated computer system for a multi-factor analysis of the abduction experience. Ultimately, it is hoped that the data will reveal the true nature of the abduction experience and be able to answer many of the questions researchers have about the beings and their purpose. Through February 1996, Wright had accumulated 750 transcripts involving 215 separate cases detailing abductions going back to the 1940s. Although this represents a massive amount of data, it is clear that the project is in its infancy and that many more cases are needed to reach the point where the resulting analysis will have scientific validity. Even so, it is the best information available regarding the nature of the beings and of their activities to date and deserves close attention.

At the 1995 MUFON Symposium held in Seattle, Wright summarized the project's findings, which at that time consisted of only 142 cases, submitted by 15 researchers. The topics addressed in his presentation included the means used by the beings to capture and transport subjects, the layout of the ships, appearance of the entities, behaviors and emotions displayed, reproductive and other procedures conducted, the presence of "hybrid" beings and other humans seen on board, physical effects discovered after the abduction, etc. Excerpts from Wright's presentation give us a few clues as to the nature of the phenomenon.

An "away team" of very short, whitish, grayish or bluish beings take the person from his home, car or other location. In 45 of the cases, the beings passed through solid walls or objects during the abduction and in 31 cases the witnesses were aware that they, themselves, were being passed through solid matter, such as a wall or a ceiling and then floated up to an awaiting craft. Wright reports that one of the beings heads the team and speaks for the others, always telepathically. A being who is perceived to be a doctor takes over aboard the craft. This being is nearly always taller than the others and is sensed to be male, although gender differences are not outwardly visible. "Often displaying a superior, no-nonsense demeanor, he performs intricate procedures on the subject. Other beings of nearly the same likeness serve as 'interns' or 'technicians,' helping to examine the subject. They are sometimes chastised by the doctor for lack of precision. Quite often, one of these is sensed by the abductee to be female and is given the job of comforting the subject, ensuring cooperation."

Sometimes, subjects report the presence of a tall blonde—an extremely tall male with human features that include pale skin, longish blonde hair and blue, green or hazel eyes who stands nearby, but who serves no obvious function. "Several subjects," reports Wright, "have been certain in retrospect that this was his/her real father." In some cases, a "heavily wrinkled, old one" makes an appearance, but again, does not seem to be performing any function. Two other types reported in the study were the insectoids or "praying mantis" types, which are described to have a thin, skeletal body and the face of a praying mantis, and the reptilian types, which are described as having powerful, muscled bodies, greenish or brownish, scaly skin, penetrating, yellow "cat eyes" with vertically-slit pupils and four-fingered, clawed hands with webbing between the fingers. Often these last two types are thought to be in leadership positions.[12]

Onboard Activity

Among the procedures reported are the forced ingestion of a peculiar liquid, external brain scanning, internal probing of the brain with needles or drilling instruments, implantation of small objects in various parts of the body and sampling of blood, tissue, bone marrow and bodily fluids. Forty percent reported enduring sexually-related intrusions. For the men, this entailed the placement of an apparatus over the testicles and penis for the removal of semen and for the women it usually involved the removal of ova by means of a needle through the navel. The women also reported the insertion of a very small object,

---

12. Wright, 1995, pp. 165-203.

thought to be an embryo, into the womb, and subsequently the removal of a two- to three-month-old fetus.

Wright also reports on what is one of the most disturbing elements of the abduction scenario:

> In three incidents, a woman was forced to have sexual relations with a male abductee also onboard who appeared compelled to perform the act, judging by his dazed appearance. Two subjects recounted that they were mounted and raped aboard a craft—a woman by a taller figure with grayish-white skin, and a man by a short yellowish-gray female. In a third case, a woman awoke in bed amid the throes of sexual passion to discover scaly claws at her private parts—indicative of a reptilian.[13]

In 40 cases, the experiencers received nonverbal communication in the form of visual images transmitted to them either telepathically or shown to them on a computer screen, via a holographic image. Often the images are of other planets, star systems or extraterrestrial landscapes. Five subjects received images from Earth's past, "from dinosaurs to early twentieth-century wars." While in 13 cases, there was "imagery depicting Earth's future. Without exception it was an unpleasant sight: volcanoes erupting, nuclear power plants exploding, vast regions on fire, devastated rain forests and the like."

Thirty-one subjects, both male and female, were shown a being or beings that were apparently half human and half alien. In eight cases, the person was taken to a separate room where they were shown numerous hybrid fetuses being grown in tanks filled with a liquid. "An umbilical cord connected the pre-infant to tubes, which, in turn, led to a machine. Thirteen subjects reported being presented with a "terribly pale and frail hybrid newborn and told that s/he had helped to create that child." In several cases, women abductees were handed an infant and told to nurse it. In those cases, they reported that "amazingly…her breasts were filled with milk.…" Three hybrid experiences involved children older than toddlers, one with an adult hybrid present. Eleven others described hybrids of undetermined age, but all described the hybrids as being extremely thin, having large heads with patches of wispy hair and unusually large eyes that were either all

---

13. Wright, 1995.

black, like the Grey's, or human-like. "In one case, a hybrid child, dressed in a simple gown and adjudged to be of elementary school age, approached the subject and said matter-of-factly, 'You are my mother.'"

Paranormal Aspects

A few of the subjects in the study reported events that are hard to categorize. One discovered that he was able to levitate objects with the power of his mind, while aboard the ship. Three persons said that they felt that they (their souls) had been placed somehow into the body of a gray alien. They recognized their own hands as those of a gray entity. (Since there were no mirrors available, they couldn't tell what the rest of their bodies looked like.) One commented that his body felt "much slimmer than his normal stocky frame." Two of the three remembered that the purpose of their being placed in an alien body was due to the fact that the ship was about to travel "inter-dimensionally" and a change to a body with a different vibration was necessary. These few individuals felt a strong connection with the aliens and even felt that they, in fact, had a dual existence. Sixteen of the subjects voiced a conviction that the "entities are their true forbears."[14]

Although not reported in this study, past-life memories, out-of-body experiences and increased psychic abilities are also common elements of abduction cases. Dr. John Mack, in his book, *Abduction*,[15] reports on several cases in which subjects have remembered, under hypnosis, past existences as aliens and of an agreement they made in a previous life to incarnate into their present body in order to carry out their mission as an "abductee." Although severely criticized by some UFO researchers for the lack of a "scientific" approach to his investigations, Mack broke new ground in pursuing the spiritual aspects of the experience, one that is present in every case, even if the investigator is unwilling or unable to understand it. Mack is not the only researcher who has come across such information. Other researchers have reported similar cases as well, but have been unwilling to report it because of its "unscientific" nature and because they are striving to

---

14. Wright, 1995, pp. 165-203.
15. Mack, 1994.

remove themselves from possible accusations that they are "New Age" kooks.

In addition to past-life memories, many experiencers report having had out-of-body experiences while at home, often in bed, as in the case of Michael Talbot, described in an earlier chapter. In some cases, abductees say that some of their abduction experiences have occurred completely out of body, as in the case of Betty Andreasson Luca as described previously, while others are not sure if a particular abduction occurred while in or out of their bodies. Instances in which the experiencers suddenly find themselves out of their bodies while in the company of the beings are also common. This commonly occurs when the subjects are on the operating table, observing themselves as the subject of a painful operation or procedure. Whether these experiences are spontaneous or are induced by the beings is unknown at this time. Cases have also been reported in which abductees have seen duplicate bodies of themselves and of numerous other humans, seemingly held in suspended animation in glass cases, presumably being kept for some unknown future purpose. Indeed, it would seem that the ETs have an entirely different attitude toward physical bodies than do we. To them, physical bodies seem to be only uniforms to be donned whenever they have a need to enter the physical, three-dimensional world. Whitley Strieber received this information in the form of a lesson, when, during an abduction, he was shown drawers full of alien bodies, stacked like a cord of wood, apparently in storage. Indeed, they even told him at one point that their purpose was to "recycle souls." The aliens seem to be trying to convey the idea to their human subjects that humans are more than just flesh and blood—that they are spiritual beings with a far greater importance and power than they, themselves, imagine.

Who Gets Abducted?

As comprehensive and important as the transcription project is to abduction research, because of the small quantity of data now being analyzed, it will be years before it can be used to generalize about the abduction experience. Much more work is needed to correlate the information from the thousands of cases being reported and studied. Some individuals, such as Budd Hopkins, John Mack, Whitley Strieber, Leo Sprinkle, David Jacobs, John Carpenter and others have access to information on hundreds of cases each (perhaps thousands in some cases), most of which have never been fully investigated. Yet there is no way to correlate the data they hold without a substantial investment of both time and money by someone who is so inclined to take on such a project. The one effort which has come closest to attempting such a feat was published in 1987 by folklorist Thomas E. Bullard.[16] The work, *UFO Abductions: The Measure of a Mystery,* includes data on 300 cases and serves today as one of the benchmark efforts to achieve a cross-sectional view of the abduction mystery. To his surprise, he found that one-third of the abductees in his sample had never undergone hypnosis to remember their experiences. In addition, he found that the identity of the hypnotherapist made no difference. The stories remained consistent down to minute details. He concluded that the phenomenon was not the product of hypnosis.

But again, 300 cases obtained from the files of researchers cannot be considered to be either a sufficient sample or a valid sample for such an undertaking. If there are indeed millions of abductees, as I and many other researchers believe, we will need a significantly larger and more valid sample to be able to say with any certainty what type of person has had the abduction experience and to what extent their experiences are similar. But the problem with finding a valid sample is that any sample obtained from the files of researchers is heavily skewed toward those experiencers who have been traumatized by the experience and who have therefore sought help. It would not be likely to contain many cases of persons who were not traumatized or who felt their experiences were manageable or even positive. Furthermore, every researcher conducts his or her own research according to his or her own standards. Each has his own biases and pet theories and the questions each asks his subjects may be quite different, thereby eliciting different information.

As discussed in a previous chapter, there are many experiencers who never seek help, but who, unfortunately for the researchers, would make excellent case studies. Many of these hold positions of importance or prestige in their communities. They are businessmen and women, physicians, educators, scientists and celebrities who perceive their potential loss of reputation and credibility so great that they

---

16. Bullard, 1987.

164

dare not come forward. Many of these individuals know what is happening to them. They read the books and watch the TV shows about the phenomenon, but they speak to very few about their situation. Their cases may never be studied and they may never participate in a survey. At the other end of the spectrum are those whose experiences have taken them over the edge. They are the ones who have been medicated or who have been institutionalized. They are the ones who have turned to drugs or alcohol to mask their fears. Or they may have serious psychological problems in addition to their paranormal experiences. These too tend to be screened out of the research. Finally, there are those who are in deep denial—those who simply cannot accept what is happening to them or who cannot bring themselves to change their paradigm to accept the reality of their experiences.

So, in truth, there is no way to say at this time with any certainty what kind of person is chosen for the abduction experience. Indeed, it may be that scientific methodology is simply incapable of dealing adequately with phenomena that originate in a nonphysical reality. We may in fact be spinning our wheels, so to speak, when we attempt to use science from a three-dimensional world to study fourth-dimensional experiences. The meager data at hand merely allows us to hazard guesses about the overall picture. From these studies it appears that men and women are taken in about equal numbers, that representatives of every race and religion are participants, and that children (even infants), as well as adults of all ages are involved. (It does appear that the experiences seem to dissipate the older one gets, yet there are cases in which elderly people have been abducted.) There is also a strong indication that abductees are not chosen at random from the population, but are preselected, even before birth. It may well be that they in fact preselect themselves, as previously mentioned. However, it seems quite apparent to researchers that a person's genes may have more to do with his or her involvement than anything else. This is due to the fact that the abduction phenomenon runs through families, from one generation to the next. It is well known among researchers that if you find one experiencer, you are more than likely to have found a family of experiencers, which may include some or all of the members of the immediate family, as well as members of the extended family, such as aunts, uncles and cousins, etc.

The Omega Project

Of particular interest to those who lean toward the God Hypothesis is a study conducted by a respected psychologist with no previous connection to UFO research, but who was instead interested in studying the near-death experience (NDE). Prior to his involvement in this area, NDEs had been described only in anecdotal form by various medical experts who had accumulated thousands of case studies. But it was Dr. Kenneth Ring, a professor of psychology at the University of Connecticut, who first attempted to analyze the cases scientifically in an attempt to determine if there was a psychological profile that differentiated an NDEr from nonexperiencers. Through his research, he determined that those who experience near death may be predisposed to the experience by childhood factors, which in many cases include a history of paranormal events. It was only after he had published two studies on the NDE experience that he began to take an interest in the abduction phenomenon, ultimately deciding to compare the two experiences. In his book, *The Omega Project*,[17] published in 1992, Ring explains how he first became aware that NDEs and UFO abductions were quite a lot alike, even though at first glance there seems to be marked differences. The most glaring difference is that in the NDE experience, there is frequently reported contact with a radiant, luminous figure, commonly called "a being of light," who is full of love and compassion. This did not at first sound to Ring anything like the abduction experience, which is full of hideous, buglike creatures and often feelings of stark terror.

It was only when he read Whitley Strieber's book, *Communion*,[18] sent to him by his publisher with a note to the effect that he should read the book immediately, that he began to soften his skeptical views toward the UFO phenomenon:

> ...As I got further into Strieber's story and particularly where some of the paradoxical-seeming positive aftereffects of his bizarre episodes began to emerge, the threads joining NDEs to UFO encounters like Strieber's were plain to see...these two very different types of personally shattering experiences could nevertheless apparently lead to a similar kind of transforma-

17. Ring, 1992.
18. Strieber, 1987.

tion. Indeed, when Strieber talked about the kind of self-insights he had come to through the deep exploration of his encounters, his personal values, and his fears and concerns for the ecological well-being of the Earth, and so on, he seemed to be speaking in the very phrases that I had heard so often from the lips of the near-death experiencers…. In describing the psychological and spiritual aftermath of his own encounters, he was doubtless speaking for many others.[19]

Additionally, Ring and other NDE researchers had come across some near-death cases that were totally anomalous to their data. These were the cases in which an individual, upon his death, found himself in the presence of what could only be considered ETs. As a case in point, Ring relates the case of a 39-year-old, college-educated woman by the name of Beryl Hendricks who operates a day-care center in New York state. In 1977, after discovering a golf-ball sized tumor in one of her breasts, she experienced a near-death episode, witnessed by her husband. But when she left her body, instead of experiencing the now-familiar dark tunnel and a beautiful luminous being, she found herself in a strange place:

> The next thing I remember was looking out of a round window and seeing the blackest blackness with tiny white sparkles. [I later realized I was experiencing deep space.] I felt cold—colder than I have ever experienced. I was unconcerned about my predicament, and I turned my gaze from the window…. There was a bright white light directly above me with four to seven, thin, tall figures around me. [I later realized I was on some kind of operating table.] I was given two messages, [telepathically]:
>
> 1. "Look and see—it is gone."
> 2. "Follow your husband" [We had been experiencing marital difficulty at the time.][20]

Two hours after the experience, the lump was gone and she remained in excellent health. Additionally, she reconciled her differences with her husband and found a close personal relationship with God.

---

19. Ring, 1992, pp. 10-11.
20. Ring, 1992, p. 109.

Other cases, such as this one, made Ring begin to understand that the line between alien abductions and NDEs might be quite thin. "I have found others who in describing what purports to be an NDE begin to talk about UFOs and aliens in the same context."[21] He began to see that each experience, in its own way, was a pathway to the same "psychospiritual transformation." Ring had already proposed the hypothesis that NDEs were a kind of catalyst for human evolution, and now he began to see that the abduction experience could also be serving the purpose of "jump-stepping the human race to a higher level of spiritual awareness and psychophysical functioning." He found himself asking the question: "Could phenomena so vastly different as NDEs and UFO encounters somehow both be expressions emanating from the same common source, whose intent furthermore is to strive to awaken the human species to a truth it now desperately needs not only for its own survival, but for the survival of all life?"[22]

Ring's interest in shamans and shamanistic initiations led him to compare near-death experiencers and UFO abductees to those mysterious "witch doctors" of primitive cultures known as shamans. Shamans are trained to enter altered states of consciousness in order to travel into nonphysical dimensions and to communicate with ethereal beings. To primitive cultures, it is the shaman who provides other members of the community with information and insights into the "dream" world and provides guidance in important community decisions. Such individuals hold prestigious and authoritative positions in their society and are highly respected. But, as we now know, such is not the case for the shamans of the modern age. Those who have gone beyond the familiar borders of the three-dimensional world and who dare speak of what they saw are laughed at and derided at best or discredited and ostracized at worst. Yet, as Ring points out, it is they who may hold the very knowledge so desperately needed by modern society today to move the human race forward toward its next step in the evolutionary process.

Ring's study, which included 264 NDE and UFO experiencers, was an effort to conduct a controlled examination of the perceptions of such individuals with regard to two areas: factors that might predis-

21. Ring, 1992, p. 110.
22. Ring, 1992, pp. 11-12.

pose them toward these experiences and how they were affected by their experiences. What he found was that there was a distinctive psychological profile that was common to both groups and, perhaps most importantly, that the aftereffects of the two experiences were almost identical. He found that both groups had undergone both physical changes, as well as psychological and spiritual changes. Both groups reported that after their experiences they began to notice that electronic equipment such as car batteries, lamps, vacuum cleaners, watches and tape recorders began to malfunction frequently in their presence. He also found that even though the two experiences were extremely traumatic, both the NDErs and the UFOers consistently asserted that they had undergone fundamental changes in largely positive ways. They felt they had been expanded in their "psycho-physiological functioning, cognitive processes and social values—and made more hopeful concerning the outcome of humanity's spiritual evolution."[23] Both groups came away from their experiences with a heightened psychic awareness and an intense feeling of concern for the Earth and its rapidly-depleting resources. Both had received knowledge of a coming ecological apocalypse.

In short, what Ring detected was an acceleration among the experiencers of a higher form of human evolution that led him to speculate that what he might be witnessing is the creation of a new species of humans. Ring, however, was not the first to consider this possibility. Whitley Strieber, who helped Ring with his project, lends credence to this startling conclusion:

...What we're dealing with is an exponential leap from one species to another. These beings that I have observed have properties and powers that I would suggest are far beyond what is present in normal human beings, and I would suspect that what we're looking at is the process of evolution in action.... This...process that is going on...will materially alter the nature of the human species to the extent that it will be, in effect, a new species.... I think they [the ETs] are probably midwifing our birth into the nonphysical world—which is their origin. [They] are probably an evolutionary step beyond ours

---

23. Ring, 1992, p. 191.

which has emerged into our world as a result of actions on the nonphysical plane.[24]

Ring calls this process the "shamanizing of humanity." He can see a time in the future when all humans will have achieved this remarkable transformation: "...The findings from the Omega Project suggest that we could be in the beginning stages of a major shift in levels of consciousness that will eventually lead to humanity's being able to live in two worlds at once—the physical and the imaginal.... It may be what humanity as a whole is currently learning to do, as a result of its increasing familiarization with extraordinary encounters."[25]

24. Ring, 1992, pp. 237-242.
25. Ring, 1992, p. 240.

CHAPTER 10

CONVERSATIONS WITH "HOMO NOETICUS"

"The theory of evolution is valid. But life on Earth did not evolve naturally. On Earth, certain conditions were created and life forms, suitable for survival within those conditions, were introduced. This process was repeated until the introduction of man…. If life on Earth had developed naturally, man as we know him would not yet exist."

—A praying mantis being named MU.

Praying Mantises, Reptilians and Tall Blondes

John White, in his book, *The Meeting of Science and Spirit*,[1] has named this new emerging species *"Homo noeticus,"* arguing that human development has been accelerating in the last few centuries. "We are witnessing the final phase of *Homo sapiens* and the simultaneous emergence…of *Homo noeticus*, a more advanced form of humanity…. But the forerunners of *Homo noeticus* are here now, in increasing numbers, making their presence felt, crowding *Homo sapiens*, creating their own niche in the eco-psychosystem and pointing out to him his own potential to change consciousness and thereby evolve, directing his own evolution and accelerating the process."[2] If this is so, and I believe it is, then we would be wise to consult with these individuals, these shamans, these "new humans," to find out what they can tell us about the nature of the universe in general and of the purpose of the "alien" presence in particular. For if they are truly the forerunners of a new species of humankind, they are in possession of unprecedented

---

1. White, 1990.
2. White, pp. 172, 248.

knowledge regarding the nature of the human experience and our relationship to those entities that Whitley Strieber calls the "mid-wives" of the "New Man."

The cases below were selected especially to shed some light on some of the beings alluded to in the previous chapter, which appear often in the abduction literature, but whose purpose or role is still unclear: the Praying Mantises, the Reptilians and the Tall Blondes. It is through the intimate relationships the three witnesses have with these

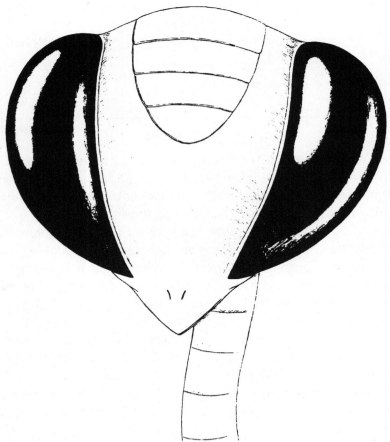

FIGURE 6. *Head of a Mantis being. A composite sketch drawn by abduction researcher, David W. Chace, based on numerous reports. (© David W. Chace. Reprinted by permission.)*

172

extraordinary beings that we may begin to understand a little about who they are, what they want and what may lie in store for the human species.

The Praying Mantises

Among the varieties of beings commonly described by abductees are those whose appearance places them squarely in the category of insectoid. These creatures are often said by abductees to look just like a giant praying mantis, with huge, black eyes, a sharp, pointy chin and a thin, skeletal body, although other varieties have been reported. These beings are more often than not reported to be lingering quietly in the background, observing the procedures being performed by the Greys or other types. The Mantis type is also reported to participate in the "staring" procedure which has been described by various researchers,

FIGURE 7. *Rita Perregrino's sketch of one of the Praying Mantis beings she saw.*

173

particularly Dr. David Jacobs of Temple University in his book *Secret Life*.[3] This procedure involves a being placing its face "nose to nose" with the abductee and engaging in prolonged staring directly into the human's eyes. The effect, as described by those who have experienced it, is totally shattering to the human ego. Abductees often comment that it is as if "my mind and my soul were completely swallowed up by those eyes." In some cases, the abductee feels that information is also transmitted into his or her brain during the procedure. Whatever its true purpose, it is another example of the strange behavior and the paranormal quality found in most abduction cases.

The appearance of advanced, intelligent, insectoid creatures is not something that anyone in the UFO community (particularly the abductees) would wish for. In fact, it is probably safe to say that no member of the human race would be too thrilled to learn that there is a race of insects superior to the human race. For this reason, the existence of the Mantis people, like that of the Reptilians, was not generally publicized until recent years. The general opinion among researchers seems to be that these enigmatic beings seem to hold a leadership role amongst the ET races and that they are endowed with a superior intellect. There is also the general feeling that they are an extremely old species, endowed with wisdom gained over thousands, or perhaps millions, of years.

One who knows these beings quite well is a 44-year-old West Virginia woman who prefers to use the pseudonym Rebecca Grant to discuss her ongoing communication with the Mantis people (and other ETs) for the past four years. Her case is in many ways typical of many abduction cases in that Rebecca was unaware that she was an abductee until she was an adult, even though she had a long history of paranormal experiences throughout her life, including missing time episodes. Yet, she had always attributed these events to "guardian angels" or "spirit guides," never to ETs or to UFOs. (In fact, this case serves to illustrate quite well how easily humans confuse alien contact with angelic contact. In point of fact, it may be that there is no difference, or that the difference is merely in the choice of words.)

In the introduction to a self-published manuscript about her experiences, Rebecca tells a story quite familiar to abduction researchers,

---

3. Jacobs, 1992.

for it includes many of the paranormal symptoms often described by experiencers:

> Throughout my life I have had odd experiences. There were nights I awakened to find "ghosts" in my bedroom. Prophetic dreams. Times I "heard" what people were thinking. Rare flashes of clairvoyance. Near accidents when something or someone intervened to protect me. Dreams of past lives. On occasion, my soul was able to leave my body. And from the age of twenty onward, I was able to speak telepathically with a group of beings I thought were spiritual guides.[4]

When, at the age of 40, they revealed themselves to her, at first only telepathically, she was shocked and confused. "At first I was dismayed and angry, but as our talks continued, my feelings changed. Week after week, month after month, for almost two years, they doled out information and explanations to me. About themselves. About their intentions. About their activities on Earth." Eventually, they appeared to her in physical form. "There were times when I awakened to find these beings in my bedroom. Usually they only made an appearance to show me what they looked like. These visits were very brief. The moment I started to get frightened, they would step back into the shadows or walk out of the room—usually through an exterior wall." (It is important to note here that Rebecca has never had hypnosis and is able to recall much of her contact from conscious memories, which she routinely enters into a journal.)

A Bug Named MU

She eventually developed a relationship to one particular Mantis being who told her not to be surprised that many of their species had evolved from forms of insect life.

"Man is a relative newcomer to the evolutionary chain," he said. She questioned him about the theory of evolution. "The theory of evolution is valid," he responded. "But life on Earth did not evolve naturally. On Earth, certain conditions were created [by the ETs], and life forms, suitable for survival within those conditions were introduced. This process was repeated until the introduction of man.... If life on

---

4. Personal files, 1996.

Earth had developed naturally, man as we know him, would not yet exist."

Rebecca was amused at this explanation for the origin of humans. "Considering the number of arrogant individuals wandering about the Earth, it was hilarious to think that the entire human race had been created by a bunch of bugs. [At the time, I was under the impression that the "visitors" were all from the praying mantis species.] They corrected me by saying, 'All life is created by God.' We merely took existing life material and made genetic alterations." (Rebecca now understands this to mean that a variety of ET types were involved in the genetic manipulation of the human species, not just the Mantis type.)

Throughout Rebecca's mental communication with this particular being, she had irreverently referred to him as a bug on many occasions. "He was very good natured about this, but after 18 months, he telepathically groaned, and said, 'It's really disgusting for a being who is master of the universe to be constantly referred to as a bug.'

"I told him to come up with a name for himself and awakened the next morning with the strong conviction that he wanted to be called MU—short for Master of the Universe. I told him I would call him MU-bug to help him keep things in perspective."

Throughout the years, Rebecca has learned, as have many abductees, that Earth isn't being visited by one alien species, or even by several. "I've seen 23 different types of aliens, and according to the aliens, this is less than a third of their true number. Many of the species...have obviously evolved from forms of insect life. Two of them appeared to have sprung from reptilian beginnings while another is human-like and Nordic in appearance. Then there are a handful whose beginnings I couldn't hope to identify. These beings say they come from a variety of places. One group said they lived on a parallel world and that there were windows between their world and ours. Others came from our universe, and one of the groups identified the star Sirius as being their star. Another group comes from a different spiritual plane than we do. This group has a physical body, but their bodies are far less dense than ours. They are almost pure spirit and are the most spiritual of the beings I have met.

"All of these beings who are now visiting Earth have reached a point in their development, either technological and/or spiritual,

176

where they are able to interact with intelligent life forms from other worlds. And they are working together, perhaps not on the same specific project, but for the same overall purpose: to help the human race."

The Extinction of Humankind

Rebecca has learned from MU what many abductees have learned: that the ETs are here because the human race is in danger of extinction. "Our visitors told me that they came here because of the ecological damage we were doing to the Earth, both to our ozone layer and to our oceans. In 1994 they told me we had, at that time, already upset the Earth's ecological balance to the point where it would no longer support human life, but they added it would be twenty years before we suffered the full extent of that damage.... Therefore, the human race is essentially, if not actually, extinct."

Rebecca learned that the ETs have the technology to save the human race and that it is their inclination to help us because they view us as a part of them. "The potential loss of any intelligent race is a loss to the entire group and cannot be ignored." However, if the ETs were to repair the Earth without making any changes in our behavior, we would simply "undo all the good they had done.... We might survive long enough to find an even grander way to destroy ourselves, one that could harm worlds other than our own. These beings feel that, by saving the human race, they would be condemning themselves to a violent confrontation with us in the future."

So, it is humankind's violent and self-serving nature, as well as his propensity to see himself as separate from and superior to other life forms, that will cause his ultimate doom, unless the ETs can find a compromise solution. This, according to MU, is what they are currently attempting. By using human DNA and combining it with the DNA of various other ET species, they have "ensured that, if they do nothing else for us, something of the human race will continue...." It was explained to Rebecca that each species has a finite life span, just like humans and solar systems. They evolve, rise to a zenith, then decline, slowly losing the ability to reproduce, and finally become extinct. Some of the species in the hybridization program are very old species, and if they are to survive, they must have "an influx of cells/life material from a younger species. They are cross-breeding with the human race to save themselves from extinction."

This may not seem like such a good solution to us, but to them it makes sense. They made it clear to Rebecca that this was the best they could do. "These beings said the human race, as it now exists and as it has existed, cannot be saved. If it were, all the problems they could foresee happening when we eventually met them in space would be inevitable, assuming we didn't destroy ourselves first." Therefore, another part of their plan is to attempt to change us in more subtle ways by means of genetic manipulation and by attempting to reawaken our spiritual values and beliefs. The more spiritual of the ETs told Rebecca that they "believe in a Godhead, a physical manifestation of God who walks among them. This Being is their King, and he was known to us on Earth as Jesus Christ.... My contact with them has completely altered my views on Christianity." (Rebecca, however, is not a member of a church and is not interested in organized religion. Negative experiences with religion in earlier years caused her to question the value of religion.)

Other groups are attempting to introduce the capacity for three-dimensional thought into the human brain. This type of thought involves all the psychic senses. "These new faculties are latent or dormant in the minds of those humans they've developed.... The visitors can switch these faculties on if, and when, they decide to do so. It is with three-dimensional thought that we become aware of our true nature which is spiritual, not physical. Their hope is that, in making us more aware of our true selves, they will move our focus away from material satisfaction and toward spiritual achievement."

When Rebecca asked if there would be a new race of humans with heightened psychic abilities, MU responded: "You [meaning the abductees] aren't the forerunners of a new race. You *are* the new race."

By now, it should be obvious to the reader that there is a high degree of correlation between the understanding that this rural West Virginia woman has of the ET phenomenon and that discovered by Kenneth Ring through his study of near-death experiences and by Courtney Brown through remote viewing. Rebecca lives an isolated life in a town of less than 3000 persons and had never heard of either Ring or Brown or their books when I interviewed her in April 1996. It is highly unlikely that either Ring or Brown has ever seen the 34-page, unpublished narrative of her experiences which she has diligently compiled. Furthermore, the essential ingredients involving the ET's

178

genetic manipulation of the human species, their concern for the survival of the human race and their efforts to awaken us to our spiritual nature are all common elements found in abduction research. It is this pattern, arising from totally disparate sources, rather than any single case, that provides researchers with the best evidence for the alien presence and begins to provide us with at least a glimpse of the larger picture of alien reality.

In any case, the wisdom and insights into the nature of the universe and of spiritual laws possessed by this high-school educated, unsophisticated woman is quite astonishing and cannot be easily explained, particularly in light of the corroborating information coming from many other diverse sources.

Spiritual Laws

Rebecca's teachings go far beyond the who and the how of the alien presence. They also delve into the spiritual and philosophical beliefs of the beings. When challenged on the issue of human rights being violated when people are abducted, the beings taught Rebecca that there are higher, spiritual laws that take precedence over the principles we understand. "Free will [as we know it]," they told her, "simply does not exist. It is the duty of all life, first and foremost, to serve the common good. This is not the complete abnegation of individual rights, but where individual rights conflict with the demands of species survival and enhancement, species needs must take precedence. Any species that does not come to this conclusion at some point within its evolution simply does not survive." The problem with humans, then, is that we think too small. Since we are disconnected from the larger picture by lack of psychic abilities and spiritual development, we can only think in terms of values pertinent to our narrow view. To the ETs, free will is a spiritual doctrine. "It has nothing to do," she was told, "with our individual right to serve ourselves, but with our right to choose whether or not to serve God. We have used [free will] as an excuse to run amuck in our daily lives." For example, MU explained that humankind has used its mistaken understanding of free will to include the right to exploit the Earth's resources without concern for our action's impact on other species. Since the beings see all other species as part of a larger whole, and thus, part of themselves, they understand that free will cannot include endangering any other species. Any species that violates this law, and indulges in this erroneous notion of free will, jeopardizes the balance of nature and is regarded by the beings as "suicidal." As a result of their larger view of reality, they do not see their "interference" in humankind's development as being wrong or immoral. Rather, they see it as their *responsibility.*

From their vantage point, they see all life forms, including humankind, as experimental. "Some survive and some don't," they casually told Rebecca. As for the human species, it has essentially been a failure because of our failure to transcend the physical plane on our own. At

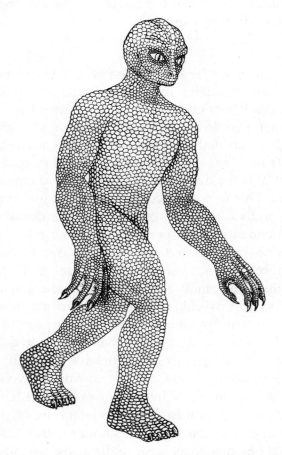

FIGURE 8. *An artist's rendering of a reptilian being based on UFO case studies. (© David W. Chace. Reprinted by permission.)*

this point, the alliance of ET species view humanity as too dangerous to be allowed to develop advanced technology. "If these beings have a prime directive," says Rebecca, "it is this: No violent race can be allowed to move more than a few steps beyond its planet of origin. They are certain that as long as we can't get along with each other, we will never be able to get along with them."

So what does MU say about the future of our species? Unfortunately, the picture is not a pretty one. They explain that the future is not absolute and they predict the future based on probability studies. However, they have told Rebecca about future ecological disasters that include the usual forecast of earthquakes, volcanic eruptions and other devastations, as well as social and political upheavals that may include the use of atomic and biological weapons. If these predictions materialize, humankind would essentially be rendered sterile from contamination. Therefore, they are prepared to "remove a group of women and children from the surface of the Earth to protect them for the purposes of procreation." Those selected would be from among those they have already genetically altered. In the event that the Earth becomes completely uninhabitable, they plan to remove the few survivors, "suspend their lives, and revive them when the Earth has renewed itself." In any event, they are determined not to allow humanity to develop higher technology. She was told that if any division of our government has developed advanced spacecraft through their association with some of the visitors, they would not be allowed to use it. They apparently are prepared to use their destructive powers to prevent this from happening. This, however, is not new. This is exactly what happened many thousands of years ago to the Atlanteans. MU explained that it was the ETs who were responsible for the destruction of Atlantis for the same reasons as are developing again today. However, the Atlanteans were considerably more technologically advanced than we are now. Because of their uncontrolled human emotions, however, the Atlanteans "degenerated into a tyrannical and corrupt race." After repeated warnings went unheeded, Atlantis was destroyed for the "greater good of the majority." They then left the human race to "develop at its own pace in the hope that we would also develop some wisdom and restraint as we developed our own technology." Unfortunately, that has not been the case.

The Reptilians

Rebecca has also been introduced to other enigmatic beings who appear with some frequency in abduction cases—those with distinct reptilian features. This group, Rebecca says, claims to have existed on Earth during the time of the dinosaurs and that they are a form of dinosaur themselves. "They said that we have discovered some of their bones, but it never occurred to us to think that they could possi-

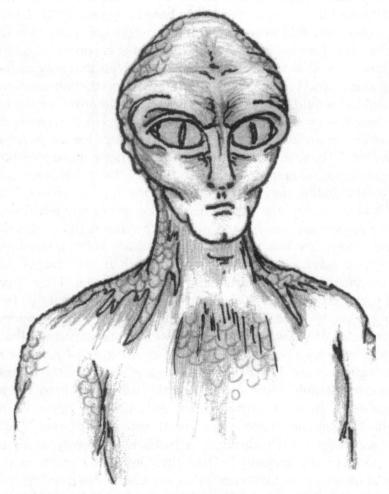

FIGURE 9. *A Reptilian, drawn by an abductee. This sketch includes many of the features often reported, such as the large head, scaly greenish skin and large, yellow eyes with vertical pupils.*

bly have been an intelligent life form." Because of their ferocity and the terror that they strike in the hearts of humans, MU has allowed her to know these creatures only through a series of "teaching dreams," similar to those commonly reported by abductees. "My feeling is that they are human size, at least six feet or taller. I also think they're bulkier or broader than a large man. I have…been shown the hands which are more like talons. I only remember seeing three fingers, but this might be because what they really wanted me to notice was the claws at the end of the fingers. [Which are two to three inches long.] Very vicious looking. The only other thing I associate with them is enormously ferocious yellow eyes. So ferocious you can't meet and hold their gaze."

"During one telepathic conversation, one of these beings deliberately attempted to intimidate me by saying, 'It wasn't so long ago we would have regarded the human race as food.' I said, 'We probably would have regarded you as food also. Hey, we still might.' Instead of being annoyed by the retort, he seemed amused, and it was on this [and only this] occasion, I felt any sexual interest coming from one of these beings. However, with MU in charge of what happens to me, I can't see this ever occurring."

Rebecca's description of the Reptilians is nearly identical to those of other abductees whose recollections are both from conscious memories and those retrieved under hypnosis. Their powerful stature, dangerous claws, scaly skin and golden eyes with vertically slit pupils present an image that easily terrifies most who have seen them, and their sexual appetite is also commonly reported. One woman who has experienced these beings suddenly awoke to find herself levitated in midair while two reptilians were engaged in sex with her.

Although she remembers the event as a traumatic experience, she added with some embarrassment that the orgasm she experienced was amazingly powerful. Others, however, report that their Reptilian contact has not included a sexual component and, in fact, has been quite positive.

Preliminary results of MUFON's Transcription Project indicate that beings with reptilian features are reported in something less than 20 percent of the cases. Project director Dan Wright commented on his findings by saying that "When a so-called reptilian is repeatedly described as having the same scaly skin tone, claws for fingers, and an extreme interest in sexuality, one must pay attention."[5]

Another researcher who has published his findings about Reptilians is John Carpenter, MUFON's director of abduction research. In the April 1993 issue of the MUFON Journal, Carpenter cautiously revealed that researchers had held back their knowledge of the "lizard creatures" from the general public for fear of being laughed at. Researchers have "a fairly large gray basket to which other alien types are presently relegated...because they are judged either too weird, too unlikely or too few to be significant." But when researchers began to share some of these findings, they discovered "amazing matches and similarities." Carpenter, who has had about a dozen cases in which his subjects have reported such encounters, reports that the creatures are often described as being "hideous, rude and aggressive." From these reports, he has fit together the following description: 6 to 8 feet tall, upright posture, lizard-like scales, greenish to brownish in color, four-fingered hands with claws and webbing between the fingers, a face that looks like a cross between a human and a snake, a central ridge coming down from the top of the head to the snout, cat-like eyes with vertically slit pupils and gold irises. Their manner is usually intrusive, forceful and uncommunicative. Often, they leave claw-like bruises and scratches on the abductees. "This weird stuff gets crammed into our gray baskets and buried!" says Carpenter. "But something is going on here that needs to be studied more openly and publicly...."[6]

"Maria" and the Reptilians

In September of 1994, the El Paso MUFON Chapter, in a joint effort with the University of Texas at El Paso Union Programs Office, invited John Carpenter to speak on the "Reality of the Abduction Phenomenon."His arrival was awaited with a combination of excitement and anxiety by Rita Peregrino (See Figure 10 on page 185.), whose story, the Maria Case, the reader is familiar with from a previous chapter. For months she had vacillated, trying to muster her courage to undergo hypnosis and now, she knew that she would have the opportunity of a lifetime—and she didn't want to lose it. Who better to do hypnosis with than John, she reasoned. Not only was he an experienced researcher in the field of UFOs, but he was actually coming to her

5. Wright, 1995, p. 167.
6. Carpenter, pp. 10-11.

184

hometown, and he had already agreed to perform the hypnosis for free. Yet, she was terrified. She knew she would have to face her worst nightmares and more than anything she did not want to see those horrible creatures again. She had spent a lifetime trying to ignore them and to push them out of her life, only to be drawn back time and time again, finding it impossible to lead a normal life. Her lifetime of experiences had affected every aspect of her life and at times it seemed that it did so only in negative ways.

She blamed them for what seemed like a lifetime of insomnia and anxiety. She felt that her ability to have serious relationships with men had been severely impaired and that her experiences had left her with

FIGURE 10. *Rita Perregrino.*

numerous strange phobias she could not understand, like an absurd fear of babies. Even though she had had a child, she had always suffered an unnatural fear of infants and could barely stand to hold one in her arms. She also had an unusual aversion to bald men—she just didn't like them to get too near to her.

In the end, hypnosis was her only choice. She was 48 years old, and although she had a good job as a youth counselor for the public schools and functioned quite well in most ways, she knew that there was a whole part of her life that was a wreck. Even as a child, her experiences caused her problems.

> When I was in the third grade, I remember getting into trouble with my teacher when she was attempting to teach the class about the five senses. I corrected her. I told her she was wrong, that there were at least twice as many senses. She looked at me as if I were crazy and tried to be kind. But out of curiosity, she asked me what other senses I knew about. I told her about our sense of knowing what was happening out in space—on other worlds, I told her about being able to talk with someone without using words. I told her about communicating with plants and animals and about knowing what would happen in the future. The more I talked, the angrier she got. Finally, she told me there must be something wrong with me and she wanted to know where I got all these ideas and that it could not possibly be true. She said she was the teacher and that I had to learn that there were only five senses.[7]

Like abductees everywhere, Rita always felt that she was living in two separate realities, and she had great difficulty in coping with her dual existence. The combination of her psychic abilities and her memories of UFOs and alien beings did not blend well with the ordinary reality in which she had to live each day.

> My teachers also got upset because during art, I drew pictures of aliens. I was told not to be drawing monsters because they don't exist. I told my teacher that I knew them and that is what they really look like. I remember one teacher sitting down next to me to help me learn how to draw human beings and telling me that is all there is.[8]

---

7. Personal files, 1994.
8. Personal files, 1994.

186

Over time, Rita learned that she was the only person she knew who had these abilities and experiences and the realization made her feel alone in a strange world. The loneliness was increased by the strong feeling that she was really not from Earth, but had origins somewhere else—somewhere far away in the cosmos. Yet, she wasn't exactly sure what was happening. There were gaps in her memories that could not be filled alone. She needed help to understand who she was and why this was happening to her and to confirm to herself that she wasn't crazy.

After her first hypnosis session, Rita was able to talk about what it was like to be aboard an alien ship as a frightened little girl. She also described more fully her first conscious encounters with the beings who had dominated her life in so many ways:

Every once in a while you get a glance at your captors, but you do not believe what you see. You think it must be a dream, but it's really happening. A few minutes ago you were outside playing with your friends and suddenly you seem frozen. All you know is that you are still alive, but everything about your life has changed. It all looks so strange, round walls, round halls, arched doorways—being floated to an open area where there is a long table in the middle of the room.... A physical exam, painful, intrusive. As a child you can't understand. However, you are aware that instruments are being used and procedures are being performed that reach inside your body, to places you can't even reach, including your head and your mind.

There were three small gray beings about four feet tall, large heads, big eyes, thin bodies—looked like bugs or ants. A taller being had a very different appearance. He looked like a monster. His head was big and seemed to come to a point toward the top. His eyes were huge and seemed to protrude from his face. There was no hair, no eyebrows, no nose, but a chin and mouth area that looked reptilian. His skin was dark gray and black and seemed leathery. He had claws for hands. He moved slowly and observed and directed the activities of the Greys.

At one point I was becoming combative, and a taller being came into the room to calm me down. This being was what I recognized as an insect that I had seen before. It was a seven-foot-tall praying mantis. (See Figure 7 on page 173.) He talked with me and asked me not to hit or hurt the Greys any more because they were just doing their job. He said it was important that the procedures be performed—all of this was very important for the future. He said I would not be hurt, and as a matter of fact, I would be protected from harm. He said that in time, as I grew older, I would come to understand the importance of their work. All this communication was telepathic.[9]

Although these three types of beings were those with whom Rita had contact, she believes there are at least seven basic types and probably as many as 50 or more variations, including nonphysical beings. She is quite sure, however, that the three that were part of her experiences were working together, although she can't be sure what the precise relationships are between them. In addition, on one occasion, she also saw a tall, blonde human-looking being who stood silently, observing her.

An interesting aside to her first remembered abduction experience was the sudden arrival, a day or so later, of a team of "government doctors," who came to the neighborhood to talk to the parents and check the children. "They said they were there because there was something wrong with the drinking water and they needed to be sure the children were okay. They checked me and asked questions. They examined my body and took a blood sample. The parents told them about the UFO that everyone had seen and my missing time experience and my mysterious scar, but they said that UFOs didn't exist. We never heard any more from them or about any problem with the water."

Visits to Other Worlds

More than six months passed from the time of her first hypnosis with John Carpenter before Rita mustered up enough courage to try it again. This time she was better prepared for the shock of reliving the traumatic events of her childhood, and she felt more comfortable with the process. She realized there was still a lot to know, and many questions had been left unanswered. She knew that hypnotic regression was the only way. By this time, I had completed my certification

---

9. Personal files, 1995.

course in hypnosis and had sat in on nearly a dozen sessions conducted by local hypnotherapists, as well as the one conducted by Carpenter. Rita asked me if I would do the hypnosis, and I agreed, provided that psychiatrist Dr. Roberta Fennig would be available to serve as an observer. In the last week of April 1995, the three of us met in Dr. Fennig's office at the El Paso Medical Center for what would be the first of a series of three sessions extending through the end of October—sessions that would shock and astonish all of those present and lead us all to the conclusion that there was a profound spiritual aspect to the amazing phenomenon we were studying.

The April 25th session began with the reliving of an experience that occurred in 1958 when Rita was about 10 years old. She remembered that she had gone to visit a girlfriend a few blocks from her home and had been told that the friend could not play. Disappointed, she headed back home in the early afternoon, passing by the neighborhood Catholic church. Her next memory was that it was dark and that she was disoriented and also that there was a glowing ball of light, about the size of a cantaloupe, floating in the air above her and seeming to follow her.

Under hypnosis, Rita was surprised to remember that, as she passed the church, she suddenly found herself being levitated high into the air. Later, she recalled her memories. "I tried to get myself to go down, but I couldn't. Instead, I became fascinated with the view. I could see the top of the church, the railroad tracks and the area that had been cleared for the new freeway that was coming through. It was broad daylight, and I was flying through the air just a block from the church." (Researchers speculate that such abductions are conducted with the use of some type of force field which renders both the craft and the abductee invisible.)

Once aboard the ship, the now familiar beings told Rita that they had come to take her to see other worlds. "They wanted me to learn about other places and about how easy it was for them to come and go from Earth to distant places." This was the beginning of a series of experiences in which young Rita would be taken to numerous strange worlds, "some of which were incredibly colorful and alive with sounds, while others seemed barren and desolate," she said. In one case, she was taken to an underground world inhabited by beings that looked like insects. "There were developed societies with living quarters that looked like hives, honeycombed—with tall arches. The beings

189

and these creatures were in commerce with each other." On another world the inhabitants were very much like humans, but had the ability to levitate and fly at will. Their homes were tall buildings that stretched high into the sky, glistening with white light. "Their sole purpose was to care for plants and animals that were brought to them from other worlds. They would prepare them so that they could repopulate new worlds." (Note: It is not uncommon for abductees to report having been taken to other planets.)

There was one world in which all the inhabitants lived underwater because the surface of their planet had become uninhabitable. They adjusted well, but their appearance changed. "They looked like humans and fish at the same time. They lived in individual structures, but worked together to provide for the common good. The beings told me that they had assisted this race when the environment on their planet changed."

Rita began to realize that they wanted her to be aware of the diversity of life in the universe and that Earth was only one of many worlds with intelligent life. They also gave her insights into her own life. "On many occasions they told me that they have known me for a very long time, and I got the feeling that they were talking about not only my present life, but also past lives and possibly future lives. As a result, like many abductees, Rita struggles with the knowledge of her dual identity—trying to reconcile her human and non-human natures.

A Sense of Mission

One of the most astonishing hypnosis sessions any of us had experienced occurred on August 9, also at Dr. Fennig's office. On this occasion, Rita appeared to slip easily into a state of deep relaxation as I helped her to get to that "safe" place in her mind in which she would imagine a beautiful, peaceful scene. This standard procedure used in hypnotherapy allows the conscious mind to relax so that the subconscious can take over. Rita was now quite at ease with this procedure and could achieve trance state easily. But as the questioning began, it was apparent by the tone of her voice that she was not in a trance. Rather than the soft whispers we were accustomed to, she spoke in her normal tone of voice. In a short while, she opened her eyes and began to explain what had happened.

"I was imagining myself walking along…a shoreline. The sun was shining, and it was nice to have my feet in the sand…and then I looked up and there was a being—not a Grey or a reptilian, just a being…kind of like a translucent light. I knew we were supposed to discuss certain matters." The being appeared on Rita's "safe" beach to let her know that there was no place that she could hide from them and that access to her memories was in their control. "I had recently been having a dialog with the beings about my role and my identity." She explained that she was having doubts about continuing with her plans for speaking about her experiences and for writing a book and a play. She was suspicious about the motives of the ETs and unsure if she should go along with their plans for her. Their response was to admonish her during her hypnosis session. "They know my thoughts. If I don't want to do it by the numbers [their way], they can cut me off from my memories. Only those who are going to continue [on their mission] can know that kind of information. There are a lot of things going on that they don't want people to know about yet. They don't know how that information would be handled by others." When she communicated her doubts to the being on the beach, he told her, "It's okay to question, but I can't run away from it [her mission]. There is no safe place."

At this point, we decided to try once again to put Rita into a trance, but this time with the intention of speaking to the being directly if he showed up. Shortly after entering the trance state, Rita began to sob deeply, as if experiencing some powerful emotion.

Joe Lewels (JL): What's happening?

Rita(RP): *[still weeping and in a whispered voice]* I'm home, I'm home.

JL: Where is home?

RP: They let me go home…. We're all together.

JL: What is it like there?

RP: *[regaining some composure]* It's nothing physical. It's just like a feeling, like a connection of thoughts.

JL: Is this an existence…before this life?

RP: Before everything.

JL: What do you look like?

RP: A bright light.

JL: Do you have a physical body?

RP: No…kind of like when you see lightning—there's a spark. These beings were sent here…because they knew what was going to happen. They usually don't have form. They told me that I had to be involved with the other group [the ETs] to know what they are doing."

They further explained to Rita that when her mission is complete she will be able to go "home" again, something she finds very alluring. After this, Rita's memories were unblocked, and she was able to remember an additional experience—one with profound implications. It seemed as if Rita's understanding of who she really was made her realize the importance of her current mission.

A Lesson About Death

Rita was now able to remember the details of a time when she was taken to a world where she was shown something like a zoo, full of exhibits of strange animals of all sizes and shapes, unlike any she had ever seen before. (In a previous session she had remembered this incident, but it was so traumatic that she could not deal with it.) In this case, she remembered that she was accompanied by three reptilian-type beings (the ones she calls the "ugly ones.") They took her from one exhibit to another, giving her a close look at each of the creatures. In one particular area, there were a group of large, buglike worms with dangerous-looking pincers. She began to describe what happened in childlike whimpers, between deep sobs and obvious fear.

RP: *[weeping]* They were taking me to all these places, and they always took good care of me. We went to this place…and they left me alone…. They had to go do something…and these animals came over and they started eating me…. They attacked me! They started biting me! The beings came back and saw what was going on, but they didn't stop it. I died. They killed me! *[crying and scared]*

JL: Just go through the experience. You can see it objectively.

RP: The bugs ate me! They tore me to pieces! I went up [out of her body] and I could see the bugs eating my body.

JL: What happens?

RP: *[now in control and in a more adult voice]* The beings, the ugly things, they changed. They came up, but as they came up they changed. They look like ghosts—whitish color—

192

they're not bodies anymore. If I didn't know better I would think that they're angels.... They changed their physical bodies into transparent bodies.... There seems to be love there. They're up where I am, and they hold me. I tell them I'm angry with them because they didn't protect me. They're trying to explain that nothing really happened. I said, "Yes, the bugs ate me!" *[weeping again]*

I want my body back! I'm just a child. I don't know about this stuff. They told me they could make me "me" again. I said, "This is too crazy. I don't understand." They said, "Don't worry, we're going to make you 'you' again, and then we're going to take you home."

JL: How do they get you back together?

RP: They said they have duplicates, spares of everybody—that they do that to everybody—that a person isn't just one person. You can be many people...and you can be in different places at the same time! And that I should not be concerned [about her old body] and that they can get me a new body. They ask me if I want anything special in this new body and I said "No, I want the old body." They said, "Okay."

JL: Go forward now.

RP: They got lots of things...like a warehouse and all this stuff.

JL: Do you see where they get your new body?

RP: I wasn't looking.... It was lying down, and they brought it for me to look at. They're doing stuff to it. They tell me to look at and accept it as my own. That even though my new body was there and I was over here, that it was the same. I don't understand.... This is real strange. They say they do this all the time. There's nothing strange about it.

JL: How do you get into the body?

RP: All I had to do was think myself as that body, and it takes care of itself...just think of being one.... Once I got into the body that I would still remember what happened and that I would be healthy.... I'm afraid my family won't recognize me. I'm afraid they're going to see something different.... I want to be the same. *[weeping]*

(Rita then began to understand the lesson she had just been taught.)

RP: It's okay to be in another body if you're the same person. You can die, but you don't die. They are the keepers of knowledge. They know a lot of things. They chose their bodies for specific reasons.... They never thought of themselves as ugly. They're kind of like lizard-looking—slimy. I don't like looking at them. They tell me not to be angry with the bugs because they were just hungry....

After the session, Rita was able to see her experience more objectively. "They taught me a lesson on death, that death is not a problem. It may have seemed cold hearted [the way they did it], but I had to understand and accept this process—of our lives coming to an end. The body rests, and the spirit moves on. Now, I'm not afraid of death anymore."

Duplicate Bodies

As remarkable and strange as this experience may seem, it is by no means the only case of its kind. Other abductees have reported seeing human bodies in suspended animation aboard alien craft. Others have reported being shown their own duplicate bodies. In one case, a woman endured an operation in which the entire bottom half of her body was removed and replaced by a duplicate half. In another, an individual remembered lying on an operating table and looking down at her body only to realize that she was seeing a reptilian body.

But perhaps the most startling example is the one provided by the late researcher and abductee, Dr. Karla Turner, in her book, *Masquerade of Angels*.[10] The book is a case study of an abductee by the name of Ted Rice who remembered an experience with reptilians quite similar to that of Rita's. Although the book was published in 1994 and I had read it prior to Rita's session, I was certain that Rita had not read the book and that she was not aware of its contents.

Ted's case has many elements with which we are, by now, familiar. In early childhood, Ted, who was raised in rural Alabama, developed psychic abilities and grew up believing that he had "spirit guides." But as an adult, his experiences began to parallel those of UFO abductees and included night visitations by beings who walked through his bedroom walls and spirited him away. As he slept, a particular entity

10. Turner, 1994.

named Volmo would appear and instruct him in spiritual truths. Gradually, he became aware that Volmo was a very unusual spirit guide. As he began to explore his experiences more fully with a spiritualist named Marie, he realized just how different Volmo was:

> This spirit, or whatever Volmo is, just isn't human.... The shape of his head and everything about him isn't human.... He's really tall.... I reckon he's six and a half feet tall...and massive. He's got a strong, powerful body, and it's dark colored, dull gray or olive brown.... Volmo's God-awful ugly!... His eyes don't look human.... They're dark, sort of yellow-gold...but his mouth is the worst part.... It looks like a big fish mouth, with sharp teeth.... There are only three or four fingers on each hand, and I think they're webbed. The hands look clawlike, because he's got these long, pointed nails on each finger. [11]

Neither Ted nor his friend Marie had ever heard of reptilian beings at the time, nor had they any idea that they were dealing with a case of UFOs and alien abductions.

Later, with the help of Karla Turner and hypnotherapist Barbara Bartholic, Ted was able to explore more fully his lifetime of abduction experiences. One of these, an abduction that took place when he was eight years old, is of particular interest. Ted was placed on an operating table and was forced by the beings to drink a strangely glowing, green liquid. The liquid made him violently ill, and in a short time he was floating above his body, watching it lying motionless. Then a strange thing happened. "Something cloudy and formless began to rise up from the small body.... 'It's my soul,' he thought in amazement."

One of the beings then attached wires to the body and to a rectangular black box, and Ted's "soul" was slowly sucked into the box. Next, the being used a laser-like instrument to decapitate his body, allowing the blood to drain into a vat. Another being went to a locker and removed a body identical to his, completely naked

> The beings moved this body over to the tilted table...brought back the black box and set it on the...chest....
> He could see the naked body suddenly begin to jerk in short

---

11. Turner, p. 47.

spasms. After that, the chest started to rise and fall, as if the body was now breathing.[12]

After having needles inserted into the bottom of each foot, the chest and the back of the head and some drops placed in his eyes, Ted found himself in his duplicate body. Then, a tall, blonde, human-looking man arrived and explained to him that the procedure was necessary for Ted to fulfill his purpose in life. He understood that he was part of "an experiment for the continuity of life, in some way involved with the final stages of growth."

The Case of the Tall Blondes

Shona Bear Clark is a 48-year-old Native American woman living in Santa Fe, New Mexico, who was born and raised on a Creek Indian reservation near Oklahoma City. Her tall stature, light skin, high cheek bones and fine features, she says, are typical of her people. Because she comes from a long line of medicine women, she is skilled in the ritualistic healing arts of her tribe. Perhaps because of this, she is normally withdrawn, secretive and mysterious. Immersed since childhood in the ancient knowledge and traditions of her people, she has lived her entire lifetime aware of the existence of other realities and of strange, magical beings that could traverse the dimensional barriers and enter her world. These are things that Native Americans rarely speak about to white men, but in October 1995, all that changed when a series of experiences frightened and distressed her so badly that she became desperate for help. Her call for help was made to the national headquarters of MUFON, and she was referred to the El Paso Chapter and to me in particular. Her call to me that October evening had the familiar tone of quiet desperation, embarrassment and caution I have come to know quite well.

Shona (S): I need to know what is happening to me.

JL: Tell me about it.

S: It's pretty strange.

JL: Don't worry, I hear a lot of strange things.

S: I need to know if I'm crazy or if this is real. I need to be able to sleep at night.

---

12. Turner, pp. 200-202.

JL: Do you think your experiences have something to do with UFOs?

S: I don't know, but I don't know where else to go. I went to a psychiatrist and asked him to lock me up for observation, but when I told him my story, he told me I wasn't crazy and that I needed to go to someone who knew about this stuff.

JL: Well, give me an example of something that has happened to you.

S: Okay, but before I do, I have to ask you something. Are you a Christian?

JL: Yes, I am

S: Good, that's important to me. I was raised a Christian on the Indian reservation where I grew up. MUFON gave me the name of someone in Santa Fe, but I don't want to deal with anyone up here—there's too many new-age kooks here.

JL: I understand. Why don't you tell me about your experiences.

S: Okay. Last summer I woke up in the night, it was 3:32 A.M. according to my clock, and my room was all lit up, but the lamp wasn't on. At first I thought the light was coming from outside, but then I realized it wasn't. I looked down at my foot and there was a piece about one-inch deep and three inches long missing. The inside of my foot looked silver, but there was no blood. Then I realized that there were two men standing next to me, one on each side. They were standing right through the bed. They had blonde, shoulder-length hair and blue eyes and looked to be about 50 years old. Their skin was a bronze color, like they had good tans. They wore robes. One robe was red and white with gold roping around the collar, and the other was blue and white with gold roping. The man in the blue took his hand and went over my foot and said, "Shona, you are completely healed." The other man put his hands on each side of my head without touching me and said, "We will be back when you need us." Then they disappeared. My foot was back to normal, but the light stayed until around six in the morning, and I felt as if I was being bathed in love.

After telling me more about her life and her experiences, she agreed to come to El Paso to meet with me and with Dr. Roberta Fennig. It was agreed that if Dr. Fennig thought it appropriate, we would conduct a hypnosis session.Two weeks later, Shona and a friend drove the more than five-hour drive to El Paso and checked into a motel where we taped the official interview. It was then that we learned the full extent of her lifetime of paranormal experiences.

"When I was a little girl I had scarlet fever and I was kept in a darkened room for several years. My mother was told that I could go blind if I was exposed to sunlight. During that time, little white children would come into my room at night, right through the walls, and

FIGURE 11. *One of the tall, blonde beings who appeared in Shona Bear Clark's bedroom on several occasions. This drawing is by Shona Bear Clark.*

play with me. They had blonde hair, and they would take me out of my body to go play outside. All of my life I have left my body to go places, but I haven't tried to do it. I also saw the blonde men twice when I was a child. In one case, one saved my life when I was badly injured on the reservation. Then, when I was 43, I went to check on my father because he was very ill with pneumonia. When I got to his house there was a white man standing in the front yard. I thought he was a preacher. He also had blue eyes and shoulder-length blonde hair. He had on a light blue suit and what seemed to be a clergyman's collar and black, patent-leather shoes.

"I passed within three feet of him, and I asked him who he was. He just smiled and said, 'Everything is all right. Everything is going to be fine.' Then I blinked and he was gone. He just disappeared. I went in to see my father, and he was in the kitchen making coffee. He was perfectly well. I asked my mother who the white man was, and she thought I was crazy. I told my father about what had happened, and he just laughed and said, 'Maybe it was my guardian angel.' I went back outside to look for him again, but there weren't even any tracks in the snow."

When Shona was 25, she and a large group of friends and family were driving to the hospital in a caravan of four cars because her small daughter had been bitten badly by a dog. On the way, at about 2 P.M. in the afternoon, they all saw a saucer-shaped object come down from the sky and hover a short distance above them. "It was silver and looked like two saucers put together with a line around the middle, and it had a row of windows and red, yellow and green headlights. We could see figures standing in the windows. Everyone got scared and left, but my daughter and I stayed to look. It didn't do anything; it just sat there, and when it left, it went up and disappeared, like there was a hole in the sky. (Under hypnosis, Shona was able to remember that she and her daughter were taken out of their bodies into the craft. The same blonde men were able to examine the injured girl and determine that it was not a serious wound.) Two nights later it came back and stayed over my mother's house for nearly two hours. We weren't afraid. My mother told me then that her mother had a problem with spirits coming to her. She would put tobacco and other herbs out around the house to keep them away. I have also talked to spirits, and they have taken me out of my body and taken me places."

Near-Death Experience

As a young woman, Shona died from uncontrolled bleeding during childbirth and had a near-death experience. Because she has Rh-negative blood, a donor was difficult to find. As her life drained out of her, she suddenly shot out of her body. "I was up on the ceiling, and I was in a warm light made of pure love. I had vision from every way you can have vision. It was amazing. I knew the secrets of the universe. Then I could feel that the doctors were tying a tag on my toe and that they were saying the Lord's Prayer. I died for seven minutes, and they pronounced me dead. I could see them from above, but I could feel my toe. Then, all of a sudden I went back into my body and it felt like I was breathing through clay because I wasn't getting enough air.

FIGURE 12. *Shona Bear Clark.*

While I was dead, I didn't see or hear anyone in the light, but ever since then, I have been able to hear people thinking and I can see a person's spirit or soul floating above his head. It gives me information about that person."

As varied and numerous as her experiences had been, it was events that occurred only a few weeks before our meeting that drove Shona over the top and to finally seek help. "Three weeks ago I woke up around 11:30 P.M., and there was a man standing in my room. He was wearing a white robe with gold roping around the neck and also had blonde hair to the shoulders and blue eyes. He said, 'We are giving you back your memories.' And that's all he said. He stood there all night as I slept on and off. After that I began leaving my body regularly. It's almost like looking into the future. It scared me. They came back a week later and did some kind of surgery on my back. This time it was hazy—like I had been drugged. They told me they had to do the operation because it was necessary—'because you need it.' They did something to my spine in the middle of my back. One of them showed me a little metal object they were going to put in my back, but it didn't leave any scars."

Shona's Hypnosis

After conducting her evaluation, Dr. Fennig was in agreement with the previous psychiatrist's diagnosis. "Shona does not suffer from any mental illness and she is not hallucinating," says Fennig. "The visions she describes are too real, consistent and detailed to be hallucinations. Shona questions her sanity and the reality of what she is seeing with a lot of conflict and emotion. This is typical of the abductees I have examined. Psychotic people accept their hallucinations as real with very little or no emotion and will insist that they are not insane. Shona functions normally in all other areas of her life. Her ego and her self image are very strong, but when she tries to fit these unusual events into her everyday life, she experiences a feeling of conflict which produces severe anxiety and fear. These symptoms are very treatable by emotional support and validation of the person's experiences through participation in a support group and through the use of regressive hypnotherapy. This helps the person make the connection between two different realities, thereby reducing the conflict."

Dr. Fennig concluded that Shona was not mentally ill and that hypnosis could be helpful in relieving her anxiety. This time, Dr. Fennig conducted the hypnosis herself, using the same technique of relaxation discussed previously. After a hypnotic induction of about 20 minutes, Shona demonstrated the signs of being in a highly relaxed state, and Dr. Fennig began the questioning, beginning with the incident in which she found part of her foot missing. As soon as she was asked to remember what happened that night, Shona began to sob and shake:

Shona (S): They healed my foot…. They have great power and they want me to know.

R. Fennig (RF): Is this a lesson for you?

S: I know it.

RF: How do you know this?

S: Because they gave it to me…when I was born…. They were there.

RF: Can you go back to a time when you first knew these beings?

S: They have always been here.

RF: Can you ask them what their purpose is?

S: They're here to help…. They don't live here.

RF: Where do they live?

S: Another place. It's pretty there. The air's good, and there's no disease and it's never dark.

RF: Have you been there?

S: [choking back tears] Yes. I was a boy…. [crying] When I lived there I was a boy. [deep sobs and moans]

RF: What's happening now?

S: [fighting back sobs] They want me to go away. They're sending me away…. I have to go to the Earth. I don't want to go.

RF: Why did they send you here?

S: To help…. He's my daddy.

RF: Who's your daddy?

S: The man in red.

RF: How do you feel about him?

S: I like him.

RF: Does he have a name?

S: He has a name, but I don't know it.

202

RF:	Do you know what they call that place they come from?
S:	...It had two suns. There's trees and rivers.
RF:	And how do they get from that place to this place?
S:	They come by ships.
RF:	Have you ever been on one of those ships?
S:	Yes.
RF:	When was the last time?
S:	Last week.
RF:	And who do you see on those ships?
S:	They're all blonde headed [with] blue eyes. Some wear robes, some wear uniforms.... My father and his father....
RF:	Was it your father who sent you here?
S:	Yes.
RF:	When they were there at your birth, do you know what they did?
S:	They made sure I got here all right.... I was five when they sent me here. But when I woke up, I wasn't five.... I was a baby.... They brought me here in a tube.... I want to go home. *[tearfully]* They say I have to stay.... They're coming here.
RF:	They're coming to visit you?
S:	No, they're coming to take a lot of people away.
RF:	Are they taking them back to where they live?
S:	They're taking them back there.
RF:	Why are they taking them?
S:	This world is no good. It's no good to live here.
RF:	When they said they would give you back your memories, what did that mean?
S:	I can remember my home.... They're going to let me go visit. There are things I have to learn...about how to help the people. They don't understand what they're doing, they're destroying everything.... They don't understand nothing. They don't care.
RF:	Have you ever had contact with other types of beings?
S:	Yes. *[becoming agitated and crying]* They're tall and wear black robes. They don't have a sun.... They hate the light.
RF:	Have they taken you?

S: I don't think so. They tried.... They called me. I thought it was my mother. I was scared.... They can't get me unless I go with them. I saw the grasshoppers. [Later, she said she couldn't think of the name "praying mantis."] Their world is dying. They want women...to breed with them. They have the head like a grasshopper...with a skinny neck, long arms, skinny legs, big eyes and antennae....

(Note: Shona was not aware that other abductees had reported seeing mantis-type beings at this time.)

RF: When did you see them?
S: With those black men.... I don't like the grasshoppers.
RF: Do you remember when you saw the UFO when you were with your daughter?
S: Yes. They did something to her.
RF: Did you go on that ship?
S: Yes.
RF: Did you go in your body or out of your body?
S: Out. You don't have to take your body with you.... Bodies are nothing. They don't mean anything.
RF: What is the difference between the blonde beings and what people call angels?
S: There's no difference.
RF: Is there anything you can tell us about Jesus?
S: He flies in ships too. He lives on another world...the first world. [The blondes] live in the second world.
RF: How do we get to [his] world?
S: He's coming to take you.
RF: What about when Jesus came here?
S: He came in a tube...like a pill...a capsule.

After the hypnosis session, it was obvious that Shona's perceptions of reality were shaken. As a Christian, she had never believed in reincarnation, yet, she could not deny her vivid memories. And the idea that Jesus flies in spaceships was also alien to her way of thinking and contrary to her Christian upbringing. As with most abductees who undergo hypnosis to recover lost memories, she questioned what she had said while in a trance. Had she made it up? Where did it come from? For Dr. Fennig (who is Jewish) and myself, the session was one more challenge to our own religious beliefs and to our understanding of the UFO phenomenon. It was becoming more difficult for us to know if we were conducting a scientific investigation or if we were on some kind of spiritual journey. We both agreed that the distinction was not clear in our minds.

Additionally, we realized that there was no way to determine the answers to certain crucial questions. Were Shona's memories tainted by her Christian beliefs? If so, why would they contradict what she had been taught and what she believed? And if her memories reflected the truth about Jesus and what humans have always called angels, then how could we accept the conventional interpretations of the Bible? Our investigations were leading us to the conclusion that a completely new approach to Bible interpretation was needed—one that included flying saucers and high technology, as well as an appreciation for a strange hierarchy of celestial beings far more complex than that commonly accepted by modern-day religions.

Section Three:

Our Hidden History

CHAPTER 11

THE WATCHERS AND HUMAN ORIGINS

The whole idea stinks of UFOs or the Chariot of the Gods or other common forms of contemporary silliness. Against this I can only claim that whereas the idea has indeed many of the stigmata of science fiction, its body is a lot more solid.... Each of the details which contribute to the required scenario are based on a fairly solid foundation of contemporary science....

—Dr. Francis Crick, discoverer of DNA on his theory that life on Earth was brought here by extraterrestrials

---

Evolution or Creation?

The official, consensus story of creation as told to us by modern science goes something like this: When the Earth was formed, about 4.6 billion years ago, it was an uninhabitable mass of molten rock, under constant bombardment by meteors. It took about a billion years for the Earth to cool enough for the first signs of life to appear in the form of algae. About 2 billion years ago, the first single-celled creatures evolved, followed a half a billion years later by multi-celled algae. And that's as far as things got for nearly 2 billion years. Then, at the beginning of what is called the Cambrian period, about 600 million years ago, something remarkable (and quite contrary to Darwin's theory of evolution) happened. To the immense consternation of evolutionist, scientists have recently discovered that, in a sudden burst of creativity, "nature produced an astonishing array of multicellular animals, the ancestors of virtually all creatures that now swim, fly or crawl through the world." As *Time* Magazine reported:

> Scientists used to think that the evolution of phyla took place over a period of 75 million years, and even that seemed impossibly short. Then, two years ago a group of research-

ers...took this long-standing problem and escalated it into a crisis. First they recalibrated the geological clock, chopping the Cambrian period to about half its former length. Then they announced that the interval of major evolutionary innovation did not span the entire 30 million years, but rather was concentrated in the first third. "Fast," [observed a Harvard biologist], "is now a lot faster than we thought, and that's extraordinarily interesting."[1]

This explosion of life forms, called biology's "Big Bang" riddle, is totally unexplainable using Darwin's theory of evolution (which postulates that natural evolution proceeds at a slow pace), yet scientists continue to search for ways to justify and explain such events in order to preserve the one theory that does not require a belief in a higher intelligence.

Biologists are not alone in their attempt to fit square pegs into round holes. If biologists are confused about evolution occurring at supersonic speeds, contrary to all previously held theories, imagine the dilemma of astronomers who have now discovered stars and galaxies billions of years older than the universe itself! These discoveries completely collapse all previous theories about the age of the universe and call into question the methodology used to arrive at previous estimates. And, of course, anthropologists have for some time been perplexed by the mysterious jump in human evolution that is undeniably obvious from the fossil record. Anthropologists tell us that from the muck and brine of the ancient world, over billions of years, single-celled creatures gradually evolved into sea animals, then into reptiles and eventually into mammals and finally into humanlike creatures. Upright, bipedal apelike beings, known as *Australopithecines*, developed about 5 million years ago. By three million years ago, a creature named *Homo habilis* appeared on the scene. With his larger brain size, this primitive human was able to fashion crude stone implements to aid him in his survival. Finally, about one and one half million years ago, *Homo erectus*, a being thought to be the first human, appeared, followed in fairly close succession by *Cro Magnon* and modern *Homo sapiens*.

---

1. "Evolution's Big Bang," p. 70

But, once again, the Darwinist theory of evolution is contradicted by the facts. In his book, *The Dragons of Eden*,[2] late astronomer and scientific guru Dr. Carl Sagan recognized this uncomfortable state of affairs and puzzled over a glaring flaw in the official story of evolution: "If man had evolved naturally from reptiles," he said, "it would have taken 200 million years...." But, in fact, the evolution of mammals and particularly humans after the extinction of the dinosaurs, 65 million years ago, was exceedingly fast. The archeological record, he notes, tells another story, one of a sudden burst of evolution. He points to the fact that the appearance of stone tools does not happen gradually, but rather they appear in enormous abundance all at once. Stone implements should be scarce in the more ancient earth strata and become gradually more abundant in the higher strata. But this is simply not the case. Sagan's response to this enigma? "There is no way to explain [this] unless [early humans] had educational institutions. There must have been some sort of stone craft guild passing on from generation to generation the precious knowledge about the fabrication and use of tools."[3]

(Is this truly a plausible theory, or is this simply another example of the convoluted reasoning that scientists in all fields must resort to in order to force the evidence into their view of reality? We must judge for ourselves whether to follow the evidence and to use common sense or to abandon reason in order to nurture our strongly held beliefs. A scientist who abandons reason, logic and the evidence before him has abandoned true science, and many mainstream scientists today practice the religion of science—a form of atheism devoted to a fanatical worship of materialism.)

Sagan cites even more evidence for the unusual and inexplicable jump in human evolution. Quoting American anatomist C. Judson Herrick's comments on the sudden development of the human brain, as evidenced by the dramatic growth in cranial volume during this same, brief period, he points out that the evolution of the human skull has been spectacularly fast: "Its explosive growth late in phylogeny is one of the most dramatic cases of evolutionary transformation known to comparative anatomy," says Herrick.[4]

---

2. Sagan, 1977.
3. Sagan, p. 95.

We find, therefore, that evolutionists are quietly struggling to find meaning in these amazing anomalies that keep cropping up to challenge the theory they hold so dearly. Yet few are willing to break with the ranks and boldly consider other possibilities. For to do so would bring the whole house of cards they have constructed over the past century crashing to the floor. It would require that they admit that they have been wrong about the nature of reality and that they have failed to recognize the one piece of the puzzle they have tried so hard to disavow: the issue of consciousness—the development of the mind, rather than of the brain. Sagan himself made it abundantly clear in the introduction to his book that he simply did not entertain any notion that human consciousness is anything more than a chemical and biological process:

> My fundamental premise about the brain is that its workings—what we sometimes call "mind"—are a consequence of its anatomy and physiology, and nothing more.... I will not in these pages entertain any hypotheses on what used to be called the mind-body dualism, the idea that inhabiting the matter of the body is something made of quite different stuff, called mind.[5]

Sagan, then, was one of the last principal proponents of what we could call "scientific materialism," the Darwinist view that depends on the assumption that all existence is matter-based, and is therefore the result of random accidents that occur under highly unusual conditions. This view of reality dates back to the 17th century when philosopher and politician Francis Bacon proposed that scientific experimentation and reason should be the basis of true religion. Because of our superior intellect and our ability to reason, Bacon argued, it is our God-given right to exploit and control the Earth's natural resources and all of its living creatures. Due to his influence on the development of the scientific method, Bacon has been called the founder of the religion of scientific materialism.

Another 17th century philosopher and mathematician, René Descartes, further proposed that the universe was like a machine and that it ran according to mathematical laws. Isaac Newton then applied this

4. Sagan, p. 97.
5. Sagan, p. 7.

view to the atomic level of matter by proposing that mathematics could be used to understand the movement of atoms as well as of the planets and stars. By the time that Darwin proposed his theory of evolution in the 19th century, science had already concluded that the universe was made up of spiritless atoms that operated according to predictable, mathematical principles.

But with every passing day, new scientific discoveries, such as those in quantum physics, are destroying the world of the scientific materialists. Findings in the fossil record contradict the Darwinian view that species arise gradually over long periods of time. In fact, there is no evidence for the gradual appearance of one species out of another. There is no evidence of intermediate species, linking one form to another, as with *Homo sapiens*. Yet, old ideas die hard.

Carl Sagan epitomized what I would call the "Berlin Wall" of human understanding. And just like the real wall (which was erected to defend a materialistic philosophy), this wall is about to come tumbling down. As more and more scientists cross the line and admit that consciousness exists throughout the universe and is not based in the material world, science will, in the not too distant future, reach a critical mass, and the resulting collapse of the "Wall" will usher in a new age of human evolution and understanding. Unfortunately, just as with the real wall, it may also usher in an age of confusion and chaos if the public is not properly prepared to deal with this new understanding of multiple realities.

Directed Panspermia

Yet, as we have learned from a bug named MU, the theory of evolution is not without merit. "The theory of evolution is valid," he said, "but life on Earth did not evolve naturally." It may be a great humiliation to scientists some day to discover a bug smarter than they, but that certainly may be true. The evidence overwhelmingly supports MU's version of historical events and, furthermore, supports the theory proposed by some leading scientists that a guiding hand—an intelligence from outer space—has helped evolution along from time to time. Such an idea is not new, and the reader might be amazed at the credentials of some who have proposed it in the past.

The idea that life on Earth may have originated on other worlds was seriously proposed at the turn of the century by Svante Arrhenius, a Swedish Nobel-Prize winning chemist in his theory of "Panspermia." He theorized that the seeds of life may be constantly raining down on Earth from outer space in the form of meteorites and microorganisms—interstellar debris, if you will. He believed that such seeds could have germinated on Earth, causing life to develop. Such a notion is not so far fetched. In 1989, amino acids, necessary for the existence of life, were found in meteor craters and are thought to have originated in outer space. (The recent discovery of possible life forms in a meteorite from Mars adds further weight to this theory.) Then, in the late 1970s, Francis Crick, the Nobel laureate who discovered DNA, and Leslie Orgel, a pioneer in prebiotic chemistry, proposed the theory of "Directed Panspermia." Directed Panspermia, they said, was the notion that the seeds of life on Earth were sent here by intelligent civilizations millions of years ago in robotic spaceships.

Crick elaborated on this thesis in his 1981 book, *Life Itself*.[6] Here he explains that while unraveling the mystery of the genetic code, he discovered a surprising conformity in the DNA code of all living organisms on Earth: "...All living things use the same four-letter language to carry genetic information. All use the same 20 letter language to construct their proteins.... All use the same chemical dictionary to translate from one language to the other."[7] He began to wonder how this remarkable uniformity first arose and how the same code could be used by nature to create the myriad complex structures that make up life on our planet. If life had developed by chance—through trial and error—as Darwinists propose, then it was more likely that numerous different codes would have evolved in different parts of the world, under different conditions. Yet, there is no evidence for an evolutionary process. Using complex statistical calculations, Crick found that chance alone could not account for such a condition. Thus, he concluded that life on Earth must have originated elsewhere and been transported here. But by whom?

Crick was not ready to concede the existence of UFOs or even of ancient astronauts, yet he was willing to consider the possibility that alien civilizations might have visited Earth periodically over the millennia and that Earth may in fact be "part of a cosmic wildlife park."

6. Crick, 1981.
7. Crick, 1981, p. 47.

Perhaps we are under some sort of discreet surveillance by higher beings on a planet of some nearby star. It is not clear exactly how these cosmic game wardens would do this without our detecting them, but with a higher technology such supervision may be relatively easy.[8]

Crick was clearly uneasy with his own discovery and his extraordinary conclusion, expressing embarrassment at his unwilling association with fringe science:

The whole idea stinks of UFOs or the Chariot of the Gods or other common forms of contemporary silliness. Against this I can only claim that whereas the idea has indeed many of the stigmata of science fiction, its body is a lot more solid. It does not really have the major feature of most science fiction, which is a great leap of the imagination.... Each of the details which contribute to the required scenario are based on a fairly solid foundation of contemporary science....[9]

As correct as Crick may appear, I am sure that even he and Orgel could not have imagined the likes of MU and other strange extraterrestrials visiting our Earth today. Yet their idea, which appears to hit the nail squarely on the head, shows that scientists can be open-minded. These British-born American scientists today work at the Salk Institute for Biological Studies in La Jolla, California, and represent another example of top-ranked scientists who have boldly broken away from the consensus views of their colleagues, and because of their credentials, have survived unscathed.

Human Reptilian Heritage

Another important aspect of human evolution is our link not only to the apes, but also to the dinosaurs. As we have seen, the reptilian beings of the UFO phenomenon appear to have been involved, along with the others, in the development of the human species. It is even possible that there were, from time to time, competing and conflicting interests among the extraterrestrials with regard to human development. Human anatomy argues strongly for the conclusion that we do indeed have a reptilian heritage. Sagan pointed out that the human brain clearly shows signs of having evolved from reptiles. The center,

8. Crick, 1981, p. 158.
9. Crick, 1981, p. 149.

215

and most ancient portion, of the human brain, is commonly known among neurophysiologists as the reptilian complex, or "r" complex, and is believed to be a primitive vestige of our reptilian past. It is this portion that is believed to be in some sense continuing to perform the dinosaur functions such as territoriality, aggressive behavior and the establishment of social hierarchies.[10]

The mid-layer of the brain is known as the limbic system and is thought to be the home of our strong emotions, such as love, hate, compassion and sentimentality. But what truly sets us apart from the dinosaurs is the outer layer of the brain, called the neocortex, which represents 85% of our brain mass and is where our cognitive abilities lie. The development of the neocortex, Sagan believed, took place gradually over a period of several tens of millions of years, but "its development accelerated greatly a few million years ago when humans evolved."[11] It is the home of reasoning, deliberation and, Sagan speculated, the place where the *"knowledge of good and evil"* resides.[12] Here, Sagan, for all his materialistic view of the world, found a peculiar parallel to the Book of Genesis and the story of creation. He noted that painful childbirth, which seemed to him to be a curse reserved only for the human species, was the result of the sudden and unexplainable development of a large cranium in our species, needed to hold our much larger brains. This curious connection between the evolution of the neocortex and the pain of childbirth seems to be referred to in Genesis 3:16: "In pain shalt thou bring forth children," God says to Adam and Eve after they had eaten the fruit of the tree of knowledge. It was specifically the knowledge of the difference between good and evil that God did not want first humans to have. Yet, by developing a large neocortex, that is exactly what happened. Could the Book of Genesis have references to genetic engineering performed by extraterrestrials? If so, it would behoove us to ask who it was that gave this awesome power to the first humans, for whoever did it was bestowing on humanity godlike powers—the ability to make abstract, moral judgments and to think in ways beyond the abilities of the other animals.

10. Sagan, 1977, pp. 62-63.
11. Sagan, 1977, p. 58.
12. Sagan, 1977, p. 98.

216

Of course, we know that it was the serpent who tempted Eve to eat the fruit, and after it was eaten, God said: "Behold, the man has become as one of us [plural], to know good and evil; and now, lest he put forth his hand and take also of the Tree of Life, and eat and live forever"[13] he must be driven from the Garden of Eden. If the fruit of the Tree of Knowledge is a metaphor for the genetic engineering performed on early humans, giving them an enlarged neocortex, then what is the fruit of the Tree of Life? Was it the ability to remember our previous lives and to think three dimensionally? Is this a metaphor for telepathic and psychic abilities? If this is so, then what is happening today, as a new species of human is being created, may be that humankind is finally being allowed to eat from that mythical Tree. When and if that happens, the human race will not only have the ability to know the difference between good and evil, but also, for the first time, the ability to understand how to use its power.

And what of the serpent who violated God's will? According to the Bible, God pronounced his judgment: "Upon thy belly shalt thou go," implying that this reptilian being was not a snake, but rather a creature that walked upright. Is this another clue that points to the authenticity of what the abductees are being told about the ETs' involvement in human evolution? Perhaps, but the Bible tells very little about the creation of humanity. To find out more it is necessary to be familiar with other ancient documents, contemporary to or even preceding the Old Testament. Two such documents are the Nag Hammadi texts, discovered in 1945 in Egypt, buried in an earthenware box, and a volume of ancient Jewish legends known as the Haggadah. These ancient texts contain many little-known references to the story of humankind's creation that imply that we had a reptilian heritage. For example, the Haggadah includes this interesting description of Adam and Eve after they ate of the forbidden fruit:

The first result was that Adam and Eve became naked. Before, their bodies had been overlaid with a horny skin, and enveloped with the cloud of glory. No sooner had they violated the command given them than the cloud of glory and the horny skin dropped from them, and they stood there in their nakedness, and ashamed.[14]

---

13. Genesis 3:22.

Were the first, prototype humans part reptilian in appearance? If reptilian beings were responsible for our genetic engineering, such a conclusion would be reasonable. Certainly there is nothing in the fossil record to contradict this conclusion since bones give little clue to a being's outward appearance. Additionally, such beings may have disappeared thousands of years ago, leaving no trace. In fact, the Bible and other ancient documents tell us the great deluge was created to rid the Earth of these abominations—the progeny of the fallen angels.

FIGURE 13. *A recurring theme in ancient texts is the battle between human-looking and reptilian gods. In Judaeo-Christian beliefs, the archangel Michael was often depicted as a blonde, Nordic type slaying a dragon. Here, the Greek snake god Typhon battles with Zeus. Note the double helix-like arrangement of the serpent's tails. (Courtesy Z. Sitchin,* The Wars of Gods and Men, *© Z. Sitchin.)*

14. Barnstone, 1984, p. 34.

One researcher who is convinced that this is the true history of the human race is R.A. Boulay, whose books, *Flying Serpents and Dragons*[15] and *Dragon Power*,[16] trace the hidden history of our species. Boulay's keen analytical mind, honed through 30 years of experience as a cryptologist for U.S. government intelligence agencies, mostly with the ultra-secret National Security Agency (NSA), helped him to build a strong case for human reptilian heritage. Referring to the reptilian gods of the Sumerian stories, Boulay says:

> By combining the characteristics of the native ape man...with their own saurian nature, they produced the "Adam" of the Old Testament. This Adam was half human and half reptile....[17]

Later, he believes:

> The homosaurus was modified and given more mammalian traits. This was the Biblical "Fall of Man" where Adam achieved "knowing" or the ability to reproduce sexually.[18]

Supporting this conclusion, the *Nag Hammadi Texts* describe a different version of the story of Adam and Eve than that told in the Bible:

> She looked at the tree. And she saw that it was beautiful and magnificent, and she desired it. She took some of its fruit and ate, and she gave to her husband also, and he ate too. Then their minds were opened. For when they ate, the light of knowledge shone for them.... They knew that they were naked with regard to knowledge.... They saw that they were naked and became enamored of one another. When they saw their makers [plural] they loathed them since they were of beastly forms. They understood very much.[19]

Such a document surely was buried with good cause. Not many of us want to be told that, rather than being created by God with a capital "G," we were created by hideous creatures known in ancient times as gods with a small "g." Yet, once again the Bible gives us clues that imply that this might be true. Genesis repeatedly uses the plural when referring to God, as in: "Let us make man in *our* own image and after

---

15. Boulay, 1990.
16. Boulay, 1992.
17. Boulay, 1990, p. 9.
18. Boulay, 1990, p. 9.
19. Barnstone, 1984, p. 71.

our likeness."[20] (emphasis added) As shall be seen below, the plural is no accident, nor does it refer, as some fundamentalists avow, to the Father, Son and Holy Ghost. It is a vestige of much earlier texts that tell the story of human creation in much more detail.

Other references in the document known as the *Haggadah* may give us a further clue. First, it describes how Adam was created from dust taken from the four corners of the world:

> The dust was of various colors—red, black, white and green. Red was for the blood, black for the bowels, white for the bones and *green* for the pale skin.[21] (emphasis added)

Further, it describes the reptilians quite specifically:

> Among the animals, the serpent was notable. Of all of them, he had the most excellent of qualities, in some of which, he resembled man. Like man, he stood upright on two feet and in height he was equal to the camel.... His superior mental gifts caused him to become an infidel. It likewise explains his envy of man, especially his conjugal visits.[22]

This description, written more than 2000 years ago, is a remarkably accurate description of today's reptilian beings as described by UFO abductees and should give us pause. Perhaps the Bible does not tell the whole story of creation. Perhaps the story is much more complicated and much more repugnant than most people would like to know. And perhaps the early authors and editors of the Old Testament knew that people were not ready to know such details. Could there have been a spiritual Watergate-type cover-up in ancient times? Could there have been a conspiracy to "clean up" the official texts—sanitize them, so to speak, for mass consumption? Even today, researchers tend to edit out some of the more controversial and disturbing elements of the abduction phenomenon. It is human nature. Is it so hard to imagine that the same thing could have happened throughout the history of humankind, until much of the truth was either forgotten or conveniently put out of mind? If so, it lends new meaning to the term "Revelation" that is so much a part of the Christian doctrine. If the Revelation includes revealing to us our true origins and our true place in the hierarchy of intelligent species in the universe, then it will come

20. Genesis 1:26.
21. Barnstone, 1984, p. 26.
22. Barnstone, 1984, p 33.

220

as a great shock to a people who have been taught to believe that they are so important that they were made in the image of the Prime Creator—the All That Is. Instead, we may find that there are many layers of godlike beings between us and the Creator and that we have a long road to travel to find our way Home.

Homosaurus

Even Carl Sagan wondered out loud about the possibility that intelligent dinosaurs might have evolved. After all, dinosaurs were around for nearly 250 million years. Mammals have been around for a much shorter period of time. It is only logical to conclude that intelligent dinosaurs would have developed. Sagan pointed out that although most dinosaurs had brains with significantly smaller brain mass than mammals, there was one dinosaur whose brain density approached that of the mammals. These *Saurornithoides* were creatures about the size of an ostrich which "probably hunted for food and used the *four fingers* (emphasis added) of their hand like appendages for many different tasks. They are interesting beasts to speculate about. If the dinosaurs had not all been mysteriously extinguished some sixty-five million years ago, would the *Saurornithoides* have continued to evolve into increasingly intelligent forms?"[23]

But was it necessary for such evolution to occur naturally? With what we now know about extraterrestrial intervention in Earth affairs, it is easy to see how such creatures might have been evolved through deliberate engineering. There is no reason to doubt that highly advanced, intelligent reptilian beings have existed and still exist. It is also possible that the dinosaurs themselves were engineered by sentient reptiles from space.

Another scientist who has speculated about this very issue is Dr. Dale Russell, a former chief of the Paleontology Division of the National Museums of Canada, who constructed a life-size figure of what such a being might look like. The resulting figure resembles so closely what abductees have seen that many of them cannot bear to look at photos of "Homosaurus." The statue is of a six-foot tall, upright reptilian with large, yellow eyes and vertically slit pupils. (See

---

23. Sagan, 1977, p. 144.

Figure 14.) The greenish skin, the clawlike hands and the slight ridge coming down from the top of its large, bulbous head to the tip of its snout is precisely how abductees have described the beings they have seen.

Serpent Gods

The history and mythology of the human race is full of references to serpent gods who at times are depicted as benevolent and at other

FIGURE 14. *Homosaurus? Dr. Dale A. Russell, of the Canadian National Museum of Natural Sciences, constructed a biologically credible creature to show what evolution might have produced if dinosaurs had evolved into intelligent beings. This artist's rendition is by Maynard Demmon (©1996, imarkdesigns. See Ashpole, 1989, for a photograph of the model.)*

times, cruel and barbaric. In India, one of the oldest books known, called the Book of Dzyan, speaks of a serpent race which descended from the skies to teach humankind. These were the Nagas (this, curiously, is "Sagan" spelled backwards!), a semi-divine race of beings with human faces and the tails of dragons. An ancient Indian epic tale, the Mahabharata, includes this passage regarding the Nagas:

> The gods came in cloud-borne chariots,
> Came to view the scene so fair.
> Winged Suparnas, scaly Nagas,

FIGURE 15. *A drawing from the wall of an Egyptian tomb showing a serpent bearing the king's soul up to the heavens. (From* Flying Serpents and Dragons *by R.A. Boulay.)*

Bright celestial cars in concourse
sailed upon the cloudless sky.[24]

Note that the gods came in "cloud-borne" chariots, indicating their appearance was something like a bright cloud, yet the last line makes it clear that the sky was cloudless. This is typical of ancient texts, which often describe the chariots of the gods as clouds—perhaps because they simply had no other frame of reference.

The ancient Chinese believed that the first emperors were fathered by celestial dragons and thus the symbol of the dragon came to denote royalty and, specifically, a divine heritage. According to Chinese legend, dragons were present at the creation and were linked with the development of humankind.

In Egypt, the snake is depicted as a powerful creature, capable of carrying the soul of the Pharaoh into the heavens, to the land of immortality. Paintings depicting the Pharaoh riding to heaven on the back of a flying snake have been found in the royal burial chambers. (See Figure 15 on page 223.) The snake was adopted by them as the symbol of kingship and divine heritage and can be seen on the head dresses of their kings, protruding from the center of the forehead, home of the mysterious "third eye" in Eastern cultures. In addition, the Egyptians believed in gods who had come down from the heavens in ancient times and mated with them, creating a line of semi-divine kings. These beings were known by the Egyptians as the "Neteru," meaning "The Guardians" and were believed to have been associated with the ancient Mesopotamian city of Ur. [25]

In Mexico and South America, the Aztecs and the builders of other megalithic structures worshipped the feathered serpent gods, Kulkulkan and Quetzalcoatl, who were said to have imparted the wisdom of the sciences, particularly astronomy, to their civilizations. Today, just a short drive from Mexico City, one can go to the mysterious and ancient city of Teotihuacan and see the pyramid of the feathered serpent, dedicated to their serpent god.

---

24. Boulay, 1990, p. 108.
25. Sitchen, 1985, p. 38.

224

The Sumerian Texts.

Perhaps the most revealing of the ancient documents comes from the Earth's earliest-known civilizations—those of the region we now call the Middle East, but which in history books is called Mesopotamia. These civilizations which sprang suddenly and mysteriously from the desert sands included Sumeria (Land of the Guardians), Babylonia (Gate of the Gods) and Assyria, part of which was located under what is today the Persian Gulf, nearly 6000 years ago.

Fortunately for us, these people were prolific writers and, also fortunately, they liked to write on clay tablets, which when baked under the desert sun for thousands of years, became hard as stone and preserved much of their culture for us to examine today. Additionally, they were artists who enjoyed depicting their daily lives and their religious stories on cylinders made of hard or semi-precious stones. Tens of thousands of these have been unearthed and studied. (See Figure 16.)

Because they are written in the ancient wedge-like script known as Cuneiform, and because that language was a mystery until only recently, there are few scholars who are able to translate their meaning. One of those is a Russian-born journalist who was raised in Palestine and while there became fluent in the ancient languages, including the ancient Hebrew in which the Old Testament was originally written. Zecharia Sitchin, having graduated from the University of London in

FIGURE 16. *The gods of the ancient cultures of Persia, Sumeria, Babylonia and Assyria were often depicted roaming the skies in winged discs. (Courtesy Z. Sitchin, The Wars of Gods and Men, © Z. Sitchin.)*

225

economic history, served as a leading journalist and editor in Israel for many years, but is no doubt best known for a series of scholarly books known as *The Earth Chronicles*, in which he presents detailed translations of many of the ancient texts. Sitchin has become convinced from his translations of these documents that they refer to actual events when they tell of the gods who came to Earth to create humankind and to use Earth's resources.

According to Sitchin, the tablets tell the story of a race of gods who came to Earth more than 240,000 years ago, led by the god An (thus they were called the Annunaki) and his sons, Enki and Enlil. One of the tablets, known as the Sumerian King List, lists the god-kings who ruled the Earth long before the great flood destroyed much of humanity. (It should be noted here that the arrival of divine beings from the heavens in the time before the flood is also referred to in the Old Testament. There, they are referred to as the "Nephilim," often translated as "giants" by biblical scholars. However, Sitchin disputes this translation. He says the correct translation for "Nephilim" is "those who came down to Earth." If he is correct, then it would seem that the Old Testament and the Sumerian tablets may be referring to the same events.)

The Sumerian writings contain not only the story of human creation, but also the story of a Noah-like figure who survived the great flood by building an ark, after being warned by one of the gods. The tablets explain that the gods decided to create a worker race to help them with their efforts to mine the Earth's resources. It fell upon Enki, sometimes abbreviated as Ea, to create this hybrid race by using the raw materials (indigenous species) to combine with the essence of the gods. With this concoction of DNA, referred to in the tablets (as well as in the Bible) as "clay," the gods were said to "bind upon it the image of the gods." Most importantly for this discussion, Enki was often depicted in the Sumerian drawings as half snake and half man. If this is, in fact, a reference to a reptilian being, then we are left with the conclusion that his creations also bore reptilian features, although this is not stated explicitly. However, the tablets do tell us that these first hybrid humans were not capable of reproduction (as is the case with most hybrid species) and that they therefore must have been created as they were needed to toil on the reservation in which they were kept, known as the Garden of E Din, meaning "home of the righteous ones."[26]

Enki, the reptilian creator god, who shared power with his half brother, Enlil (sometimes abbreviated as "il") is, however, depicted as being benevolent to the human race. The other gods, led by brother Enlil, thought the hybrid creatures to be an abomination and wanted

FIGURE 17. *The snake coiled around the tree of knowledge was the symbol of Enki, the reptilian creator god. This symbol came to represent secret knowledge, specifically the knowledge of healing. It later became the caduceus of the Greeks and the logo of the American Medical Association. (Courtesy Z. Sitchin,* The Twelfth Planet, *© Z. Sitchin.)*

26. Sitchin, 1990, pp. 186-187.

the experiment kept under control by ensuring that they never be allowed to procreate. However, the experiment, in a bizarre reversal of the roles we find in Michael Crichton's popular book, *Jurassic Park,*[27] got out of control when Enki, against the wishes of his brother, gave the hybrids the ability to procreate. In the Sumerian version, as in the Biblical account, first humans were given to eat from the fruit of the Tree of Knowledge. The ancient drawings use a picture of a snake coiled around a tree, bearing the fruit of knowledge, along with a half moon for Ea and the planet symbol of Anu, as a glyph representing the creator gods. (See Figure 17 on page 227.) In some cases, the tablets depict two snakes coiled around the Tree, coincidentally reminiscent of the double helix of the DNA molecule. Even now, nearly 6000 years later, this symbol (known as the caduceus) is used to represent wisdom and healing and is used by the American Medical Association as its logo.

We might surmise that as the hybrids began to mate (probably with apelike beings that existed at the time), they gradually lost their reptilian appearance, further enraging Enlil.

Torment of the Gods

In his book on the influence of the custodial gods on Earth's affairs, titled *The Gods of Eden,*[28] William Bramley begins by saying that the idea of UFOs and celestial beings was the farthest thing from his mind when he set out to research the causes of war in the history of human civilization:

> As I probed deeper…I was compelled to face the possibility that some human problems may be rooted in some of the most utterly bizarre realities imaginable. Because these realities are rarely acknowledged, let alone understood, they are not dealt with…. I will admit that when I began my research I had a bias about what I was expecting to find: a human profit motive as the common thread which links various third-party influences in mankind's violent history. What I found instead was the UFO.[29]

---

27. Crichton, 1992.
28. Bramley, 1989.
29. Bramley, 1989, p. 4.

Bramley traces much of the strife on Earth back to the early creator gods and finds evidence that they purposely intended to keep the human spirit entrapped in the physical dimension for the purpose of using people as slaves.[30] He cites Sitchin's translation of an ancient tablet which says:

> In the clay, god [spirit] and man [physical]
> shall be bound,
> to a unity brought together;
> so that to the end of days
> the flesh and the soul
> which in a god have ripened—
> that soul in a blood-kinship be bound;[31]

and:

> With picks and spades they [humans]
> built the shrines,
> they built the big canal banks,
> for food for the peoples, for the
> sustenance of the [gods].[32]

Bramley says that beings identified with the symbol of the serpent and led by Enki were dedicated to the attainment of spiritual freedom and the "dissemination of spiritual knowledge," particularly the power of spiritual healing. (Note: this correlates with the many abduction cases in which the abductee finds that he/she has the power to heal, using psychic energies.) Bramley concludes that Enki's defeat allowed the forces of Enlil to entrap billions of spiritual beings in the physical realm and that, throughout the ages, they have tried to keep humans from discovering their spiritual and immortal nature. This has been done, he believes, by creating differences within the human race, to set people against one another in an endless cycle of violence.

Such a hypothesis turns the tables on traditional interpretation of the Bible, which depicts the serpent as evil and elevates the forces of Enlil to the level of God with a capital "G." In Bramley's scenario, the god of the Jews becomes the enslaver of humankind—the one who

---

30. Bramley, 1989, p. 46.
31. Sitchin, 1976, p. 356.
32. Lambert, 1969, pp. 65-67.

causes humanity to lose immortality by preventing him from eating the fruit of the Tree of Life. Such a conclusion seems logical based upon the role played by Enlil in the Sumerian version of creation.

He and the other gods became angry with human overpopulation and said: "Let there be a plague; let disease, sickness and pestilence blow upon them like a tornado." When these didn't work, they decided to destroy humanity in one large cataclysm—a great flood. But once again, Enki came to humanity's rescue. He gives warning to a man named Utnapishtim and tells him to build a boat so that he and his family can survive. (See Figure 18 on page 231.)

It seems obvious that much of the Old Testament is borrowed from these much older texts, but it is also clear that the stories were altered to reflect the beliefs and prejudices of the times. The Old Testament uses various terms for God. In some places it uses the term "El," but this is merely the Hebrew translation of "il," the Sumerian god. In other cases, God is referred to as "Elohim," but this is simply the plural of El and means "gods." "El" is also used in the Bible as the suffix for the archangels, as in Mika-el and Gabri-el, indicating once again that the archangels may be the same beings referred to by the Sumerians as the Annunaki—the supporters of Enlil. At other times, God is referred to as Jehovah or Yahweh, but in all cases, it seems that early Jewish writers used earlier writings from which to draw material.

Just like Enlil in the Sumerian tablets, God is given credit in the Bible for ordering a flood to destroy humanity, yet in the Bible, the story is changed. It is God himself who warns Noah and saves humankind, rather than the serpent. Jews and Christians have been left wondering for thousands of years why God would change his mind. If he had made such a terrible mistake, why save Noah and start all over again? The Sumerian account makes more sense because it is easy to see how two opposing forces might have conflicting interests.

To make matters more confusing, early Jewish writers who presumably believed in only one God, failed to edit out references to multiple gods, as in: And Elohim said, "Let us make man in our own image." As we now know, the term "Elohim" is the plural form of "El." Later, in the Garden of Eden, when the serpent tempts Eve, he says:

You are not going to die by eating the fruit. No, the Elohim will know that the moment you eat it your eyes will be opened and you will be the same as the gods in telling good from bad.[33]

Once again in Genesis 11:1-9, we are told that after the flood, the people said:

"Come on, let us build ourselves a city and a tower whose top will reach the skies." And the Lord came down to see the tower and said: "Look, the people are united and they have one language…. Now nothing will stop them from doing what they take in their minds to do. Come on let us go down there and confuse their language so they cannot understand one another's speech."[34]

If these ancient texts, including the Bible, reflect the true attitudes of the gods toward humanity, it is little wonder that their involvement in human affairs over the millennia has wreaked so much havoc and that the religions they inspired have been the cause of so much hatred and human suffering. It almost seems that one of their goals, as Bram-

FIGURE 18. *Enki as the serpent god of the Mesopotamian cultures is shown in this illustration from a cylindrical seal giving warning to man of an imminent flood. (Courtesy Z. Sitchin,* When Time Began, *© Z. Sitchin.)*

33. Genesis 3:4.
34. Genesis 11:1-9.

ley suggests, has been to keep humanity in constant war and chaos, perhaps to keep us too busy to develop our psychic and spiritual sides.

After comparing the Mesopotamian tales of creation with the much later Jewish writings that appear in the Old Testament and other documents, it becomes increasingly difficult to tell the good guys from the bad. It is not clear at all that the serpent beings are all bad and that they represent evil. Yet, the Hebrew writers seemed to have made that distinction long ago when they changed the creation story, taking sides with Enlil, against his brother Enki and changing Enki's original title of "Prince of the Earth," as stated in the Sumerian texts, to "Prince of Darkness and Prince of Evil." Whom do we believe? Was giving humans fruit from the Tree of Knowledge an inherently evil act as the Bible says? Was the serpent trying to liberate humans or trying to entrap them? It seems that we are no better off today in understanding these celestial beings than we were at the time of Noah. This may be because the writers of all the ancient texts were, after all, just human. They were writing from the human perspective, which, as we know, is often based on fear and hatred of anything we cannot understand. Additionally, human prejudices and self interests come into play as, throughout the millennia, the texts are edited, altered, hidden and destroyed to suit the beliefs of the particular time. This human element of diminished perspective must be considered as we continue to examine these lost books of the Bible.

The Books of Enoch

One of the descendants of Adam, according to Genesis 5:21-24, was Enoch, the father of Methuselah and great-grandfather of Noah. Enoch lived to be 365 years old, but did not die a normal human death: "When he was 365, and in constant touch with God, he disappeared, for God took him!" Enoch lived in the antediluvian days when Watchers or Nephilim were on the Earth intermingling with humans:

> Now a population explosion took place upon the earth. It was at this time that the beings from the spirit world looked upon the beautiful earth women and took any they desired to be their wives.... In those days, and even afterwards, when the evil beings from the spirit world were sexually involved with women, their children became giants [Nephilim] of whom so many legends are told. When the Lord God saw the extent of

human wickedness, and that the trend and direction of men's lives were only towards evil, he was sorry he had made them. It broke his heart. And he said, "I will blot out from the face of the earth all mankind that I created. Yes, and the animals too, and the reptiles and the birds. For I am sorry I made them."[35]

(Once again we see evidence of a conflict between two opposing forces of seemingly even powers. The evil spirits referred to here are the Watchers or Nephilim who are described as being spirits who have sex with human women and bear unusual children. God, it seems, is powerless to stop this activity, so he resorts to drastic measures. It should also be noted that having sex and taking wives is something that is done in a physical body and that, therefore, these spirits had physical characteristics not mentioned in the Bible.)

Although the Bible does not make it clear, the story of Enoch and his involvement in the war of the Watchers over human dominance is a long and complex one in which we are given much more information about the nature of the guardian gods. The original stories alluded to in Genesis are contained in much older documents, known as the Books of Enoch, written by anonymous authors (as is much of the Old Testament), but attributed to the Patriarch, Enoch. Parts of the Books of Enoch, written in the archaic Hebrew language called Aramaic, were found among the scraps of parchment in the caves of Qumran in 1947 on the shores of the Dead Sea. These, of course, are the Dead Sea Scrolls. They had been placed there for safe keeping by a group of radical, anti-Roman Jews, known as the Essenes, nearly 2000 years earlier, around the time of Christ. Another version of the Books of Enoch exists in Ethiopian. This is due to the fact that many Jews fled at the time of the Roman persecutions.

According to the Aramaic texts, as translated by Fr. Joseph Milik, a French priest who was among the first with access to the scrolls, "Enoch was the first among the children of men born of the Earth who had learned writing, science and wisdom" from the angels.[36] In one of the books, titled the Book of the Watchers, we learn that the Watchers are angels and that there are good and bad Watchers. We are told that the Watchers are angels of the Lord, "come down to earth to instruct

---

35. Genesis 6:1-7.
36. Milik, 1976, p. 11.

the children of men and to bring about justice and equity on earth."
But, in the case of the wicked or bad angels, the science they teach
turns to wicked ends because of their sin, which is that they permit
their sexual appetites to dominate them. "When the evil Watchers
descended and beheld the daughters of man, they began to corrupt
themselves with them. When the sons of God saw the daughters of
man, they could not restrain their inclination."[37]

These Watchers fall from grace with God when Enoch travels to
heaven in physical form to testify against them. He tells God that the
Watchers "had begun to go unto the daughters of men, so that they
became impure." As punishment for the sins of the evil Watchers on
mankind, God destroys humanity, including the hybrid race of beings
who are the offspring of humans and Watchers, by causing a great
flood. The evil Watchers are then put into a fiery pit and imprisoned
by the four chiefs of the good Watchers, the archangels Mika-el, Sari-el,
Rafa-el and Gabri-el.

The Testament of Amram

Although the Books of Enoch make vague references to "white
men" when referring to some of the Watchers, the writings are frus-
trating in their lack of descriptions of these enigmatic beings. However, another interesting reference to the Watchers was found in the
same cave as the Books of Enoch, but was not known until 1992 when
two biblical scholars, Robert Eisenman and Michael Wise, published
their book, *The Dead Sea Scrolls Uncovered*.[38] Among the 50 documents
released for the first time in this book, is a reference to the Watchers
that is unique, for it provides us with one of the few physical descriptions. The text, called the Testament of Amram, is the testimony of a
little-known Biblical character who describes an experience in which
he saw "an angel and a demon" wrestling over his soul:

"[I saw Watchers] in my vision, the dream vision. Two
[men] were fighting over me. I asked them, 'who are you that
you are thus empowered over me?' They answered me, 'We
[have been em]powered and rule over all mankind.' They said
to me, 'Which of us do yo[u] choose to rule [you]?' I raised my

37. Milik, 1976, p. 327.
38. Eisenman, 1992.

eyes and looked. [One] of them was terrifying in his appearance, [like a s]erpent, [his] c[loak] many colored, yet very dark.... [And I looked again], and...in his appearance, his visage like a viper.... [I replied to him,] 'This [Watcher], who is he?' He answered me, 'This Wa[tcher]...[and his three names are Belial and Prince of Darkness] and King of Evil.... He is empowered over all Darkness, while I [am empowered over all light]...and over all that is of God. I rule over [every] man.' I asked him, ['What are your names...?'] He said to me, '[My]three names are [Michael and Prince of Light and King of Righteousness'].[39]

There are numerous parallels in this brief passage to the tales of UFO abduction that are becoming so widespread today. First, Amram describes this event as a "dream-vision," rather than as either a dream or a vision. This is very much like the way abductees see their experiences. In almost every abduction case, experiencers report events that seemed something like dreams, yet at the same time, like real events. In fact, this researcher has heard the exact term used to describe abduction events by abductees. Secondly, the scene, which includes the forces of good and evil wrestling over a human soul, is identical to that shown to Betty Andreasson and reported in Ray Fowler's book, *The Watchers II*.[40] The hypnosis session from which that material was reported, occurred years before the Eisenman book was published, and therefore could not be the product of Betty's memory.

Thirdly, the reptilian being is said to be wearing an unusual dark cloak of many colors. ETs (including reptilians) wearing dark cloaks (sometimes with hoods) are commonly reported in abduction cases, and this detail lends credence to Amram's testimony. Fourthly, of course, is the description of the evil Watcher as having the terrifying appearance of a reptile. In this case, both the words "serpent" and "viper" are used to convey this unmistakable meaning. Note, also, the lack of description of Michael, the archangel. Yet it is clear from the passage that Michael bore no resemblance to the evil Watcher and was, presumably, not frightening in his appearance. We can only imagine the appearance of the Prince of Light, and no doubt most of us picture a tall blonde, similar to the familiar image of Michael, clad in armor,

---

39. Eisenman, 1992, pp. 155-156.
40. Fowler, 1995.

slaying the dragon, so common in religious art. And the final point of comparison with the abduction phenomenon has to do with the fact that abductions run in families. Someone who has had alien contact, in every case I have been involved with, is a member of a family of experiencers. In this case, the comparison seems valid because of who Amram was. Although the name might not ring a bell, Amram was indeed an important personage, for he was none other than the father of Moses! And, as we shall see in the next chapter, Moses may have been the most famous contactee in history.

CHAPTER 12

JEHOVAH—A POWERFUL ENTITY

...the Lord traveled before them by day in a pillar of cloud, to lead them along the way and by night in a pillar of fire, to give them light; that they might travel by day and by night. He took not away the pillar of cloud by day, or the pillar of fire by night, from in front of the people.

—(Exodus 13:21-22)

The Great Flood

As we have seen in previous chapters, the history of the origins of humanity and the evolution of the human species is a complex one that to this day has puzzled our best scientists. Occasional, perhaps even frequent, genetic manipulations by advanced ET beings have made the search for our beginnings a difficult one. Additionally, worldwide cataclysms that have rearranged the entire geography of the Earth and buried the evidence of earlier civilizations under the oceans and possibly under miles of polar ice have made it nearly impossible for us to know today (through conventional scientific investigation) our true history. However, we can surmise from the evidence at hand that about 13,000 years ago a great geological upheaval destroyed, by fire, flood, and earthquake, much of the world's population. Whether this upheaval was caused by the guardian beings known as the Watchers is uncertain, but it is a strong possibility that, as the ancient texts describe, the gods were dissatisfied with the progress of their experiment.

However, as we know, there were survivors. Some escaped by chance, while others were especially chosen by the Watchers to be survivors. If the ancient texts can be believed, these special survivors were given instructions on how to build an ark that would survive the great flood. But, given what we now know about the methods employed by the amazing guardian beings, it is highly probable that the chosen ones were simply taken aboard their ships, placed in suspended animation and then returned to Earth at a much later time (perhaps thousands of years later) when the Earth was once again suitable for habitation. These chosen humans (perhaps selected for their genetic characteristics) still maintained their knowledge of science and technology from their earlier existence, and, when returned to Earth to mingle with the descendants of the accidental survivors, were able to restore civilization within a relatively short time. This would explain how the Sumerian civilization suddenly appeared out of nowhere and why archeologists cannot find traces of Sumer's early beginnings.

If this scenario is accurate, it is exceedingly interesting that the origins of the Hebrew people (as far as we know today) lie in the Sumerian city of Ur about 4000 years ago. It was there that the earliest Hebrew writers began to inscribe the stories of early human history. But their versions of the creation and the times before the flood were written at a time when there was already a rich, written history, almost 2000 years old—a history written in cuneiform writing on thousands of clay tablets, upon which they drew heavily. In any case, the early Hebrews believed that they were chosen by God to serve a special purpose, and their earliest writings relate a long history of their relationship to a being (or beings) who (like the Sumerian gods) traveled the skies in cloud-borne chariots of fire.

By the time these earliest Hebrews committed their stories to writing, the Mesopotamian cultures had a long tradition of belief in creator gods who had come to Earth in antiquity to create the human species and who continued to descend regularly from the heavens to intervene in human affairs. Thus, it is not surprising that the early Hebrew tradition also contained many of the same elements and many of the same stories. Even though they acknowledged the ancient gods, calling them variously Watchers, Nephilim or fallen angels, what set the Hebrews apart was their special relationship with one particular entity they were told, and believed, was God—the Creator of heaven and Earth. But unlike the neutral God of quantum physics and of Eastern philosophy, the Hebrew God behaved much in the same way as the

Sumerian gods, with little regard for human life—often resorting to violence and massacres to get his way. It was this being who led them from Ur to the city of Haran in northern Mesopotamia and then towards Egypt on a long and arduous journey. Forced by starvation to enter Egyptian territory, they lived there in peace until the coming of a new king to the throne. The new pharaoh enslaved the Hebrews, and there they remained for 400 years of misery and hardship. It seems almost as if the Hebrews were chosen to survive the great flood only so they could suffer endless cruelties at the hands of almost everyone else.

Moses and the Pillar of Cloud

Most casual readers of the Old Testament, particularly those instructed by religious institutions, come away with the belief that the early Hebrews were in contact with only one God—the Prime Creator of the Universe, whom they variously called Yahweh, Jehovah or El. But a careful reading of the Bible and other ancient Hebrew texts, as we have already seen, reveals a far less consistent story—one in which a singular God is often confused with plural gods. This is often reconciled by the explanation that God has an army of angels who are often sent to do his bidding. However, the early Jews were often themselves confused about just who it was they were dealing with, at times referring to the same object in both the singular and the plural. One thing that is consistent, however, is that both angels and God were believed to travel the skies in cloud-borne chariots that glowed like fire and that these chariots regularly landed, disembarked passengers and took away into the heavens certain chosen humans. This common theme is carried through into the New Testament and is of crucial importance in the life of Jesus and in his ascension into heaven, also in a cloud.

As we have already seen, Amram, the father of Moses, reported in his testament a frightening experience he had with the Watchers, one of whom was reptilian, who claimed to have dominion over humankind. And since we today are aware that contact of this type occurs within families, over many generations (probably for reasons having to do with genetics), it is logical that at some point in their lives, Amram's children, Moses, Miriam and Aaron, would also become aware of similar experiences. For Moses, it seemed to come, as it does with so many abductees today, in middle age. As the Book of Exodus

239

explains, one day as Moses was tending the flock of his father-in-law, Jethro, on the edge of the desert near a mountain known as "the mountain of God," he encountered a strange scene:

> Suddenly, the angel of Jehovah appeared to him as a flame of fire in a bush. When Moses saw the bush was on fire and that it didn't burn up, he went over to investigate. Then God called out to him, "Moses, Moses!" "Who is it?" Moses asked. "Don't come any closer," God told him. "Take off your shoes for you are standing on holy ground. I am the God of your fathers—the God of Abraham, Isaac and Jacob."[1]

(Note: Unless otherwise specified, Biblical quotes in the remaining chapters are taken from Tyndale House Publisher's modern translation, *The Book*.[2])

It is interesting to note that the writer first says that the "angel of Jehovah appeared to him" but then goes on to describe a conversation between Moses and God, rather than an angel. Later, in the New Testament, Stephen, who is about to be stoned to death by Jews because of his Christian beliefs, says:

> Now when forty years had passed, an angel appeared to him [Moses] in the wilderness of Mount Sinai, in a flame of fire in a bush. This Moses whom they refused, saying, "Who made you a ruler and a judge?" God sent as both ruler and deliverer by the hand of the angel that appeared to him in the bush.[3]

So early in the descriptions of the Jehovah tradition, there is confusion as to whether Moses had been contacted by an angel or by God himself. Needless to say, making such a distinction, even for modern humans, would not be an easy task. Any one of us confronted by such a powerful entity would be likely to believe he was being addressed by God himself, especially if the being identified himself as God! Such a conclusion would probably have been more likely, however, in ancient times when little was known about the size of the universe, when it was believed that we were God's special creation and when people were not so skeptical.

Another aspect of this event that should be mentioned is that according to Dr. Barry Downing in his book, *The Bible and Flying Sau-*

---

1. Exodus 3:1-6
2. *The Book*, 1986.
3. Acts 7:30-35.

cers, the Hebrew word "bush" actually means a thicket. He suggests that what Moses saw was a glowing UFO that had landed in the midst of a clump of bushes, making it seem as if the thicket were on fire.[4]

It was during this experience that Moses was commissioned to serve as Jehovah's emissary to the Pharaoh and to ultimately lead his people out of slavery in a long journey known today as the Exodus. And throughout their journey, the Bible reports:

> ...the Lord traveled before them by day in a pillar of cloud, to lead them along the way and by night in a pillar of fire, to give them light; that they might travel by day and by night. He took not away the pillar of cloud by day, or the pillar of fire by night, from in front of the people.[5]

It is clear that the Jews believed that God was *inside* the pillar of cloud and fire, not that the cloud *was* God. (It should also be noted here that modern day reports of UFOs that appear cigar-shaped or cylindrical and that are covered by a thin layer of cloud are not uncommon.) There was no confusion in their minds that the oblong, glowing object was a vehicle which carried an entity they believed to be God. Later, in the book of Psalms, the pillar of cloud described as a vehicle that carries God: "...lift up a song to him who rides upon the clouds."[6] And again in Psalms 104:3 it is God who "makest the clouds thy chariot."

But since they were never allowed to see the entity on penalty of instant death, they could never be absolutely certain who or what exactly was inside. Even Moses was not permitted to gaze upon the face of Jehovah as illustrated by an event that took place on Mt. Sinai after he had walked into the cloud of the Lord:

> Then Moses asked to see God's glory. The Lord replied, "I will make my goodness pass before you, and I will announce to you the meaning of my name Jehovah, the Lord.... But you may not see the glory of my face, for man may not see me and live. However, stand here on this rock beside me. And when my glory goes by, I will put you in the cleft of the rock and cover you with my hand until I have passed. Then I will remove my hand and you shall see my back, but not my face." [7]

---

4. Downing, 1968, p. 113.
5. Exodus 13:21-22.
6. Psalms 68:4.
7. Exodus 33:18-23.

Is it possible that the real reason Jehovah would not allow the Israelites to see his face is that its countenance would have frightened them—perhaps horrified them? Lest the reader be too shocked at such a conclusion, it should be pointed out that this is not in the least an original idea. In fact, many of the ancient Hebrews themselves believed that this was the case. An early Jewish sect which held that Jehovah was not God, but rather a lesser deity, were the Mandaeans. They believed in a dualistic universe, divided equally into the worlds of light and darkness. To them, the physical world, including the Earth, was created and ruled over by the Lord of Darkness, a reptilian being born of a terrifying female deity known as Hewat/Ruha (hewat meaning beast or reptile.) This ruler, variously called Snake, Dragon, Monster and Giant, was thought to be the true creator of humanity.[8] At the same time they believed in the realm of light and life, populated by spiritual beings (elementals) who sought to help liberate souls from the world of darkness. Such a paradigm, similar to that found in quantum physics, pits the forces of light (the positive) against the forces of darkness (the negative) in an eternal struggle designed for a higher purpose by a neutral intelligence called God. Being beyond good and evil, God may in fact be responsible for occurrences that our limited understanding interprets as painful and nonsensical, such as suffering and death.

Was Jehovah perhaps a reptilian or even a praying mantis being? There is, of course, no way to be certain about his appearance, but given the facts we now have regarding the guardian beings, we must harbor some suspicions about the hidden identity of the Hebrew God. However, one thing was certain—this particular being (if indeed it was only one being) considered the Hebrews his special people and he was determined to mold their beliefs and their behavior in such a way that they would be forever separated from the rest of humanity. Much like a shepherd or rancher who keeps track of his herds by fencing them in, branding them and monitoring their breeding to ensure that the best genetic traits are passed on to future generations, the angels, Watchers or Jehovah, as the case may be, made sure that their flock did not go astray.

---

8. Couliano, 1990, p. 38.

Creating a Religion

From the beginning of his relationship with the Hebrew people, Jehovah used every means at his command to exert authority and control over his flock. In the book of Genesis, God made Abram an offer he couldn't refuse:

> I will prepare a contract between us, guaranteeing to make you into a mighty nation. In fact you shall be the father of not only one nation, but a multitude of nations! ...And I will continue this agreement between us generation after generation, forever, for it shall be between me and your children as well. It is a contract that I shall be your God and the God of your posterity. And I will give all this land of Canaan to you and them, forever.... Your part of the contract is to obey its terms. You personally and all your posterity have this continual responsibility: that every male among you shall be circumcised.... This shall be proof that you and they accept this covenant.... Your bodies will thus be marked as participants in my everlasting covenant. Anyone who refuses these terms shall be cut off from his people; for he has violated my contract.[9]

The offer seemed simple enough at first. Multiple kingdoms, vast lands and great riches were offered to Abram and his heirs if only he agreed to obey the terms of the contract and have all the male children circumcised. "What's a little piece of skin?" Abram must have thought to himself. But, in fact, the symbolic act of circumcision was a form of branding that would set Jewish men apart from all others for thousands of years. From that point on, it would be impossible for any Jewish man to hide his identity, for it was not likely that non-Jews would consider such an operation.

Another way in which Jehovah exerted control was through demonstrations of awesome powers that drove fear into the hearts of all who witnessed the events. In the book of Exodus, God prepares a demonstration of his powers by telling Moses:

> Give these instructions to the people of Israel. Tell them you have seen what I did to the Egyptians, and how I brought you to myself [to Mt. Sinai] as though on eagle's wings. Now if you will obey me and keep your part of my contract with you, you

---

9. Genesis 17:2-14.

shall be my own little flock from among the nations of the earth.... I am going to come to you in the form of a dark cloud so that the people themselves can hear me when I talk with you and then they will always believe you.... So Moses went down to the people.... He told them, "Get ready for God's appearance two days from now...." On the morning of the third day there was a terrific thunder and lightning storm, and a huge cloud came down upon the mountain, and there was a long, loud blast as from a ram's horn; and all the people trembled.... All Mt. Sinai was covered with smoke because Jehovah descended upon it in the form of fire; the smoke billowed into the sky as from a furnace, and the whole mountain shook with a violent earthquake.... The Lord told Moses, "...warn the people not to cross the boundaries. They must not come up here to try to see God, for if they do, many of them will die. Even the priests on duty must sanctify themselves or else I will destroy them."[10]

This passage illustrates several important elements regarding the nature of Jehovah and his relationship with Moses and the people of Israel. First, it indicates that Moses was lifted physically to the top of the mountain by God. Whether this was through levitation or aboard the "cloud" is not clear, but it specifically states that he was taken "as if on eagle's wings." This is only one of many examples in the ancient texts in which humans are taken bodily into the heavens by the gods, the angels or God. In the book of Kings, for example, Elijah was taken up to heaven in physical form while he was walking with his successor, Elisha: "And as they went on and talked, behold, a chariot of fire and horses of fire separated the two of them. And Elijah went up by a whirlwind into heaven."[11]

Secondly, Jehovah emphasizes to Moses that he considers the Israelites his own, special "little flock," separate from other humans. Thirdly, a dramatic display of power in the form of the dark cloud, thunder, lightning and earthquake was clearly meant to scare and intimidate the people into submission. And finally, the threat of death to anyone who should disobey, particularly those who attempted to get a close look at the being within the cloud, served to inspire loyalty.

10. Exodus 19:3-22.
11. II Kings 2:1.

244

Clearly, the people did not believe the cloud itself was God, for they were tempted to climb the mountain to see what was inside.

Rules to Live By

Other ways in which Jehovah sought to isolate and differentiate the Jewish people was by instituting traditions, rigid rules of behavior and religious practices that would bind them together as a social group and make them stand apart from all others.

Aside from the commonly known Ten Commandments, the Old Testament contains long lists of rules and laws laid down by Jehovah to govern Hebrew society in its everyday activities. Some of these, as found in chapter 21 of the book of Exodus, tell a great deal about the Jewish God and how he viewed human civilization:

> If you buy a Hebrew slave, he shall serve only six years and be freed in the seventh year, and need pay nothing to regain his freedom....
>
> If a man sells his daughter as a slave, she shall not be free at the end of six years as the men are. If she does not please the man who bought her, then he shall let her be bought back again; but he has no power to sell her to foreigners....
>
> Anyone who hits a man so hard that he dies shall surely be put to death. But if it was accidental...then I will appoint a place where he can run and get protection....
>
> If a man beats his slave to death...that man shall surely be punished. However, if the slave does not die for a couple of days, then the man shall not be punished—for the slave is his property....
>
> If a thief is captured, he must make full restitution; if he can't, then he must be sold as a slave for his debt....
>
> A sorceress must be put to death....
>
> If you lend money to a needy fellow-Hebrew, you are not to handle the transaction in an ordinary way, with interest....
>
> You must be prompt in giving me the tithe of your crops and your wine and the redemption payment for your oldest son....
>
> Be sure to obey all these instructions; and remember— never mention the name of any other god.[12]

This sampling of Jehovah's laws gives us an idea of the detail to which he was involved in dictating the daily behavior and beliefs of the Hebrews and, to some extent, the agenda he followed. To be sure, many of the rules of behavior were humanitarian and instructed the Jews against injustice, against taking bribes, against making false charges and against oppressing foreigners, yet Jehovah's laws clearly prescribe a standard of behavior that would be difficult today to attribute to God. Slavery and sexism were accepted and condoned, the death penalty was meted out casually to include a wide variety of crimes, including the crime of being a "sorceress," although the term was not defined, and Jews were taught to treat their slaves and non-Hebrews in an inferior manner.

One can argue that times were different in those days and different rules applied, but is that really a valid argument? True universal and spiritual laws, as we have seen, apply to all species and all peoples at all times and cannot be bent or adjusted to fit a particular situation or culture. Were these the laws of God—the Prime Creator of the Universe, or were they the rules of subordinate gods—the Watchers—carrying out their duties according to some cosmically-divined master plan that is still unfolding today? Obviously, this is a difficult question to answer, particularly for Jews and Christians whose religions are both based on a belief that the God of the Old Testament was indeed the one true God. Yet, perhaps the time has come to review the ancient interpretations of these events with modern eyes and to ask once again the fundamental questions that have guided much of the behavior of the human race for thousands of years and which continue to impact social and political decisions today. In order to do this we must cast aside our emotional responses to religious issues and see clearly and objectively. If we are sincere in our desire to do so, then we must admit that there is no better way to judge a person, extraterrestrial or otherwise, than by his actions—and the actions of the God of the Old Testament were quite peculiar and highly suspect for one presumed to be the Prime Creator.

---

12. Exodus 21 and 22.

Parting the Red Sea

After accepting his mission to lead his people out of slavery, Moses went back to Egypt to meet with the Pharaoh and to demand the release of the Jews, but, of course, the Pharaoh would not relent in spite of several demonstrations of Jehovah's power. So the God of the Hebrews prepared more powerful demonstrations to convince the Egyptians once and for all that Jehovah's powers were far greater than those of the gods they worshipped. One after another, plagues and disasters were rained down on Egypt in the form of hailstorms, hordes of frogs, lice, locusts and flies, but still the Pharaoh would not relent. So Jehovah sent a plague upon the animals and caused boils to appear on the Egyptians, but none of the animals belonging to the Israelites were affected. In each case, however, "Jehovah hardened Pharaoh in his stubbornness, so that he refused to listen...."[13]:

> Then the Lord said to Moses, "Go back again and make your demand upon Pharaoh; but I have hardened him and his officials, so I can do more miracles demonstrating my power. What stories you can tell your children and grandchildren about the incredible things I am doing in Egypt! Tell them what fools I made out of the Egyptians, and how I proved to you that I am Jehovah."[14]

In other words, the entire story of the departure of the Jews from Egypt and their journey to the promised land was much like a play with a detailed script, plotted out by God and his angels. Because Jehovah could control the Pharaoh's reactions, he knew exactly how the story would unfold, long before the events took place. After hardening the Pharaoh's heart, Jehovah then planned his final, deadly demonstration of power—the killing of Egypt's first born males:

> About midnight I will pass through Egypt. And all the oldest sons shall die in every family in Egypt, from the oldest child of Pharaoh, heir to his throne, to the oldest child of his lowliest slave; and even the firstborn of the animals. The wail of death will resound throughout the entire land of Egypt; never before has there been such anguish, and it will never be again.[15]

---

13. Exodus 9:12.
14. Exodus 9:12. (Check)
15. Exodus 11:4-6.

This event so crushed the will of the Pharaoh that he finally relented and allowed the Israelites to leave Egypt, following their God, who led them from within his cloud. But where did he lead them? He led them directly to the shores of the Red Sea—which he certainly must have known was a dead end. But, of course, he had a plan—a plan that would free his chosen people and punish the Egyptians even further.

> Tell the people to turn toward Pihahiroth between Migdol and the sea, opposite Baal-Zephon, and to camp there along the shore. For Pharaoh will think, "Those Israelites are trapped now, between the desert and the sea!" And once again I will harden Pharaoh's heart and he will chase after you. I have planned this to gain great honor and glory over Pharaoh and all his armies, and the Egyptians shall know that I am the Lord.[16]

Jehovah then instructed Moses on the next part of the plan, which included making it appear that Moses was participating in the miracle about to occur, when in fact it was Jehovah in his cloud that was responsible.

> The Lord will fight for you, and you won't need to lift a finger! Use your rod...hold it over the water, and the sea will open up a path before you, and all the people of Israel shall walk through on dry ground! I will harden the hearts of the Egyptians and they will go in after you and you will see the honor I will get in defeating Pharaoh and all his armies....
> Then, the Angel of God, who was leading the people of Israel, moved the cloud around behind them, and it stood between the people of Israel and the Egyptians. And that night, as it changed to a pillar of fire, it gave darkness to the Egyptians but light to the people of Israel! So the Egyptians couldn't find the Israelis![17]

After the sea had been parted for them, the Hebrews proceeded through the opening, followed by the Pharaoh's armies, so that the final blow could be struck to the Egyptians:

> But in the early morning, Jehovah looked down from the cloud of fire upon the array of Egyptians, and began to harass

---

16. Exodus 14:1-4.
17. Exodus 14:14-20.

them. Their chariot wheels began coming off, so that their chariots scraped along the dry ground. "Let's get out of here," the Egyptians yelled. "Jehovah is fighting for them and against us." [18]

But it was too late. Jehovah had sprung his trap:

When the Israelites were on the other side, the Lord said to Moses, "Stretch out your hand again over the sea, so that the waters will come back over the Egyptians and their chariots and horsemen." Moses did, and the sea returned to normal beneath the morning light. The Egyptians tried to flee but the Lord drowned them in the sea. The water covered the path and the chariots and horsemen. And all of the army of Pharaoh that chased after Israel through the sea, not one remained alive. [19]

Dr. Downing's analysis of the above passages is one of an open-minded cleric with a strong scientific education:

The text suggests that some sort of UFO, totally under its own control, led the Israelites out of Egypt to the Red Sea, and then as Pharaoh's army closed in, the UFO moved from the front to the rear of the army of Israel and kept the two camps separated during the night. [20]

Thus, on the basis of the Biblical text it is quite permissible to argue that the UFO hovered over the sea in order to cause it to part.... [21]

A Substitute God

Once free from Egyptian bondage on the other side of the Red Sea, the Israelites found themselves in an arid wilderness with no means of support. There, led by the cloud, they journeyed for forty years, always with the promise that a land of milk and honey awaited those who obeyed and worshipped their God. At this point, something strange seems to have occurred. Jehovah passes on responsibility for leading the Jews out of the wilderness to a subordinate:

See, I am sending you an Angel before you to lead you safely to the land I have prepared for you. Reverence him and

---

18. Exodus 14:24-25.
19. Exodus 14:26-28.
20. Downing, 1968, p. 82.
21. Downing, 1968, p. 90.

obey all of his instructions; do not rebel against him, for he will not pardon your transgressions; he is my representative—he bears my name. But if you are careful to obey him, following all my instructions, then I will be an enemy to your enemies. For my Angel shall go before you and bring you into the land of the Amorites, Hittites, Perizzites, Canaanites, Vivites, and Jebusites, to live there. And I will destroy those people before you. You must not worship the gods of these other nations, nor sacrifice to them in any way, and you must not follow the evil example of these heathen people; you must utterly conquer them and break down their shameful idols.[22]

So, from here on, it is clear that it is not Jehovah, but his representative, who is leading the Hebrews. Yet, there is no explanation for why this substitution occurred, and there is no discernible difference between the physical appearance and mannerisms of the new leader to that of Jehovah. Again we see how easy it is to mistake an "angel" for "God." According to the Old Testament, both traveled inside of "clouds" or "chariots of fire," and an "angel" could speak for God and, in fact, act like God, carrying out his instructions. The ancients seem all too willing to accept any being who rode in a "cloud" as God, thus the concern by Jehovah that the Hebrews worship no *other* god.

You must make no covenant with them, nor have anything to do with their gods. Don't let them live among you! For I know that they will infect you with their sin of worshipping false gods, and that would be an utter disaster for you.[23]

After being told this, Moses was instructed to ascend the mountain together with some of the elders:

Moses alone shall come near to the Lord; and remember, none of the ordinary people are permitted to come up into the mountain at all.[24]

Then Moses went up the mountain and disappeared into the cloud at the top. And the glory of the Lord rested upon Mt. Sinai and the cloud covered it six days; the seventh day he called to Moses from the cloud. Those at the bottom of the mountain saw the awesome sight: the glory of the Lord on the mountain top looked like a raging fire. And Moses disappeared

---

22. Exodus 23:20-24.
23. Exodus 23:32, 33.
24. Exodus 24:2.

into the cloud-covered top, and was there for forty days and forty nights.[25]

As one can see, the new, substitute god, the Angel of the Lord whom Jehovah appointed to take his place, seems to have been quickly accepted by Moses and the Israelites. While Moses was with him in his cloud on top of the mountain, he gave Moses complex instructions on how to build a strange structure, a tent-like pavilion meant to serve as a home for the new substitute God who was quickly settling in as leader of the Hebrew nation. The first order of business was to be the gathering of a special offering from the people—an offering of gold, silver, precious stones, fine cloths, spices, oils and fragrances for the purpose of building "me a sacred Temple where I can live among them."[26] In addition to the pavilion, or Tabernacle, as it was called, the Angel instructed Moses to build a golden box, called the Ark of the Covenant, in which to store the stone tablets he would be given upon which were written the Ten Commandments. The instructions for building these structures and the ceremonies attached to each were so detailed and lengthy that they occupy all the rest of the book of Exodus, chapters 25-40, and cannot be dwelt upon here in any length. However, it is worth the reader's time to review these chapters in his own Bible, for their detail argues convincingly that such structures were actually built at some time in the distant past.

Burnt Offerings

An amazing thing happened when the Tabernacle was completed:

> Then the cloud covered the Tabernacle and the glory of the Lord filled it. Moses was not able to enter because the cloud was standing there, and the glory of the Lord filled the Tabernacle. Whenever the cloud lifted and moved, the people of Israel journeyed onward, following it. But if the cloud stayed, they stayed until it moved. The cloud rested upon the Tabernacle during the daytime, and at night there was fire in the cloud so that all the people of Israel could see it. This continued throughout all their journeys.[27]

---

25. Exodus 24:15-18.
26. Exodus 25:9.
27. Exodus 40:34-38.

JEHOVAH—A POWERFUL ENTITY

Clearly, the ancient Hebrews were not saying that a regular, cumulus cloud, like the ones we see in the sky every day, was what they were seeing. They knew full well even then that clouds are insubstantial and are incapable of the behavior attributed to this object they believed housed their God. If the above passage leaves no doubt that the "glory and cloud" of the Lord was a real, physical object, then the next book, Leviticus, leaves little doubt that there was a real, physical being inside of the "cloud."

This book was meant to be a handbook for the Hebrew priests known as "Levites" (thus the name Leviticus). It sets down the regulations needed to guide the life of the Israelites on a daily basis and specifically, the rules governing sacrifice and worship:

> The Lord now spoke to Moses from the Tabernacle, and commanded him to give the following instructions to the people of Israel: When you sacrifice to the Lord, use animals from your herds and flocks. If your sacrifice is to be an ox given as a burnt offering, use only a bull with no physical defects. Bring the animal to the entrance of the Tabernacle where the priests will accept your gift for the Lord. The person bringing it is to lay his hand upon its head, and it then becomes his substitute: the death of the animal will be accepted by God instead of the death of the person who brings it, as the penalty for his sins. The person shall then kill the animal there before the Lord, and [the priests] will present the blood before the Lord, sprinkling it upon all sides of the altar at the entrance of the Tabernacle. Then the priests will skin the animal and quarter it, and build a wood fire upon the altar, and put the sections of the animal and its head and fat upon the wood. The internal organs and the legs are to be washed, then the priests will burn them upon the altar, and they will be an acceptable burnt offering with which the Lord is pleased.[28]

At the risk of offending Christian and Jew alike, the author feels compelled to make the observation that the process of bringing burnt offerings to the being inside the craft, as described in the above passage, could easily be interpreted to mean that they were bringing food to their deity. The list of offerings acceptable to the Lord reads much like a cookbook of his favorite recipes:

---

28. Leviticus 1:1-9.

If anyone wishes to use a bird as his burnt offering, he may choose either turtledoves or young pigeons. A priest will take the bird to the altar and wring off its head and the blood shall be drained out at the side of the altar. Then the priest will remove the crop and the feathers and throw them on the east side of the altar with the ashes. Then grasping it by the wings, he shall tear it apart, but not completely. And the priest shall burn it upon the altar, and the Lord will have pleasure in this sacrifice.[29]

Anyone who wishes to sacrifice a grain offering to the Lord is to bring fine flour and is to pour olive oil and incense upon it. Then he is to take a handful, representing the entire amount, to one of the priests to burn, and the Lord will be fully pleased.... If bread baked in the oven is brought as an offering to the Lord, it must be made from finely ground flour, baked with olive oil but without yeast.... If the offering is something from the griddle, it shall be made of finely ground flour without yeast, and mingled with olive oil. However it is prepared—whether baked, fried or grilled—you are to bring this grain offering to the priest and he shall take it to the altar to present it to the Lord.... Every offering must be seasoned with salt, because the salt is a reminder of God's covenant.[30]

Offerings were required constantly for all types of reasons. There were offerings of thanksgiving, offerings for unintentional sins, offerings of guilt and special peace offerings. All of this ensured that a constant stream of foodstuffs were constantly making their way into the Tabernacle for the pleasure of the Lord.

Claiming the Promised Land

The road to the Promised Land was nothing short of one bloody massacre after another, if the Old Testament is to be believed. Time and time again, at the urging of the being in the cloud, the Israelite army was dispatched to vanquish and, in some cases, to annihilate those who occupied the lands granted to the Jews by Jehovah or who violated his strict codes. One of these unfortunate peoples were the Midianites whom Jehovah accused of leading the Hebrews into idolatry. To exact vengeance, Moses assembled an army of 12,000 men and, led by

29. Leviticus 1:14-17.
30. Leviticus 2:1-13.

253

priests carrying the Ark, they proceeded not only to win the battle, but to wipe out the men of Midian:

> And every man of Midian was killed.... Then the Israeli army took as captives all the women and children, and seized the cattle and flocks and a lot of miscellaneous booty. All of the cities, towns and villages of Midian were then burned.... But Moses was very angry with the army officers and battalion leaders. "Why have you let all the women live?" he demanded.... "Now kill all the boys and all the women who have had sexual intercourse. Only the little girls may live; you may keep them for yourselves."[31]

Similar consequences lay in store for the other cities lying in the wake of the Israelite army which was urged by Jehovah's spokesman (the substitute God) to be ruthless:

> When the Lord your God delivers them over to you to be destroyed, do a complete job of it—don't make any treaties or show them mercy; utterly wipe them out. Do not intermarry with them, nor let your sons and daughters marry their sons and daughters.[32]

> You must destroy all the nations which the Lord your God delivers into your hands. Have no pity, and do not worship their gods....[33]

> The Lord your God will go before you as a devouring fire to destroy them so that you will quickly conquer them and drive them out.[34]

The Lord even prescribed the specific strategy that the invading army was to use as it approached a new target:

> As you approach a city to fight against it, first offer it a truce. If it accepts the truce and opens its gates to you, then all its people shall become your servants. But if it refuses and won't make peace with you, you must besiege it. When the Lord your God has given it to you, kill every male in the city; but you may keep for yourselves all the women, children, cattle and booty. These instructions apply only to the distant cities, not to those in the Promised Land itself. For in the cities

---

31. Numbers 31:7-18.
32. Deuteronomy 7:2-4.
33. Deuteronomy 7:16.
34. Deuteronomy 9:3.

within the boundaries of the Promised Land you are to save no one; destroy every living thing. Utterly destroy the Hittites, the Amorites, the Canaanites, the Perizzites, the Hivites and the Jebusites.[35]

With such instructions, the Hebrew army set forth into the Promised Land and one after another, destroyed the cities and the populations that stood in their way, including, as in the case of Jericho, the animals as well:

So when the people heard the trumpet blast, they shouted as loud as they could. And suddenly the walls of Jericho crumbled and fell before them, and the people of Israel poured into the city from every side and captured it! They destroyed everything in it—men and women, young and old; oxen; sheep; donkeys—everything.[36]

So Joshua and his army conquered the whole country—the nations and kings of the hill country, the Negeb, the lowlands, and the mountain slopes. They destroyed everyone in the land, just as the Lord God of Israel had commanded....[37]

A Master Plan

Certainly, to the people who occupied the Promised Land, the God of Israel appeared more like a demon than a god. The Bible tells us that these people were being punished for their disobedience to the Lord, but if this is so, then what of the children and the animals? Had they also been disobedient? Had they also earned their punishment? Looking at the events of the Old Testament with the perspective of several thousand years and with the knowledge we now have regarding the custodian beings known as the Watchers, we might surmise a different purpose behind the actions of the Hebrew God. It seems more likely that the custodian gods were carefully implementing a systematic plan that was meant to have far-reaching implications for all of mankind and which continues to be implemented to this very day. First, he and the other guardian beings were devoted to creating differences among the human races by confusing their languages, creating different religions, races, nationalities, customs and traditions. This would ensure

35. Deuteronomy 20:16, 17.
36. Joshua 6:20, 21.
37. Joshua 10:40.

that the human species was forever pitted against one another in an endless series of wars. Perhaps the reason for this was to attempt to control the human population, or perhaps it was to create an environment rich in opportunity for human souls to learn to choose between good and evil.

To this end, the God of the Hebrews, by instilling in the Jews the idea that they were special and that they were different from all others and by causing them to ruthlessly conquer so many peoples, ensured that the Jewish religion would persist and that the Hebrew people would remain in a state of permanent isolation from the rest of humanity. One can easily see from a careful reading of the first five books of the Bible that Jehovah and his angels had a master plan—one in which the outcome of events was already predetermined. Time and again, Jehovah manipulated the minds of humans to achieve his desired results. In the case of the Pharaoh, Jehovah ensured his defeat by hardening his heart against the terms of Moses. In the case of the Canaanites, they were slaughtered for the same reason:

> ...it was the Lord God who hardened their hearts that they would go against Israel in battle, that he might destroy them utterly, and that they might find no favor, but that he might destroy them....[38]

If Jehovah knew in advance the outcome of the events he masterminded and if he was a being who had access to a master plan for the entire human race, then is it not possible that his plan extended even into the present time? Perhaps the events of the Old Testament were designed for the specific purpose of creating a nation of Israel that would be pitted against its Islamic neighbors in a final cataclysmic war that would signal the end of one phase of human existence and usher in a new one. This, of course, is precisely the point of the New Testament and it seems to be the direction in which UFO researchers are being led—one hesitant step at a time. If so, then the lesson of the UFO might be that we who are alive at this particular time may bear witness to the final chapter in a master plan designed by the highest authority and carried out by the guardians of the Earth—those godlike beings known in days of old as the Watchers.

---

38. Joshua 11:19, 20.

256

CHAPTER 13　　　　THE STORY OF JESUS

After Jesus' birth in Bethlehem...astrologers from the east arrived one day in Jerusalem inquiring, "Where is the newborn King of the Jews? We observed his star at its rising and have come to pay him homage." ...Herod called the astrologers aside and found out from them the exact time of the star's appearance.... After their audience with the King, they set out. The star which they had observed at its rising went ahead of them until it came to a standstill over the place where the child was.

—(Matthew 2:1-9) The New American Bible

Healed By Jesus

Shortly after the death of my father, I had the opportunity to sit at leisure with my aging mother, reminiscing about old times when I was little and living on the third floor of an old, decrepit apartment building along the Rio Grande, just a stone's throw from old Mexico. And as it has on many past occasions, the conversation turned to the secret we have shared for so many years—the time Jesus came to heal me.

"Tell me the story again," I urged, "about the time I was healed."

A pensive expression flashed across her face and then she took a deep breath.

"What do you want to know?" she asked.

"Start from the beginning. Tell me the whole thing."

"Well," she began, "you were only three years old when I began to notice that something was wrong with you. Your ankles would turn under you when you walked and your knees would knock when you were walking or running. I took you to Dr. Bennett, our pediatrician, and he felt how soft the bones in your head had become. He said you had rickets—a vitamin D deficiency—that was the result of not getting enough sunlight. I felt so bad because we were afraid to let you go out to play because of the railroad tracks across the street."

257

"Yeah," I said, "I remember that my ankles would do that, and I remember playing on those tracks, too."

"I was scared because he said it was serious and that you would never walk normally again. He told me the damage had been done, but that I should take you out every day and give you cod-liver oil."

"I remember that, too."

"Later your uncle, who was a heart surgeon in Mexico, also examined you and confirmed what the doctor had told me. I was so scared that I prayed day and night for you. I begged God for a miracle. Then one night while your father was traveling, it happened. It was like a dream or a vision—it was more than a dream. Jesus was standing by the bed. He was wearing a red robe and he had light brown wavy hair down to his shoulders. He sat down on the bed and called to you with his hand to come to him. Your sister and I were over to one side, watching. Then I told him about your condition. He listened to every word, then, without saying a word, he put his hand on your head. That's all I remember."

"What happened then?"

"When I woke up in the morning, I knew that you had been healed. As soon as the doctor's office opened, I rushed you down there and we waited until he could see you. I asked him to examine you, and he said you looked fine to him. It had been several months since he had seen you and he had forgotten what he had told me. I asked him about the rickets and he acted like he didn't know what I was talking about. But I made him check his records and, sure enough, he found it. He just shook his head like he didn't know what was going on. Later, your uncle examined you again and said it was a miracle. You never had any trouble after that."

Although I have no memory of that event, the certitude and the emotion with which my mother told me the story when I was young and the knowledge that I had indeed recovered from the condition from which I had suffered, made a deep impression on me very early on. For me, Jesus was always very real and my relationship to him very special. (Only in recent years did I discover that stories of Jesus-like figures who heal people are a fairly common ingredient in UFO investigations.) In any case, because of this, the story of Jesus and the mystery of who he was, how he arrived on Earth and how he ascended into heaven was more than just a passing interest for me.

Unlike many who are able to consign these matters to faith, or those who have let them rest as impenetrable mysteries, I, on the other hand, have never stopped searching for answers—first in the New Testament, then in the Old and eventually in other ancient texts. Throughout this search, Jesus has remained an elusive enigma. Efforts by archeologists to uncover the true Jesus have been fruitless. Excavations of those sites mentioned in the Scriptures have produced nothing that proves that Jesus ever lived at all. Although there were excellent historians who published voluminous accounts of the period in which he lived, none of them even mention Jesus or anyone who fit his description, even though other familiar names such as Pontius Pilate, Herod and Caiaphas (the Jewish priest who condemned Jesus) are mentioned.

Shortly after Jesus' time, much of the evidence of that period was eradicated as the Roman army destroyed the Jewish Temple, wiped out revolutionary groups such as the Essenes, and caused the Jews and early Christians to flee and disperse throughout the Middle East and Europe. During this time of turmoil, important documents inevitably were destroyed and valuable witnesses were put to death. It is highly likely that both Roman and Jewish leaders attempted to systematically erase all evidence of the life of Jesus for their own political gain.

Today, as tourists walk the streets of Jerusalem to see the famous sites—the sacred tomb, the Mosque of the Ascension, the Garden of Gethsemane and the streets on which Jesus carried his cross, they are in fact seeing only monuments commemorating those events. The real sites have been lost to antiquity and lie under 10 to 15 feet of soil and rubble. Yet, in spite of this, what I have found is convincing evidence that Jesus did exist. For just as the Jewish people and the state of Israel stand today as evidence of the existence of a real being named Jehovah, the many millions of Christians today and the vivid legacy of his teachings bear witness to the very real events that occurred two millennia ago. And, when one learns to look at the evidence in light of what is now known about the UFO phenomenon, one begins to see that there is a different way of thinking about and seeing the New Testament. And just as with the previous discussions of Jehovah and human origins, this interpretation is not likely to entirely satisfy either the materialists, the theologians or the fanatical true believers.

This view, as you might have guessed, revolves around an age-old debate about the role of the Watchers—the angels if you will—in the birth, life, death, resurrection and ascension into heaven of the man called Jesus. My search for answers led me to the discovery that early Jewish and Christian leaders had grave misgivings about things many take for granted today, such as the "anthropomorphism" of God: some early Jewish sects argued that God, the Creator, should not be endowed by humans to have human or physical form. To them, it was clear that the world and its life forms were created not directly by God, but by an angel of God. They believed in a vastly superior, nonphysical Creator and also in inferior deities who created humans.[1] Thus, they did not believe that the Old Testament God was the Prime Creator. As early as 85 A.D. Christian scholars questioned the connection between Jesus and the Old Testament God. Marcion, a formidable scholar of scripture, believed that the kind and good Jesus couldn't possibly be the son of the wrathful, vengeful and materialistic God of the Hebrews. He believed, as did the Mandaeans and other Gnostic sects, that Jehovah was the creator of the physical world, while Jesus was the Son of the Prime Creator. His denial of Jesus' connection to the God of the Hebrews, of course, outraged the Christians of Rome, whose views ultimately became the consensus Christian doctrine.[2] Marcion and his followers believed that Jehovah was in fact evil incarnate. They reasoned that if Satan tempted Jesus with earthly power and riches, and if the material world is Satan's domain, then the creator of the world, (the Old Testament God) was, in fact, Satan. They noted that Jehovah had tempted Abram, the Hebrew patriarch, with lands and riches and made a pact with him to deliver to him the Jewish people. Such a bargain would only be made by the ruler of the physical world, not the Prime Creator. Marcion's perspective, as unpopular as it may have been in his time and today, is very much in line with today's efforts to reexamine the Bible with modern eyes and with an objectivity tempered by several thousands of years of perspective. Reconsidering this ancient argument may help us achieve a better understanding of the true identity and purpose of the person we know as Jesus.

1. Couliano, 1990, p. 119.
2. Pagels, 1979, pp. 28-29.

The Colossian Heresy

A similar debate revolved around the story of Jesus in the early days of Christianity. This debate has been called by Bible scholars the "Colossian heresy" and is referred to in the New Testament in the letters of Paul to the Colossians. In his epistle, Paul, the fanatical Jewish persecutor of Christians whose miraculous conversion to Christianity caused him to become an equally fanatical Christian, warns early Christians against "false teachers" who are teaching that angels served as agents in the creation of humanity and in the giving of the law.[3] Although Paul does not name these false teachers, it is believed that their views had origins in the writings of an ancient Jewish sect, known as the Gnostics. (The word "gnostic" means "knowledge" and Gnostics were those who held sacred, secret knowledge.) These early Jewish teachers held that Genesis implies that human creation was carried out by angels because of the plural references: "Let us make man as one of *us*..." and "Let us make man in *our* own image."[4] They believed that it was these lesser gods that gave the Judaic law to the Hebrews. The keeping of Judaic law was regarded by these teachers as a tribute of obedience to those angels and breaking their law incurred their displeasure and brought the lawbreaker into their debt and bondage. These angels were believed to be elemental beings ("stoicheia") who were lords of the planetary spheres, sharers of the divine plenitude ("pleroma") and intermediaries between heaven and Earth.[5] Additionally, they believed that these beings controlled the lines of communication between God and humans, that they controlled all revelation from God and that worship of God could only be successful as a result of their mediation.

In this view of reality, Christ himself must have had to submit to their authority on his way from heaven to Earth and presumably at the time of his resurrection and ascension. This early view of Christianity has been traced back to the Essenes, a radical Jewish sect thought to be the authors and caretakers of the Dead Sea Scrolls. And it is this secret knowledge that was taught and believed by many early Christians as a

---

3. Paul's conversion appears to have been a UFO event. While traveling at night on a lonely road, he is suddenly engulfed in a light from above. He interprets this event as a direct contact with Jesus.
4. Genesis 1:26, 3:22.
5. Bruce, 1977, p. 414.

261

form of advanced teachings for the spiritual elite. Teachings about the power of the angels were used as a means of exploring the deeper mysteries through a series of initiations with the goal of obtaining perfection ("teleiosis"). Christian baptism was only the first step. Those who were deemed worthy and who wished to reach the realm of light (the ultimate result of enlightenment) had to pursue an ascetic life by shunning material wealth, until they became citizens of the spiritual world.

To the Gnostics, Jesus came from the realm of light and incarnated, with the help of the good angels, to liberate those who had become imprisoned in material bodies (the lower world of darkness) by imparting to them the knowledge of the truth. This is in contrast to the orthodox belief that Jesus came to save humanity from its sins. The Gnostics believed that those who receive gnosis find God through inner spirituality, thereby making the Church, along with its priests and bishops, irrelevant. But to the apostle Paul and other orthodox Christians, the gnostic teaching was heresy, not only because it would usurp the power of the Church, but also because it implies that Jesus had to relinquish some of his authority to the angels. Obviously, to Paul, since Jesus was God, he wouldn't need the help of the angels at all. To him it seemed that belief in the powers of the angelic realm was dangerous because one might conclude that the elemental beings were as powerful as Jesus and, thus, should be worshipped. In Paul's view, belief in Jesus is all that is necessary to reach the realm of light, and, thus, the sacred knowledge taught to the elite was irrelevant. Paul's belief, in contrast to that of other early Christians, was that Jesus, not the angels, was the sole mediator between God and humans—and that, in a nutshell, is the essence of modern Christianity today. In fact, it has been argued that modern Christianity is, in truth, "Paulism," because of the extent to which Paul's interpretations of doctrine has prevailed. Far from believing in the power of angels, modern Christians have adopted Paul's view that Jesus himself was the one through whom all things were created. His death and resurrection were his proof that he was their conqueror. Thus, the angels, in Christian theology, were reduced to the status of "weak and beggarly elemental spirits."[6]

---

6. Galatians 4:9.

But such a distinction does not explain away the abundance of evidence to the contrary—that angels (godlike beings) have played a powerful role in the history of the Earth and of humankind. Paul's fanaticism, inherited by modern Christianity, seems, in light of the lessons learned thus far, to favor blind faith to intellectual pursuit of knowledge and it is through his influence as the primary architect of the Christian religion that we have been left today ignorant and confused about the true nature of God and of the universe.

Angels and the Life of Christ

Although these "lords of the planetary spheres," as they were called by the Gnostics, were for the most part ignored and forgotten over the last 2000 years, some students of the UFO/abduction phenomenon today, and many of the "experiencers," are convinced that it is time to renew this ancient debate. The increased and more open appearances of the Watchers since the beginning of the atomic age compels us to reopen the case files on the lords and to re-examine the role they played in the life of Jesus as related in the New Testament. This is done with full knowledge that the factual accounts related therein are considered by experts to be unreliable. However, it is this writer's belief that many of the main elements of the life of Jesus described in the Bible bear some element of truth, even if there are embellishments and contradictions. Furthermore, it is my contention that these events can be more easily understood in light of what we know today of the Watchers and UFO phenomena.

The term "angel" in the Bible is said to mean "messenger," a rather benign and neutral term that belies the true importance of these secretive beings. The Old Testament portrays them as supernatural beings, ranking only a little higher than humans. We are told that angels are created beings[7] who are without bodily organism, but who upon occasion reveal themselves in bodily form to humans. Jesus said that they do not marry and do not die.[8] They are described as beings with personalities, not merely abstract personifications of good and evil. Although possessed of superhuman intelligence and more powerful than men, they are not believed to be omniscient or omnipotent.[9] They

---

7. Psalms 148:2-5
8. Luke 20:34-36.
9. Matthew 24:36; I Peter 1:12; Psalms 103:20; II Peter 2:11.

THE STORY OF JESUS

are said to exist in great numbers, both good and evil, be highly organized and of different ranks and endowments.[10] Although they were
created holy,[11] after a period of probation, some fell from their state of
innocence[12] due to a deliberate, self-determined rebellion against God.

With regard to the life of Jesus, angels played critical roles in connection with his birth and their appearances to Mary, Joseph and the
shepherds; in ministering to him after he was tempted in the wilderness; giving him strength in the garden; rolling away the stone from
his tomb; and being with him at the ascension. In addition, appearances of a "bright cloud" at major events in the life of Jesus imply that
angels were present at other times as well. In fact, it is the appearance
of the mysterious "clouds," similar to the one(s) that appeared to the
Jews of the Exodus, that firmly links the story of Jesus to the Jehovah
of the Old Testament. Nowhere is this connection made more explicit
than in the story told in Matthew. Just before Jesus was to be crucified,
he took Peter, James and John to the mountain where a mysterious
event took place, known as the "Transfiguration":

> ...and as they watched, his appearance changed so that his
> face shone like the sun and his clothing became dazzling white.
>
> Suddenly Moses and Elijah appeared and were talking
> with him. Peter blurted out, "Sir, it's wonderful that we can be
> here! If you want me to, I'll make three shelters, one for you
> and one for Moses and one for Elijah."
>
> But even as he said it, a bright cloud came over them, and a
> voice from the cloud said, "This is my beloved Son, and I am
> wonderfully pleased with him. Obey him."
>
> At this the disciples fell face downward to the ground, ter-
> ribly frightened. Jesus came over and touched them. "Get up,"
> he said, "don't be afraid." And when they looked, only Jesus
> was with them.[13]

Although Bible scholars are highly suspicious of this passage, considering it a fabricated event by early Christian zealots who sought to
connect Jesus directly to the God of the Old Testament, it does demon-

---

10. Col. 1:16; Jude 9; Romans 8:38; Eph. 1:21; 3:10; Col. 1:16; 2:15.
11. Genesis 1:31.
12. II Peter 2:4; Jude 6.
13. Matthew 17:1-8.

264

strate the continuing belief by Christians in the cloudlike chariot of the Lord. Barry Downing points out the importance of this connection:

> The fact that Moses and Elijah were supposedly present at the Transfiguration obviously points to the unity between the Old and New Testaments, as does the presence of the UFO. Whether or not Jesus was associated with—indeed sent by— the God of the Old Testament is of course the most important question which could confront any Jew—and the disciples were Jews.[14]

To many, this passage is simply too convenient. Not only does it connect Jesus with the God of the Old Testament through the presence of the cloud and the voice (similar to the voice heard by Moses) which identifies Jesus as his son, but also through the actual appearance of Moses (who had presumably been dead for hundreds of years) and Elijah (who had been taken physically from the Earth in a cloud). Additionally, Jesus is described as having "shone like the sun," in a similar way that Moses' face shone when he came down from Mount Sinai.[15] Casting further doubt on the event is the fact that it was witnessed only by Peter, James and John, but was only described in detail by Matthew, Mark and Luke. In Peter's brief reference to the event he (or those who related the story for him in later years) makes it clear that this was a real event:

> For we did not follow cleverly devised myths when we made known to you the power and coming of our Lord Jesus Christ, but we were eyewitnesses of his majesty. For when he received honor and glory from God the Father and the voice was borne to him by the Majestic Glory, "This is my beloved Son, with whom I am well pleased," we heard this voice borne from heaven, for we were with him on the holy mountain.[16]

Interestingly, the term "Majestic Glory" here is clearly used as a euphemism for the vehicle or "cloud" which God occupied when he communicated his message. So, the vehicles of the angels and of God are variously referred to as "pillars of cloud," "pillars of fire," "clouds", "bright clouds," "chariots of fire," "the majestic glory," "the throne of the Lord," "the spirit of the Lord," or simply "the glory of

---

14. Downing, 1968, p. 128.
15. Exodus 34:29.
16. II Peter 1:16-18.

God," throughout the Bible and other ancient texts. Once the reader becomes accustomed to these terms and understands what they refer to, the true meaning of the ancient religions begins to become clearer, and it allows one to read the Bible with "modern eyes."

The Star of Bethlehem

In approximately 65 A.D., two Gospels credited to Matthew and Luke were written which tell the story of the miraculous birth of Jesus and the role of the angels in this event. Matthew, who was a tax collector called by Jesus to follow him, was obviously not a first-hand witness to the events, but nevertheless would have known the participants and the basic facts.

> These are the facts concerning the birth of Jesus Christ: His mother, Mary, was engaged to be married to Joseph. But while she was still a virgin she became pregnant by the Holy Spirit. Then Joseph, her fiancé, being a man of stern principle, decided to break the engagement but to do it quietly, as he didn't want to publicly disgrace her. As he lay awake considering this, he fell into a dream, and saw an angel standing beside him. "Joseph, son of David," the angel said, "don't hesitate to take Mary as your wife! For the child within her has been conceived by the Holy Spirit. And she will have a Son, and you shall name him Jesus [meaning 'Savior'], for he will save his people from their sins. This will fulfill God's message through his prophets."[17]

Once again, God's message is received through a dream-vision, and, in typical fashion, the appearance of the angel is not provided. The absence of any description leaves us wondering if the angel's appearance merited any special recognition or if, in fact, the angel merely looked like a man, as in other cases described in the Bible. In any case, the angel imparted several important pieces of information: that the Holy Spirit had impregnated Mary, that the child would be a boy, that his name would be Jesus, and that he would be the Savior of prophecy.

17. Matthew 1:18-22.

266

Luke, who was a physician and a traveling companion of the Apostle Paul, relates a different story with regard to the role of the angels:

...God sent the angel Gabriel to Nazareth, a village in Galilee, to a virgin, Mary, engaged to be married to a man named Joseph, a descendant of King David. Gabriel appeared to her and said, "Congratulations, favored lady! The Lord is with you!" Confused and disturbed, Mary tried to think what the angel could mean. "Don't be frightened, Mary," the angel told her, "for God has decided to wonderfully bless you! Very soon now, you will become pregnant and have a baby boy, and you are to name him Jesus. He shall be very great and shall be called the Son of God. And the Lord shall give him the throne of his ancestor David. And he shall reign over Israel forever; his Kingdom shall never end!"[18]

Again, Gabriel's appearance is not described in this scene during which Mary is given the same information received by Joseph at a later date. There is no account in either story regarding the actual moment of impregnation, and we are left to assume that it was a miraculous event. However, understanding the long tradition of the Watchers and their reputation for being superb genetic engineers, we must now consider the possibility that Mary was, in fact, artificially impregnated with a special embryo, as when women abductees today are being made pregnant. This special embryo would have been genetically designed especially to house the soul of a master teacher who would have unusual psychic abilities necessary to carry out a dramatic and important plan—a plan that started with an amazing display of aerial phenomena.

That night some shepherds were in the fields outside the village, guarding their flocks of sheep. Suddenly an angel appeared among them, and the landscape shone bright with the glory of the Lord. They were badly frightened, but the angel reassured them. "Don't be afraid!" he said. "I bring you the most joyful news ever announced, and it is for everyone! The Savior—yes, the Messiah, the Lord—has been born tonight in Bethlehem!..." Suddenly, the angel was joined by a vast host of others—the armies of heaven—praising God: "Glory to God

18. Luke 1:26-33.

in the highest heaven," they sang, "and peace on Earth for all those pleasing him."[19]

The reader by now can see the truth of this event. The angel that appeared to the shepherds is referred to as "the glory of the Lord," which we know to be a term often used to describe a vehicle, rather than a being. In this case, the vehicle cast a bright light upon the landscape, as many UFOs do. The voice seems to have come from the craft, as is often case throughout the Bible. Then, it appears as if the craft is joined by a flotilla of other craft which put on an impressive aerial display. At about the same time, in a distant land, another craft appears:

> At about that time some astrologers from eastern lands arrived in Jerusalem, asking "Where is the newborn King of the Jews? For we have seen his star in far-off eastern lands, and have come to worship him." King Herod was deeply disturbed by their questions, and all Jerusalem was filled with rumors. He called a meeting of the Jewish religious leaders. "Did the prophets tell us where the Messiah would be born?" he asked. "Yes, in Bethlehem," they said.... Then Herod sent a private message to the astrologers, asking them to come to see him; at this meeting he found out from them the exact time when they first saw the star. Then he told them, "Go to Bethlehem and search for the child. And when you find him, come back and tell me so I can go and worship him too!" After the interview the astrologers started out again. And look! The star appeared to them again, standing over Bethlehem.[20]

In the New American Bible, the last line is translated as: "The star which they had observed at its rising went ahead of them until it came to a standstill over the place where the child was."

For nearly 2000 years Bible scholars and astronomers alike have puzzled over these few lines, offering every conceivable explanation for this mysterious aerial phenomenon reported by the ancients. Was the mystery star a comet? Was it an unusual alignment of the planets? Perhaps it was a super nova. About the only explanations that have not been put forth have been that it was a weather balloon or swamp gas, but then again, no one has asked the Air Force for its opinion.

19. Luke 2:8-14.
20. Matthew 2:1-9.

However, on examination of the little evidence we have available of this sighting, we must conclude that the strange object could not have been any of the above. The magi, or astronomers, certainly would have been familiar with comets, planets in unusual alignment and super novae. Yet, they identified it as a star. Obviously, stars do not appear for short periods of time. Nor do they appear only to some and not to others. The magi say they first saw the star in a far-off land, yet Herod and all his experts were baffled by their description. They obviously had not seen the star from their location. The priests had to tell Herod where the Messiah was prophesied to be born. Thus, Herod had not been able to determine where the star was in the heavens. The star then surprises the magi by appearing to them again and leading them to the town of Bethlehem, over which it apparently hovers.

This description qualifies the object as what ufologists today would call an "unknown" or "CE-I" (close encounter of the first kind)—something unexplainable that does not correspond to any known natural phenomenon. In its strictest sense, then, the Star of Bethlehem is an Unidentified Flying Object—a UFO. Furthermore, we can now say with some degree of assurance, given the aerial displays put on by the angels of the Lord in so many other cases, that the mysterious star was in all probability a ship which made itself visible to the wise men for a specific purpose. That purpose appears to have been to advertise the birth of Jesus to specific, chosen individuals who would convey the message to a wider audience, including King Herod. Interestingly, it seems as if only the Magi were permitted to see the ship, for if the general public had seen it, throngs of people would have shown up to see what was going on, including Herod's men.

It seems quite clear that the Star of Bethlehem was a very special "star" that did not fit into any known category of natural phenomena, and that it serves as one more example of the many times that UFOs are seen and described by the ancients in their writings. And if this conclusion is correct, it means that Christians today continue to use the ancient symbol of the UFO as part of their annual ritual in celebrating the birth of Christ. Every time a star is placed atop a Christmas tree in lands around the world, Christians are paying homage to the chariots of fire used by the angels of God—The Watchers—to travel the skies while keeping vigil over their flocks.

The Baptism of Jesus

The baptism of Jesus by John the Baptist was considered by early Christians to have been a highly significant event, even a turning point, in the life of Jesus. All four gospels refer to this event, which was highlighted by the appearance of an object which apparently lifted him up physically and took him away to the wilderness where he was tempted by the devil:

> Then Jesus went from Galilee to the Jordan River to be baptized there by John. John didn't want to do it. "This isn't proper," he said. "I am the one who needs to be baptized by you." But Jesus said, "Please do it, for I must do all that is right." So then John baptized him. After his baptism, as soon as Jesus came up out of the water, the heavens were opened to him and he saw the Spirit of God coming down in the form of a dove. [Or as in the New American translation: "...he saw the Spirit of God descend like a dove and hover over him."] And a voice from heaven said, "this is my beloved Son, and I am wonderfully pleased with him." Then Jesus was led out into the wilderness by the Holy Spirit, to be tempted there by Satan.[21]

According to Barry Downing, after Jesus was baptized:

> ...some sort of UFO apparently entered the situation for some reason. What did the UFO look like, and what was its mission...? Matthew, Mark and John say in effect that Christ saw the Spirit "descending like a dove." The fourth Gospel says that John the Baptist "saw the Spirit descend as a dove from heaven, and it remained on him." This is important, for the Biblical witness as a whole suggests that the "Spirit" was some concrete reality....[22]

Downing concludes that the object did not look like a dove, but rather descended from the sky like a dove, with wings spread and motionless. Such a description is entirely consistent with the way UFOs are reported to behave. Again, we might conclude that, even though it is reported that the voice of God emanated from heaven, the object was in fact piloted by physical beings—the angels of the Lord.

---

21. Matthew 3:13-17, 4:1.
22. Downing, 1968, pp. 135-136.

At this point, it seems as if the craft took Jesus physically to the wilderness, just as Elijah had been taken up to heaven when the chariot of fire appeared, carrying him away "by a whirlwind into heaven."[23]

In the wilderness, Jesus ate nothing for forty days and forty nights. Then Satan tempted him to get food by changing stones into loaves of bread. "It will prove you are the Son of God," he said.

But Jesus told him, "No! For the Scriptures tell us that bread won't feed men's souls: obedience to every word of God is what we need."

Then Satan took him to Jerusalem to the roof of the Temple. "Jump off," he said, "and prove you are the Son of God; for the Scriptures declare, God will send his angels to keep you from harm…they will prevent you from smashing on the rocks below."

Jesus retorted, "It also says not to put the Lord your God to a foolish test!"

Next, Satan took him to the peak of a very high mountain and showed him the nations of the world and all their glory. "I'll give it all to you," he said, "if you will only kneel and worship me."

"Get out of here, Satan," Jesus told him. "The Scriptures say, 'Worship only the Lord God. Obey only him.'" Then Satan went away, and angels came and cared for Jesus.

Here we see that Satan, who is said to be a fallen angel (Watcher), has the power to offer Jesus earthly riches, once again establishing that he is the lord of the physical world, and Jesus, in resisting worldly trappings, demonstrates the central purpose of his incarnation—to liberate humankind from the material world. This is the complete antithesis of what Jehovah had taught the Jews in the Old Testament. Also in this passage, we find the angels, now associated with the removal of Jesus from the site of his baptism in physical form, playing an important role in protecting and caring for him. Undeniably, the angels were looming constantly in the background during the entire story of Jesus, like stage hands behind the scenes, or special effects masters, creating the desired effects, but rarely showing themselves. In this instance, the

23. II Kings 2:11-14.

angels seemed to have taken Jesus to the wilderness, cared for him after his ordeal and, presumably were prepared to come to his aid, should he have needed their assistance. Such a role argues strongly against Paul's position that the angels were of minor importance in the life of Christ. But perhaps the strongest case for the power of the Watchers can be made through a close examination of their role in the one event that sets Jesus apart from all others—his resurrection and his ascension into heaven.

The Resurrection

No other event in the Bible has been more controversial than the story of Jesus' resurrection from the dead. Such a seeming impossibility has caused even the most devout Christians to hesitate in their acceptance of the New Testament as a record of literal truth. And it is the requirement, at the insistence of both the Protestant and Catholic Churches (which adopted the teachings of Paul) that its members accept this belief through faith alone, that has made many turn their backs on Christianity. Official Christian doctrine holds that Jesus' resurrection proves that he is God and anyone who does not believe this, cannot rightly call himself a Christian. Those who cannot accept this basic tenet, but who can accept his teachings of love and forgiveness, are considered to be doomed to eternal damnation.

For this reason, it is essential that the issue of the resurrection of the dead be understood for what it really is—a marvel of advanced, spiritual technology possessed by the guardian beings who created us and who assist us in our evolutionary journey. As we have seen previously, resurrecting the dead is not considered by the Watchers to be an unusual event. Through what appears to be advanced cloning technology, and through their amazing ability to control and process souls, these beings are able to resurrect anyone. It would not be a great challenge for them to land on the White House lawn and disembark Abraham Lincoln and George Washington, or even the crew of the Challenger disaster, should they find a need to do so. If we can accept and understand this fact, then we are a step closer toward understanding the single most important event of the Bible.

The crucifixion was the culmination of a well-orchestrated melodrama produced by the Watchers (those representing the nonphysical world) for the purpose of helping humans find the path of spiritual enlightenment through which they might escape the lower world of darkness. As an exclamation point to their message, they produced a final scene that would not be easily forgotten—a scene that would demonstrate clearly the reality of life after death.

On what we now call Palm Sunday, Jesus entered Jerusalem in his third year of ministry to play out the final scene in his life. After being arrested and tried, he suffered the gruesome, but quite common, fate of those who stirred the ire of the Roman authorities—he was nailed to a cross and left to die. After his death, he was taken to a tomb hewn from the side of a hill and laid to rest. A large stone wheel was rolled in front of the opening to seal it, and Roman guards were stationed to prevent anyone from tampering with the body.

Here is where the story begins to get confusing, with each of the Gospels describing the events of the resurrection in slightly different ways. Matthew writes that:

> Early on Sunday morning, as the new day was dawning, Mary Magdalene and the other Mary went out to the tomb. Suddenly there was a great earthquake; for an angel of the Lord came down from heaven and rolled aside the stone and sat on it. His face shone like lightning and his clothing was a brilliant white. The guards shook with fear when they saw him and fell into a dead faint. Then the angel spoke to the women.
>
> "Don't be frightened!" he said. "I know you are looking for Jesus, who was crucified, but he isn't here! For he has come back to life again, just as he said he would. Come in and see where his body was lying.... And now go quickly and tell his disciples that he has risen from the dead, and that he is going to Galilee to meet them there...."
>
> The women ran from the tomb, badly frightened, but also filled with joy, and rushed to find the disciples to give them the angel's message. And as they were running, suddenly Jesus was there in front of them! "Good morning!" he said. And they fell to the ground before him, holding his feet and worshipping him. And Jesus said to them, "Don't be frightened! Go tell my brothers to leave at once for Galilee, to meet me there."[24]

From this description of the events, it appears that the angels had a great deal to do with the resurrection of Christ. Not only were they

---

24. Matthew 28:1-10

present, but they rolled back the stone covering the entryway to the tomb and seemingly caused the guards to go into a deep sleep. It should be noted that the angels did not have wings, but instead wore brilliant white clothing, similar to what the tall blondes of UFO fame are said to wear. It also appears that Jesus was already out of the tomb when the stone was rolled away because the women were invited in to see that it was empty. Given the ability of the Watchers to pass through solid objects and to cause abductees to also pass through walls and ceilings, this should come as no great surprise to those familiar with the abduction phenomenon.

Mark's Gospel tells a similar tale,[25] but in his narrative there are three women, Mary Magdalene, Salome and Mary the mother of James, who go to the tomb. He mentions no earthquake, and he reports that the tomb was already open when they arrived. When they entered, they saw "a young man clothed in white," who told them that Jesus was alive and on his way to Galilee. His report says that Mary Magdalene was the first to see the resurrected Jesus, but he does not describe their encounter.

Luke, on the other hand, says that the three women who went to the tomb were Mary Magdalene, Joanna and Mary, the mother of James. In his version, the tomb was already open when they arrived, but the tomb was completely empty when they entered. While they were in the tomb, the angels appeared: "Suddenly two men appeared before them, clothed in shining robes so bright their eyes were dazzled." The women in this case rush off to Jerusalem, rather than Galilee, to tell the disciples. Instead of appearing to Mary Magdalene, he appears first to Peter and to two men who are described as followers of Jesus—one whose name was Cleopas.[26]

John gives a different account of the events that Sunday morning:

Early Sunday morning, while it was still dark, Mary Magdalene came to the tomb and found that the stone was rolled aside from the entrance. She ran and found Simon Peter and me and said, "They have taken the Lord's body out of the tomb, and I don't know where they have put him!"

25. Mark 16:1-11.
26. Luke 24:1-32.

We ran to the tomb to see; I outran Peter and got there first, and stooped and looked in and saw the linen cloth lying there, but I didn't go in. Then Simon Peter arrived and went on inside. He also noticed the cloth lying there, while the swath that had covered Jesus' head was rolled up in a bundle and was lying at the side. Then I went in too, and saw, and believed— for until then we hadn't realized that the Scriptures said he would come to life again!

We went home, and by that time Mary had returned to the tomb and was standing outside crying. And as she wept, she stooped and looked in and saw two white-robed angels sitting at the head and foot of the place where the body of Jesus had been lying.

...She glanced over her shoulder and saw someone standing behind her. It was Jesus, but she didn't recognize him! When she finally recognizes him, she reaches for him, but Jesus warns her: "Don't touch me, for I haven't yet ascended to the Father. But go find my brothers and tell them that I ascend to my Father and your Father, my God and your God."[27]

This version includes an interesting aspect regarding the resurrected body of Christ—that it may not have been a physical one. What would have happened had she tried to touch him? Would her hand have passed through him? Was this merely an embellishment added by religious zealots or is it possible that she was, in fact, seeing a holographic image? Jesus' resurrected body seems to have varying appearances during the days that followed. In some cases, his body seems physical as when he allows Thomas to touch his wounds and at other times, it seems so changed that his disciples, and even his own mother, do not recognize him. It seems as if this is meant to be a period of transition, during which the apostles learn that there is another realm where physical bodies, as we know them, are not needed and where material possessions are irrelevant and insignificant.

In any case, all of the above passages, which describe the singular, most important event of the New Testament, present great difficulty to those fundamentalists who preach that the Bible is the unerring word of God. Obviously, all four Gospels tell a different story, and they can't all be right. Either the Bible was written by humans who make mis-

---

27. John 20:1-17.

takes or it was written by God who does not. And if the Bible was written by humans who make mistakes, then we must deal with it as merely one of many other documents written by men. We must study it objectively and unemotionally and make intellectual judgments about its worthiness and its validity. These stories remind me of what it was like to be a journalism teacher. When I would assign a class of 20 students to attend an event and to write a news story including the basic information (who, what, when, where, how and why), I would invariably get back 20 different accounts. That didn't mean the event didn't happen, only that people make mistakes when reporting on events. The conflicting reports of the resurrection do not, as some have asserted, prove that the authors were fabricating the story, only that the people of the time were no different than people today. In fact, their all-too-human reporting errors lend credence to the conclusion that the event actually occurred, even if we can't be sure today of all the details. However, if the event did occur, one of the consistent elements in the different accounts was the fact that the angels played an important and mysterious role in the resurrection, and, as we shall see, an equally important role in Jesus' trip back to heaven.

The Ascension

During the forty days following the resurrection, Jesus sometimes appeared to the apostles and to others to preach. According to Luke, when the apostles were assembled with Jesus on the Mount of Olives:

It was not long afterwards that he rose into the sky and disappeared into a cloud, leaving them staring after him. As they were straining their eyes for another glimpse, suddenly two white-robed men were standing there among them, and said, "Men of Galilee, why are you standing here staring at the sky? Jesus has gone away to heaven and some day, just as he went, he will return!"[28]

Clearly, Luke believed the ascension into heaven was a physical event. It seems to describe Christ's levitation into a ship which gradually rose and diminished in size, so that it became difficult and then impossible to see with the naked eye. It was then that the angels appeared and predicted that someday he would return, "just as he

---

28. Acts 1:9-11.

went," in a cloud. This brief description of one of the most dramatic events in the Bible is all we have (aside from two other brief mentions) today to decide for ourselves what actually happened. However, when placed in context with all the other miraculous events of the Old and New Testaments, the picture becomes clearer. Angelic beings, traveling the skies in vehicles that defied understanding and description by the peoples of the time were interacting with selected humans, just as they are today, to help direct their spiritual growth.

In the case of Jesus, his purpose is to be found in his words and in his actions, just as Jehovah's actions spoke for him. And it would be hard to imagine any two more opposing views. While Jehovah was the God of the physical world, granting lands and riches to a people he sought to separate and alienate from the rest of humanity, Jesus represented unity of all peoples. Although born a Jew, his ministry was for all humanity and his words and actions were meant to unite the human race, not to divide it.

"Love thy neighbor as thyself"; "Turn the other cheek"; "Forgive those who trespass against you." This is the message of unconditional love for all living things. It is a message that says we are all one with God. It speaks of the interconnectedness of all things, and is a message that could only have come from someone who understood the true nature of reality and of the universal consciousness we call God. It seems also that the life of Christ was meant to demonstrate the reality of the nonphysical world—a higher, more beautiful world that is closer to the Creator. His message was clearly that the physical world is but a trap for human souls and that it is within our grasp to transcend this world and to rediscover our immortality. By forsaking material things such as wealth and power, he sought to set the example for all of us to follow and to make it clear that material possessions are insignificant compared to what awaits us in heaven.

By dying a dramatic and very public death and then ascending into the heavens, he left a powerful message that has affected human affairs dramatically for 2,000 years. And by speaking of his eventual return, he has kept his image and spirit alive to this very day. The second coming of Jesus is mentioned more than 300 times in the New Testament, and must therefore be taken as an important aspect of his message. The night before his crucifixion he told the apostles that he would come again and that he was preparing a place for them in heaven:

"Let not your heart be troubled. You are trusting God, now trust in me. There are many homes up there where my Father lives, and I am going to prepare them for your coming. When everything is ready, then will I come and get you, so that you can always be with me where I am."[29]

Jesus here seems to refer to a very real event in which humans in the future (perhaps not the apostles themselves) are to be taken away to another place, perhaps even another planet. If so, it coincides with what many UFO experiencers and researchers have discovered—plans for an evacuation of an Earth that is no longer inhabitable.

Later, Peter tells the apostles what had been prophesied:

In the last days, God said, "I will pour out my Holy Spirit upon all mankind, and your sons and daughters shall prophesy, and your young men shall see visions, and your old men dream dreams.... And I will cause strange demonstrations in the heavens and on Earth—blood and fire and clouds of smoke; the sun shall turn black and the moon blood-red before that awesome Day of the Lord arrives."[30]

Can it happen? Of course. All the Bible miracles can be explained through an understanding of UFO phenomena. If UFOs are real, then there is every reason to believe that the events described by the ancients were, in fact, real events. Thus, the events foretold in the Bible can also come true. Indeed, the above passages seem to be referring to things that are already happening today. Increased UFO activity over the last 50 years, global warming and unusual weather patterns could certainly be described as "strange demonstrations in the heavens," and increased volcanic and earthquake activity create "fire and clouds of smoke." And as we have seen, UFO researchers have found that abductees and their children demonstrate increased psychic and clairvoyant abilities. Is this what was meant by "your sons and daughters shall prophesy and your young men shall see visions"? If so, the UFO message could be that the day of Jesus' return may in fact be near. But, if so, it will be far different than that imagined by those whose belief rests on faith alone, for it will be a day when the skies are filled, not with clouds, but with spacecraft—those celestial chariots of fire described in the ancient texts and by UFO witnesses everywhere.

---

29. John 14:1-3.
30. Acts 2:17-20.

CHAPTER 14

A NEW BEGINNING

Then the seventh angel poured out his flask into the air; and a mighty shout came from the throne of the temple in heaven, saying, "It is finished!" Then thunder crashed and rolled, and lightning flashed; and there was a great earthquake of a magnitude unprecedented in human history. The great city of Babylon split into three sections, and cities around the world fell into heaps of rubble; and so all of Babylon's sins were remembered in God's thoughts, and she was punished to the last drop of anger in the cup of the wine of the fierceness of his wrath. And islands vanished, and mountains flattened out, and there was an incredible hailstorm from heaven; hailstones weighing a hundred pounds fell from the sky onto the people below; and they cursed God because of the terrible hail.

—(Revelations 15:17-21)

The Apocalypse

Two thousand years ago, the Apostle John described a terrible vision of a violent battle known as the Apocalypse, in which angels and demons clash in a struggle for dominion over the Earth and its inhabitants and in which worldwide devastation and pestilence heralds the second coming of Christ.

In the 16th century, the great astronomer and prophet, Nostradamus, wrote a four line description of his vision of the end of the world which he believed would occur at the end of this millennium:

A great spherical mountain of [about a mile]
At a time when peace will give way to war
Famine and flooding
It will roll end over end, sinking great nations.[1]

---

1. Arvey, 1992, p. 34.

In the 1930s, the great American prophet, Edgar Cayce, prophesied great Earth changes during the last decade of the 20th century which included great shifts in the Earth's land masses, earthquakes, volcanic eruptions, flooding and, around the year 2000, a sudden shifting of the Earth's axis. And now, as the final few years of the millennium slip away, thousands of abductees, near-death experiencers and gifted psychics are warning of their own similar visions.

Is this the ranting of the mad or of the foolish who materialize every so often to warn of the end of the world, only to fade into obscurity when the fateful day passes and the Earth is still here? Is this simply the result of some strange psychosis called "millennium madness" that will subside once the new millennium has begun?

If it is some strange form of mass hysteria, as many believe, then it is a highly contagious disease which seems to have infected many of the world's most respected scientists, and it is also one capable of manifesting frightening, deadly and very real events that seem to confirm its reality. There is hardly a human alive today who is not aware that the Earth's climate has taken a turn toward the violent and unpredictable. Our nation's newspapers and network news programs are daily echoing the concerns of puzzled scientists who seem to be finding ample evidence to support the shamanistic warnings of humanity's imminent extinction.

Earth Changes in Science

One of the more alarming reports came from a 1992 Danish study that warned that humans are already losing their ability to reproduce. In reviewing more than 60 scientific studies dating back to 1938, the authors discovered that sperm counts today are about half of what they had been 50 years ago. Additionally, the study noted increased rates of testicular cancers, undescended testes and penile defects in newborn males. These findings caused the World Health Organization to revise its standard for what it considered a normal sperm count, from 100 million to 50 million per ejaculation.[2]

But the danger is not limited to the human population. Scientists are pointing to a threat to all living things on Earth due to the effects of chemical pollutants that have worked their way into the Earth's water

2. Gannett News Service, 1996.

280

supplies, food chain and atmosphere. These chemicals, they believe, disrupt the action of hormones that regulate almost all bodily activities. The result is decreased fertility and increases in diseases that endanger the reproductive process. In 1994, the Environmental Protection Agency (EPA) released a major report on the effects of dioxin, one of the suspected chemicals, which is a waste by-product of many industrial processes and is now found in most of the world's water supply. The report linked dioxin to a potential threat to the reproductive ability of humans.[3]

In the late 1980s it was discovered that the young of 16 predator species inhabiting the Great Lakes region, including birds, reptiles and mammals, were failing to survive to adulthood and could not reproduce if they did. This is due to the fact that their main food supply, the fish in the lakes, has been contaminated with hormone-like chemicals. Furthermore, mortality rates have soared in numerous animal populations in areas where contamination is greatest. In 1996 the National Academy of Science began debating the concern that common synthetic chemicals used in various household and industrial products are endangering life on Earth.[4] The alarm was sounded by a crusading zoologist, Theo Colburn, in her frightening book, *Our Stolen Future,*[5] in which she claims that scientists have been oblivious of the growing threat of human extinction.

But as obvious as the problem seems to some, there are many other scientists who continue to argue that there is not enough evidence to merit changing public policy at this time. The American Council on Science and Health, which is publicly funded by industry groups, began to attack Colburn's book even before it was published. By secretly obtaining copies of the galley proofs, the organization was able to prepare an eleven-page rebuttal by the time the book hit the stores.[6] But even as industry braces itself for the fight to ban potentially dangerous chemicals, scientists studying the Earth's climate have begun to issue dire warnings about another side effect of pollution—the rapid increase in the Earth's temperature, known as the greenhouse effect. They warn that increased levels of carbon dioxide in the

---

3. Waldholz, 1996, p. B-1.
4. Lemonick, 1994, p. 68.
5. Colburn, 1996.
6. Crossen, 1996, p. B1

Earth's atmosphere, which traps the sun's heat, have presaged disastrous changes in the Earth's climatic history.

As if dangerous chemicals were not enough of a problem, the growing threat of radioactive contamination of the Earth's environment presents an even greater dilemma. Since the world's first nuclear explosion on July 16, 1945, there have been 2045 additional detonations, for an average of one test every nine days for the past 51 years. More than 500 of these were carried out in the open atmosphere, spreading radioactive fallout around the globe. Today, every human being has traces of deadly Strontium 90, the fusionable material used to detonate atomic bombs, in his bones. All efforts to arrive at a nuclear test ban treaty thus far have failed, and more and more nations are on the verge of acquiring nuclear capability.[7]

Global Warming

In November 1995, a panel of scientists representing more than 80 nations accepted a United Nations sponsored report which officially declared that global warming is a human-made problem. Panel members agreed that, due to the burning of fossil fuels and deforestation, humans have caused the Earth's temperature to rise to its highest level since people began taking readings, around the year 1400. Unless worldwide emissions of greenhouse gases are reduced to much lower levels soon, they warn, the amount of carbon dioxide in the Earth's atmosphere will double in the next 100 years. This would cause temperatures to rise another 2° to 7° and cause untold disasters in the form of massive flooding of the coastal areas, droughts, forest fires, earthquakes and increased volcanic activity.

Oceanographers are already concerned about the rapid rise that is occurring in the water of the world's oceans and seas. In March 1995, scientists discovered that part of the Antarctic was breaking away at an awesome speed. They discovered that a giant section of the Larsen Ice Shelf, 23 miles wide and 48 miles long, (about the size of the country of Luxembourg) had broken off.[8] "For the first time in recorded history," says Mike Thompson, a scientist with the British Antarctic Survey, "you could circumnavigate Ross Island," which has been

---

7. Associated Press, Sept. 11, 1996.
8. Lemonick, Mar. 20, 1995, p. 65.

under ice since Antarctica was discovered. Over the past 50 years the average temperature on the Antarctic Peninsula has risen 2.5°, a much higher rate than anywhere else on Earth. Not only are ice shelves turning to slush, but a new abundance of plant life is emerging at an amazing rate. In some areas, vegetation has increased 25 fold. Additionally, the ice next to the area where the "big one" broke away, is now showing signs of another massive break up.

And while scientists debate whether such dramatic changes are human-made, insurance companies are bracing themselves for massive claims due to weather-related losses. Property and casualty losses, after the nastiest winter on record hit the East Coast in January and February 1994, caused Aetna Life and Casualty to announce a quarterly earning's plunge of $120 million. After massive losses caused by winter storms in 1993 and 1994, by hurricanes Andrew and Iniki in 1992 and the 1995 record hurricane season, American insurance companies had to scrap their carefully calculated predictions of future claims.[9] For them, the changing Earth is a very real threat that must be understood and dealt with immediately. Regardless of the cause, they know only too well that the threat of natural disaster is increasing. Natural disasters were 94% more frequent in the 1980s than in the 1970s. And the 1990s are proving to be even worse. Although some scientists still insist that weather goes through natural cycles, and that such changes are in all likelihood simply part of the Earth's normal climatic pattern, many others see the changes as evidence that environmental warnings are alarmingly on target.

Killer Storms

Environmental scientists tell us that as warming heats the oceans, the areas of water warm enough to produce hurricanes, and other dangerous storms, expand, producing bigger and greater numbers of storms. Such areas, we now know, have already expanded by one-sixth in the past 20 years. As the ice caps melt at unprecedented rates and as ocean temperatures increase, expanding the volume of water, sea levels rise. Over the past 100 years, sea levels have risen one foot along the Atlantic Coast and caused beaches to erode more than 200 feet. Stephen Leatherman, the director of the University of Maryland Labo-

---

9.   Linden, 1994, p. 79.

ratory for Coastal Research, is alarmed at the rapid rise in sea levels, which he says are now at their highest mark in the past 5,000 years. Furthermore, the seas are rising 10 times faster than before.

Franklin Nutter, president of the Reinsurance Association of America puts it quite bluntly in speaking for his industry: "It is clear that global warming could bankrupt the industry." With sea levels rising at a rapid rate, there is $2 trillion worth of insured property on the Atlantic and Gulf coasts at risk. One massive hurricane that hit both Miami and Fort Lauderdale head on could cost the insurance industry $100 billion and with 50% of the U.S. population living within 50 miles of the coastline, such dramatic changes in climate can wreak untold damage to modern society.

For the many countries in Asia, the Earth changes are already causing unheard of havoc in the form of massive flooding. Studies issued in 1994 by the Climate Institute, a Washington-based advocacy group, warns that coastlines in Asia are particularly threatened by global warming. By the year 2070, according to the Institute's worst case scenario, millions of residents of Indonesia, Vietnam, the Philippines and India could be forced to permanently evacuate their homes and relocate, due to rising waters. The study did not even include China, where flooding has already become a serious issue.[10] Making matters worse is the fact that the Asian-Pacific region, which has 75% of the Earth's population, will soon be the largest source of greenhouse emissions in the world.

Giant Earthquakes

Many people do not realize that there are other serious side effects to global warming that can cause disaster. As the external temperatures increase, so do temperatures within the Earth, causing internal pressures to build. Ultimately, these pressures cause breaks in the Earth's crust and become evident as active volcanoes and earthquakes. Few scientists are as concerned about the potential dangers to human life as are seismologists and geologists who are convinced that the possibilities of devastating earthquakes and volcanic explosions of unprecedented magnitude are increasingly likely in the near future. This is particularly true in the area surrounding the Pacific Ocean,

---

10. Lachica, 1994.

284

known as the "ring of fire," which includes the western coasts of North and South America and the Asian countries of the Pacific rim. Recently, American and Canadian geologists have made an abrupt change in the way they perceive the risks to the Northern part of the U.S. Pacific coast, which most people had assumed was fairly safe.[11] Using new techniques to measure the size and frequency of quakes in the area in historical times, they discovered evidence that clearly demonstrates that large earthquakes have plagued the region in the past at fairly regular intervals. They are now convinced that giant earthquakes of magnitude nine on the Richter scale could strike at almost any time in that area. There have only been two quakes of this size ever recorded—one in 1960 in Chile and one in 1964 in Alaska. After such a quake, most coastal sites would be one to two meters lower and five to 10 meters seaward of where they are now. The damage to even those cities not immediately on the coast, such as Seattle, Vancouver and Portland, would be substantial.

Overpopulation

At the core of the global warming and pollution issues lies the real culprit—human overpopulation that has stretched the world's resources to their limits. To be sure, the world's human population has grown exponentially in the modern era, doubling from about 2.5 billion in 1950 to 5 billion in 1991, and estimated to hit 10 billion by 2010. During the first half of the 20th century, we consumed more non-renewable resources than in all of our previous time on Earth, stretching the planet's carrying capacity to its limits. In 1994, Worldwatch, a private, non-profit research group that monitors population growth and natural resource supplies, issued a report that warned of potential food shortages in the years ahead. "As a result of our population size, consumption patterns, and technological choices, we have surpassed the planet's carrying capacity." Their study indicated that the slow growth in the world food supplies is evidence that the planet's biological limits have been reached. This is in sharp contrast to what mainstream science has been telling us. In spite of such warnings, many scientists continue to say that the world can continue to produce

---

11. Hyndman, 1995, pp. 68-75.

enough food to feed all its inhabitants, due to improved agricultural technology.

But the Worldwatch report says that such technology cannot keep up with the population explosion in third-world nations. They point out that fish harvests from the world's oceans have leveled off at about 100 million tons a year and may possibly not be exceeded. As more bodies of water become highly polluted, freshwater shortages are beginning to occur around the world. Grain production has slowed dramatically in the last few years, and in some cases, as with rice, corn and wheat, the per capita output has fallen since 1984. Even with massive programs of deforestation in many areas of the world, crop land has only increased 2% in the last decade as topsoil has disappeared and farmland has given way to factories.[12]

Deadly Diseases

In spite of efforts by mainstream science to minimize the dangers brought about by Earth changes, one cannot ignore the fact that today these changes have affected each and every one of us. It has become increasingly difficult in the past decade to enjoy such things as a walk in the woods (lyme disease), a hamburger (mad cow disease or E coli bacteria), making love (AIDS), going to the beach (skin cancer) or taking a cruise (Legionnaires' disease). Travelling to third-world countries today requires careful consideration in light of cholera and tuberculosis outbreaks occurring at alarming rates. All this in spite of the fact that medical researchers told us only two decades ago that humanity had been victorious over infectious diseases, conquering polio, smallpox, diphtheria, malaria, tuberculosis and many others. Yet today, the medical field is in a near panic in its efforts to deal with not only a resurgence of old diseases, many of them showing resistance to antibiotics, but also new, unheard-of diseases such as those caused by Ebola, Saba and Hanta viruses that seemed to have popped out of nowhere. One virus, known only as "X," emerged from the rain forest in southern Sudan in 1993. It killed thousands of people and then mysteriously disappeared. Scientists are at a loss to predict when it might strike again. Even more alarming is the fact that nearly every disease

---

12. Associated Press, Jan. 16, 1994.

organism we know about has become resistant to at least one antibiotic, with several resistant to more than one.[13]

As the battle against AIDS continues to baffle the scientific community, it is becoming ever more evident that our war against microscopic viruses is escalating. Laurie Garrett, in her book, *The Coming Plague,* concludes that AIDS may be only the beginning of a long series of modern-age epidemics. It seems almost inevitable that in the years ahead, the predictions of widespread pestilence, disease, famine and devastation made by scientists and psychics alike, are likely to materialize unless the human race can make drastic and sudden changes in its perceptions and in its way of life. If not, the path that it is on seems clearly marked. It is a path of ultimate self-destruction.

Indigenous Peoples

As entire species of plants and animals are disappearing from the face of the Earth at an unprecedented rate, environmentalists and anthropologists alike are keeping an anxious and vigilant eye on the indigenous peoples of the world—those gentle spirits whose way of life has nearly vanished and who are innocent of any contribution toward the conditions that threaten to eradicate them. In 1994 in a remote Indian village an hour outside Rio de Janeiro, Brazil, the first World Conference of Indigenous Peoples convened an assembly of tribal leaders to discuss, in their own inimitable way, the issue of their own extinction. They hoped to encourage world leaders and scientists in attendance to save the natural world from its imminent destruction. One of the leaders, a shaman clad only in red shorts, flip flops and an arm band of pink parrot feathers, began the meeting by performing a shamanistic ritual. He began singing guttural chants and pacing up and down while beating his chest. His singing eventually changed to choking fits and bodily contortions which lasted for more than an hour. Finally, his incantations reached an hysterical climax and suddenly, as he wandered off mumbling, an amazing thing happened. Science writer Stephen Mills, who was covering the conference, reported in *Omni* Magazine that: "The entire hut and its occupants rose slowly as if on a cushion of air and hovered two feet off the ground—for this observer, anyway.... Eerie, uncanny and downright spooky. This had

---

13. Lemonick, Sept. 12, 1994, pp. 65-68.

to be some kind of trick of the mind, but I could have sworn.... Stumbling as I tried to step two feet down onto the ground only confounded my disbelief."[14] While the tribal leaders seemed unshaken, exchanging knowing glances, the Western observers were dazed and confused and in some kind of trance:

> Some remained in denial, unable to accept their own metaphysical encounter. But many others wanted to believe, and everyone's story was different. "It was as if I turned into an exotic bird and flew off into the forest," remarked one colleague, while others spoke of leaving their bodies, as in astral travel.... But what exactly had happened, and just what was the message to the rest of the world? In essence, the tribal leaders' message was simply that only spiritual reverence for the Earth would save it—and to fail would be fatal. As [the organizer] remarked, "We can speak for the Earth because we have treated it well."[15]

It seems as if the indigenous leaders understand all too well the source of their problems. They know that "civilized" man's disconnection from the spiritual world is what causes him to destroy God's creation. By not understanding that he is part of that creation, he casually creates conditions, technology and government policies that will, in the end, destroy himself. How could they get this message across to Western scientists and politicians? No amount of discussion would convey the message in a meaningful way. No research report could convince them of the nature of the problem. There was only one way. Each person present had to experience the spiritual realm. Each one had to be transformed. Instinctively, the shaman devised a plan to alter and to realign the paradigm of each one present so that never again could they see the world the same. He knew that the only solution to the world's problems was to transform enough people so that spiritual, rather than technological, solutions might be forthcoming.

But how is it that indigenous people of the world—the aborigines of Australia, the bushmen of the Kalahari, the people of the Amazon and the Native Americans, to name a few—were able to remain connected to God and to nature, while another branch of humanity became separated and lost sight of its true nature? And how did "civi-

14. Mills, 1994, pp. 63-64.
15. Mills, 1994, p. 64.

lized" man become so arrogant that he came to view the native peoples as little more than animals and thereby lacking legal rights to their ancestral homelands? Wherever they exist throughout the world, they have all suffered the same fate, being forced from their lands and watching helplessly as intruders destroyed their forests and killed their animals. Yet these people hold the secret of how to live in harmony with nature without destroying their environment and without allowing the survival of their species to infringe upon the survival of others. Because they remain connected to God and continue to serve Him, they instinctively follow the spiritual laws that Western society has forgotten.

For example, the Australian aborigines follow spiritual laws they receive while in hypnotic states they call "dreamtime." In these deep trance states they commune with spirit entities, remote view distant places and times and understand the laws of nature. These laws they understand to be inviolable and absolute for there to be harmony in the world. As Robert Lawlor states in his book on Aborigine culture, *Voices of the First Day*:

> The Aborigines possess a sacred science, one that seeks to fuse the energies of the Earth and humanity to those of the cosmos.... This science of attunement opens their consciousness to enable them to communicate with the memory and mind of the Earth.[16]

For the aborigines, the acquisition of land and the subjugation or destruction of competing tribes has never been considered as a course of action. Lawlor states:

> The lack of any form of agriculture in Aboriginal Australia is now fully recognized as the result of conscious choice. It is not, as Darwinian experts previously claimed due to "primitivism, racial deficiencies," or the result of environmental hardship. Rather it was an active choice of Aboriginal culture to adhere to their ancient Dreamtime Law.[17]

In addition, their deeply spiritual communion with the cosmos provided them with the knowledge that the gathering of material possessions was also unnatural and contrary to spiritual law. The aborigi-

16. Lawlor, 1991, p. 111.
17. Lawlor, 1991, p. 59.

nes baffled early explorers by their complete lack of interest in possessing material things.

As we learn more about the reality of indigenous cultures, we begin to see that modern society has been misled by our scientists and our religions into believing that the native peoples were inferior and in need of our help to raise themselves to our level. Today even some scientists are beginning to realize that we (civilized societies) are the fallen ones. This revelation caused physiologist Jared Diamond to state that "Agriculture is the worst mistake in the history of the human race." Anthropologist Leslie White suggests that "Hunting and gathering society was unquestionably the most satisfying social environment man has ever lived in."[18]

Such an understanding causes us to question the motivations of science and religion, both of which have treated the native peoples as inferior. In each case, such an attitude protected a self-serving agenda. For science, it was to defend and justify the Darwinian/materialistic belief that life forms evolve from primitive to superior states in a linear progression, with modern humans at the top of the heap. For the church, it served to justify the destruction and eradication of competing religions—in this case the nature-worshipping (Pagan) cultures—in favor of its monotheistic view of reality. In so doing, both science and religion acted jointly to destroy human understanding of the very sacred science that is being rediscovered today.

The Kalahari Bushmen

There may be no other record of the ways of the indigenous peoples more insightful or more moving than that written by Laurens Van der Post who lived with the Kalahari Bushmen in his native South Africa. He learned, first-hand, the remarkable spirituality that guides what remains of Bushman culture after 200 years of systematic extermination by Europeans and other African tribes. His book, *Lost World of the Kalahari*, describes in stirring prose how these diminutive and shy people survive in a land so harsh that few outsiders dare enter:

...the Bushman's relationship with the animals and birds of Africa was never merely one of hunter and hunted, his knowledge of the plants, trees, and insects of the land, never

18. Lawlor, 1991, p. 60.

290

just the knowledge of a consumer food. On the contrary, he
knew the animal and vegetable life, the rocks and the stones of
Africa as they have never been known since.... He and they all
participated so deeply of one another's being that the experience could almost be called mystical. For instance, he seemed
to know what it actually felt like to be an elephant, a lion, an
antelope, a steenbuck, a lizard, a striped mouse, mantis, baobab
tree, yellow-crested cobra or starry-eyed amaryllis, to mention
only a few.... His killing, like the lion's, was innocent because
he killed only to live. He never killed for fun or the sake of killing, and even when doing it, was curiously apprehensive and
regretful of the deed.[19]

Time and again, Van der Post and the members of his expedition
were amazed by the psychic abilities demonstrated by the natives who
seemed so interconnected by some invisible force that they, in fact,
acted in unison. In one instance, after having made a kill of a great
eland far from the Bushman encampment, he turned to his guide and
asked:

"I wonder what they will say...when they learn that we've
killed an Eland?"

"Excuse me, master...they already know."

"What on Earth do you mean?" I asked.

"They know by wire," he declared....

"Wire?" I exclaimed.

"Yes. A wire, Master.... We Bushmen have a wire here," he
tapped his chest, "that brings us news."

More than that I couldn't get out of him, but even before we
were home it was clear that our skeptical minds were about to
be humbled. From afar in the dark, long before our fires were
visible...the black silence was broken by a glitter of new song
from the women. "Do you hear that, oh, my Master?... They're
singing 'The Eland Song.'"[20]

Van der Post also discovered how, by following nature's laws, the
Bushman was always assured that his species would never overpopu-
late his territory. The lesson came during a period of extensive drought
that threatened the survival of the community:

19. Van der Post, 1986, pp. 15-16.
20. Van der Post, 1986, pp. 260-261.

> [They] told us that the little man's women folk would become sterile during periods of drought and until the rains broke would cease to conceive.... That was one reason why the Bushman had such small families.... If a woman had conceived in a fall of rain that was not maintained and bore a child in a period of drought which threatened the survival of all, immediately at birth the child was taken from her, before.... "It could cry in her heart," and was killed by the other women. The anguish and bitterness with which those who loved children performed this deed...proved how necessary it was.[21]

As the Van der Post expedition parted company with the Bushmen after many weeks of living and hunting with them, he asked what would become of an ancient couple:

> They'll go as far as they can.... But a day will come when they can't go on. Then, weeping bitterly, all will gather around them. They'll give them all the food and water they can spare. They'll build a thick shelter of thorn to protect them against wild animals. Still weeping, the rest of the band, like the life that asks it of them, will move on. Sooner or later, probably before their water or food is finished, a leopard, but more commonly hyena, will break through and eat them.[22]

Civilized Humans

For modern humans, the life of the Bushman seems abhorrent. Yet the Bushmen, and all other indigenous humans, lead their lives in tune with nature, taking only what they need, leaving behind no pollutants that poison the soil or the waters, and loving and caring for all of God's creation. Without religious institutions, they instinctively live by the spiritual laws of the universe and practice a spirituality that makes them one with their Creator. They run naked, without shame or sin, in the garden God provided for them, and they do not make conscious decisions about which species around them should live or die. Somehow, they were not endowed with the ability to know good from evil in the same way modern humans do. For them, that knowledge is rightfully reserved for the Creator.

---

21. Van der Post, 1986, p. 263.
22. Van der Post, 1986, p. 277.

In sharp contrast are the ways of the modern human, who denies his psychic abilities, has no idea what it is like to be an animal, would never kill a baby to save his community and seeks to prolong life beyond the limit that God gave it. To a great extent, the perception that modern humans have of their place in the universe has been guided by their belief in the commandment of an ancient God:

> Multiply and fill the Earth and subdue it; you are the masters of the fish and birds and all the animals. And look, I have given you the seed bearing plants throughout the Earth and all the fruit trees for your food. And I have given all the grass and plants to the animals and birds for their food. Then God looked over everything he had made and it was excellent in every way.[23]

Following that commandment, modern man has, for the past 8000 or more years, multiplied and filled the Earth. He has seen the Earth and its plants and animals as his personal property, to own and to do with as he wished. He has looked upon nature as his adversary—as something to be conquered and subdued. He has taken the knowledge of growing seeds for food—the science of agriculture (taught to him by the gods)—and recklessly destroyed the forests to make room for more farmland, so that his species could enjoy unfettered growth at the expense of all other living things. As he began to perceive himself as master of his environment, he lost his spiritual connection to plants and animals, as well as to his fellow man and to the Creator. He forgot he was an immortal, spiritual being. And now he is finding, perhaps too late, that there is a price to pay.

This way of thinking occurred at some point in the distant past in the land of the Guardians—the Fertile Crescent of the Middle East— where anthropologists tell us humans first began to till the soil. It was then that something happened that split the human race into two groups. Those who remained connected to the spiritual world—the hunter-gatherers and the herdsmen—continued to live the life that they had always lived. But one branch of humanity seemed to the rest to go insane. They began to act like gods and to make decisions about who should live and who should die. Previously, only the Creator (nature) decided the fate of the animals and of entire species. But now,

---

23. Genesis 1:28-31.

a group of people, emerging from that area of the world, called in the Bible the Garden of Eden, began to systematically clear the land of its forests, its animals and its herdsmen to build their cities and multiply their numbers. They had decided that their own kind was more important than all others and their knowledge of the science of agriculture gave them the power to expand their numbers, ultimately crowding every corner of the globe.

What caused such a split to take place? The Bible tells us that this occurred when the serpent gave first humans to eat from the fruit of the tree of knowledge so that he could know the difference between good and evil. With this knowledge, humans would be able to think and "see" in a more godlike way. They would be able to make conscious decisions about what was right and what was wrong. But the serpent's gift was incomplete. Just like a recipe that lacks the secret ingredient and fails to satisfy, the gift, disguised as a delicious fruit, lacked the secret ingredient that would allow humans to know how to judge right from wrong. The fruit, which only allowed humans to imagine that they were godlike, was in fact deadly. By not allowing first man and woman to partake also from the fruit of the tree of life, the Watchers sealed humanity's doom by putting us on a path of certain self-destruction. When the serpent told Adam and Eve that the fruit would not kill them, as the other gods had said, he was only telling the partial truth. Although the fruit did not kill them, by eating it, they assured the eventual death of all their kind.

Having eaten the forbidden fruit and no longer being able to enjoy nature's bounty by living as one with the plants and animals, God banished them from nature's garden:

And to Adam, God said, "Because you listened to your wife and ate the fruit when I told you not to, I have placed a curse upon the soil. All your life you will struggle to extract a living from it. It shall grow thorns and thistles for you, and you shall eat its grasses. All your life you will sweat to master it until your dying day."[24]

This passage from the book of Genesis describes in mythical form how that fateful split took place. Adam and Eve and all their progeny were cursed to live a life of toil. They were cursed to live a life in which

24. Genesis 3:17-19.

294

they had to grow their food, rather than simply gather it from the bountiful supplies provided for them. Agriculture, in other words, was a curse, not a blessing as most people today believe. Furthermore, it was the Watchers who taught the ancient peoples the sciences, particularly that of agriculture. We learn this in the Sumerian texts, in the Books of Enoch and in the mythology of peoples of MesoAmerica. There seems to have been a concerted effort on the part of the Lords of the Planets to aid and abet humanity in its march toward certain doom.

Cain and Abel

For Daniel Quinn, author of *Ishmael*, a powerful novel about the history of the world as seen through the eyes of a wise, telepathic gorilla, the split between the "Leavers" (those who leave nature undisturbed) and the "Takers" (those who take from nature, but do not replenish) is alluded to in the story of Cain and Abel in chapter four of the Book of Genesis. Adam and Eve, we are told, had at first two sons, Cain being the first. Cain became a farmer and Abel became a shepherd.

> At harvest time Cain brought the Lord a gift of his farm produce and Abel brought the fatty cuts of meat from his best lambs, and presented them to the Lord. And the Lord accepted Abel's offering, but not Cain's. This made Cain both dejected and very angry. [25]

In his anger and jealousy, Cain, the farmer, killed his brother, the shepherd, and for this he was marked with an identifying mark [which Quinn believes was the whiteness of his skin] by God and banished. He was forced to become a fugitive and a wanderer.

For Quinn, this story is about the beginning of the expansion of the territory of the farmers (the Takers) and the annihilation of the herdsmen (the Leavers). In his book, the wise gorilla (Ishmael) teaches his naive and rather dense human pupil the truth about his own culture and why the human race has brought disaster upon itself. He asks his pupil to try to see the expansion of the agriculturalists through the eyes of the Semite herders of the Middle East whose lands were gradually taken from them thousands of years ago. Ishmael believed that it

---

25. Genesis 4:3-5.

was the herdsmen who must have started the story that the people of the Fertile Crescent had eaten from the fruit of the tree of knowledge, because they were acting like gods in taking away their lands.

Ishmael asks:

"Where did the Semites get the idea that people of the Fertile Crescent had eaten at the gods' own tree of knowledge?"

"Ah," I said. "I would say it was a sort of reconstruction. They looked at the people they were fighting and said, 'My God, how did they get this way?'"

"And the answer?"

"...Okay," I said...,"Here's how it would look to the Semites, I think. What's going on here is something wholly new. These aren't raiding parties. These aren't people drawing a line and baring their teeth at us to make sure we know they're there. These guys are saying.... `Our brothers from the north are saying that we've got to die. They're saying Abel has to be wiped out. They're saying we're not to be allowed to live. Now that's something new, and we don't get it. Why can't they live up there and be farmers and let us live down here and be herders? Why do they have to murder us?... They're saying, 'Nobody eats but us. All this food belongs to us and no one else can have any without our permission.' ...They're acting as if they were the gods themselves."[26]

The history of the human race as seen through the eyes of this sad but sage gorilla makes us see the truth about ourselves. It makes us see the horrible wrongs we as a species have committed against the sacred laws of nature and further, how we are still oblivious to this truth even as the world is crumbling around us. While modern humans see agriculture as the prelude to their ascent as mighty rulers of the Earth, Ishmael rightly sees it as the curse of the fallen who have been cast from the garden of the Creator.

Ishmael's solution to the world's dilemma is as follows:

"...The story of Genesis must be reversed. First, Cain must stop murdering Abel. This is essential if you're to survive. The Leavers are the endangered species most critical to the world—not because they are humans but because they alone can show the destroyers of the world that there is no one right way to

---

26. Quinn, 1992, pp. 176-177.

296

live. And then, of course, you must spit out the fruit of that for-bidden tree. You must absolutely and forever relinquish the idea that you know who should live and who should die on this planet."

His student protested: "One thing I know people will say to me is 'Are you suggesting we go back to being hunter-gather-ers?'"

"That of course is an inane idea," Ishmael said. "The Leaver life-style isn't about hunting and gathering, it's about letting the rest of the community live—and agriculturalists can do that as well as hunter-gatherers…. Your task is not to reach back but to reach forward."

"But to what? We can't just walk away from our civiliza-tion…."

"That's certainly true…you must be inventive. You're an inventive people, aren't you? You pride yourselves on that don't you?"

"Yes."

"Then invent."[27]

Saving the Future

Can the human race be saved? Or was the Mantis being MU telling the truth when he told Rebecca Grant that it's already too late? In a recent letter, Rebecca commented on this point:

Maybe they only want to frighten us into acting in our best interest while there is still time to act. The predictions might be nothing more than scare tactics designed to make us examine the problems we're creating for ourselves and correct them while they can be corrected…. If they're lying and their lies compel us to act in our own best interest, I think those lies are not only worth telling but worth repeating. Over and over again.[28]

Rita Perregrino, whose experience with the Reptilians has trauma-tized and changed her profoundly, still holds hope that the human race can reach a critical mass and change the world, if only they will listen and understand. She recently sent me a book, suggesting I read it and

---

27. Quinn, 1992, pp. 248-250.
28. Personal files, 1995.

contact the author to ask him to speak in El Paso. The book is *The Silva Mind Control Method*[29] by Jose Silva, a Texas native who, after two decades of research, developed a technique of self-hypnosis that helps people solve everyday problems, learn more easily and deepen their spiritual awareness. In short, he found a way to help anyone develop his psychic abilities by teaching him to use both hemispheres of the brain, while maintaining full awareness. Rita, who took the course and was disappointed only because she found she already possessed psychic abilities more advanced than what the basic course was teaching, nevertheless recommends it because she sees it as "part of the answer to what will happen in the future—aside from the physical Earth changes," which she sees as inevitable.

In another of Silva's books, written with Robert B. Stone, *You The Healer*, the authors describe what the world would be like if everyone used their psychic abilities:

> Can you imagine how life on Earth would be if everybody used both brain hemispheres? What would the effect be on world peace if differences between individuals—including world leaders—were addressed subjectively, Higher Self to Higher Self, and not as matters of *who* is right but of *what* is right? How would it be if geologists and other scientists were able to determine psychically the location of energy and mineral sources at will? What would bicameral business management be like, with executives being able to make dependable key decisions intuitively? What would the health-care profession be like if doctors switched their emphasis from treating illness to keeping patients healthy, and used the power of their minds more than chemicals and medications to make them well?[30]

Silva believes that at the present time only about 10% of the human population is now able to go within and use both hemispheres of the brain, but that once a critical number of humans have attained this ability, a miraculous change will occur on Earth, putting humanity back on the right path. He believes those who learn his system can train others, particularly their children, thus accelerating the process. Once the critical mass is reached, the human race will begin to resolve

29. Silva, 1972.
30. Silva, 1994, p. 220.

the world's ills by changing its ways and developing Earth-friendly technologies to feed the people without endangering other life forms and to clean up the Earth's environment. For Silva, the story of Adam and Eve refers to our inability to use the right hemisphere of our brain:

> Humanity has descended so deeply into the material, left-brain realm that our connection to the spiritual, right-brain realm has been left behind. Perhaps the first false step was taken in the Garden of Eden, when humanity first ate of the tree of the knowledge of good and evil. This is the material polarity on which the left brain thrives.... The fact remains that, however we reached this pass, today we are left-brained people, deaf to the voice of the Father within us. When the greatest healer of all time, Jesus, was asked where he obtained certain information, his reply was, "From the Father." He had never lost his connection to the Father.... Jesus exhorted us to seek the kingdom of heaven within us...and to function within God's righteousness, taking care of God's creatures with forgiveness, love and trust. If we did so, He promised, "And everything else will be added unto you." ...Can you imagine what would have happened here on Earth if we had understood Jesus' message originally? We would be living in paradise now. [31]

Hope for the Human Race

Is there hope for the human race as it exists today? Is it possible for people to change to the extent necessary to avert what seems to be an inevitable cataclysm? Or is violence and trauma necessary before our species can take its next leap in evolution? One thing is sure, the human race as we know it cannot continue for long on its present course. One way or another the human race will change. We must realize the disconcerting truth that evolution did not stop with our creation, as we have been led to believe by our religious and scientific institutions. We must learn to accept that we are not exactly the crowning glory of God's creation, but that we are, in fact, a defective, experimental prototype for some future, more advanced model yet to be unveiled.

31. Silva, 1994, pp. 225-226.

It is only when we accept the reality of who we are and where we fit into the hierarchy of God's creatures that we will be able to deal with who the extraterrestrials are and what they are doing to us. Those who see the "alien presence" as evil because of the liberties they take with us, the procedures they perform on us and the lack of respect they show us have not taken responsibility for what the human race has done to this Earth and to all of its other life forms. In contrast to the aliens who are abducting humans in the still of the night, using them for their purposes, erasing their traumatic memories and gently tucking them back in bed, the human race's behavior is by far the more reprehensible and barbaric. Those who have condemned the aliens for killing our cattle and other animals and surgically removing organs for their purposes have not fully considered what humans do to animals every day as we destroy their habitats and casually use them for our sustenance.

And those who worry that the aliens are here to enslave us have not yet considered the possibility that we are already enslaved on the lowest rung of existence—the dark world of the physical universe. Finally, those who believe that aliens are all Satanic, representatives of the fallen angels, have not accepted that we are also fallen creatures, who when given the secret of our own salvation, chose to ignore it, misrepresent it and worship it, rather than embrace it and live it.

For the abductees, to whom this book is dedicated, there is a parting message. You should know that in the past, when you have felt that you were going insane, it was only because the world was insane and you were different. It is in you, and others like you who are connected to the Father, that our hope for a better future lies. Your knowledge and special perspective is needed now more than ever before. You are needed. Your fellow humans need you to stand up and speak about your experiences and to teach the rest of us how to reconnect to the spiritual world. There is much to do and little time. Your wisdom far surpasses that of the scientists on TV, the ministers who preach from the pulpit and the professors who lecture at our universities. Have confidence in what you know—do not be afraid to make yourselves be heard.

An abductee who has never told her story publicly, and who is riddled with insecurities and fears, recently wrote to me from her home state of Indiana to share with me her profound experiences and insights. Her words, like those of the other experiencers I have encountered, are full of wisdom and secret knowledge, consistent with what so many others have revealed to me:

> It is predicted by religious men that the Earth will come to an end when the demons and the angels fight a war in heaven. Well, the planet will not blow up, but life, here as we know it, will end. This has already begun to happen. There is a deep unrest in the Earth and in the people; there are fires, earthquakes, floods, human destruction of the environment, the social structure, morals...so much power and greed trying to control everything and everybody. If we don't stop it, it will be done for us, and our slate will be wiped clean, *again.* Yes, there could very well be a war fought over us. Too much time and effort has been put into creating us that the spiritually intelligent guardians will fight to keep the bad races from destroying it all. When the planets begin lining up and devastating changes begin happening on Earth, we will be vulnerable to everything. Whether we live through it or not, our hybrid children are the future, our species will live on through them. This world has been through it several times before, and we keep coming back to begin again...each time we are advanced a little more, we get closer to our original purpose, "being one with God." Each of us carries within us a piece of God—that common, spiritual thread that ties *all* life together, no matter who we are, what we are, where we come from. We are all of God.[32]

This, in the final analysis, is the message of the UFO. At the core of its mystery lies the secret of the evolution of the human spirit—that eternal journey that each soul makes to find its way back to the light from which it came. We cannot study the UFO without studying ourselves and facing who we are, where we came from and where we are going. And we cannot understand the UFO if we do not understand what the shamans are telling us—that we are all of God.

---

32. Private files, 1994.

CHAPTER 15

AFTERWORD

"Darwin's theory of evolution is more than a hypothesis."

—*Pope John Paul II*

The Coming Transformation

Whether we agree with the concept of the God hypothesis or not, those of us fortunate enough to be living at the end of the second millennium must at least agree that these are exciting times. For thousands of years, change for the human race occurred slowly, biding its time until the next great leap in human evolution. But now, with advanced technology that allows information to be transmitted around the globe almost instantaneously, change is occurring at a dizzying speed, making it difficult to keep up with new discoveries and new ideas. Some of these, such as the discovery of other worlds outside our solar system and of evidence that life once existed on Mars, have begun to cause a rapid change in perception about the nature of the universe, the nature of reality and the nature of God.

As I write these words in February, 1997, there are already millions of persons in the U.S. alone who have begun to understand that this change in perception is but the beginning of a major transformation of human society that will inevitably sweep the globe in the coming years. Whether it is seen as a passing fad or something more significant, the current "UFO mania" that grips society and is manifested through a media blitz of movies, TV shows, books and magazines is raising our awareness at a rapid pace. The world is awakening to a new reality in which humanity, rather than being the epitome of God's creation, is instead on the lower rungs of the evolutionary ladder, surrounded by highly advanced, alien-looking life forms. To make this revelation even more ego-shattering for us is the understanding that these often grotesque and frightening beings consider themselves our caretakers, and perhaps even our owners. If such awareness had been sprung on the human race suddenly, it would no doubt have shattered our reality so profoundly that it would have done irreparable damage to our social and political structures. Instead, this awareness has been brought about gradually over a period of at least 50 years, so that now, for those who are prepared to accept it, the knowledge that we are not alone and that we have never been alone is available. Those who resist accepting this knowledge risk having their realities shattered more violently later on, as events unfold, making denial all but impossible. Whichever way the psyche is transformed to this new reality, the result is the same. Each person must individually confront the same issues and try to resolve the same questions regarding God, the universe and the nature of reality.

Demystifying God

Perhaps the greatest impact of the God hypothesis, for those who accept it, is that it, to a great extent, demystifies the enigma of God and of those Biblical events held sacred by religious institutions. Some might argue that religion without mystery is not religion at all, but something else entirely—more akin to science. In fact, the God hypothesis is the result of a re-examination of ancient doctrines through modern, scientific eyes. It is an attempt to address the issues of God and spirituality with a degree of scientific objectivity. In the end, the result is a little like finding out that there is no Santa Claus, and that instead of being made by elves in the North Pole, Christmas toys are manufactured in China by slave laborers. At first, the disappointment is crushing, but soon the child realizes that the spirit of Santa remains intact. For the knowledge that his parents were the real Santa all along, and the realization that it was through their love that the gifts magically appeared on Christmas morning, makes the demystification of the experience an even more profound and beautiful revelation.

304

The term "revelation" in this context seems exceedingly appropriate and pertinent to the current examination of the UFO mystery and its impact on humanity. It seems all too obvious, in light of the previous discussion, that the human race is even now being presented with a grand revelation of Biblical proportions. This is a time when we must confront the reality of who we really are and of our true relationship to the Creator. The truth, when it is recognized, may be crushing to our egos, but in the end we are left with the knowledge that there is a God and that there are indeed angels—it's just that they're not exactly what we expected. Many of us would prefer angels to have wings and God to be an old man with a long beard sitting on a cloud. Not many will be eager to accept that angels and demons ride in flying saucers.

Aliens or Angels?

For those who crave mystery in their religion, there is still plenty of mystery left to resolve. Aside from the awesome mystery of the nature of the Creator, we are still left with many other unresolved and currently unknowable issues. The God hypothesis does not answer one of the crucial questions regarding those beings who have been variously called gods, angels, aliens, demons and extraterrestrials. It gives no definite answer to the question of where their physical bodies originated. Are the reptilians, the mantises, the Greys and the blondes a product of evolution? The God hypothesis does not explicitly contradict many of the other popular UFO theories. It is possible that the beings are gods, aliens and interdimensional travelers all at the same time. It is also possible that they, at one time, passed through the same trials and tribulations that humans are going through today. We must consider the possibility that the human species (or some advanced model of ourselves) might some day advance toward their higher level of existence. In that case, they may simply represent life forms that have evolved so far beyond our understanding that to us they can only appear to be godlike.

But if that is so, it must still be recognized that membership in their club requires knowledge of advanced spiritual laws and a more sophisticated understanding of the creative, universal consciousness that we call God. Without such knowledge, they would have long ago used their incredible technological powers to eradicate competing species, just as we have here on Earth. Instead, what we find is a kind of

305

mutual respect and an alliance that operates within a set of spiritual laws that are obvious to all those with advanced psychic abilities.

On the other hand, it could very well be that these beings were all created at a higher level than humanity from the very beginning and that a natural hierarchy of intelligences is necessary to maintain balance in God's amazing universe. Such a conclusion makes it more difficult for us to consider them merely as aliens from other planets, and it makes such terms as "angels" and "gods" seem more appropriate.

To be sure, the God hypothesis does have its limitations. As a scientific theory, however, it seems to answer many questions about the nature of humanity and about the current course of human events. By merging science and religion, we can begin to see that there is a middle ground between the seemingly irreconcilable positions of Darwinism and Creationism. It provides us with logical and elegant answers to many of the mysteries of science and religion that have puzzled our best minds for centuries—mysteries regarding the existence of the soul and of our innate psychic abilities. Its predictive capability can be used to explain other phenomena and to foresee the course of future events. By understanding that the UFO mystery is in fact part of the great Revelation prophesied in the Bible by ETs who could predict that the human race would be in its current predicament at this particular point in time, we can begin to see that forecasting future events is not so difficult. Most obviously, the theory suggests that the Watchers are correct about the damage we have inflicted on the Earth's ecosystem. The ecological damage appears to have reached a state of crisis in which all life forms on the planet are endangered. Although this may seem abundantly clear to some already, evidence of this should become increasingly more obvious during the next 10 to 20 years. Disruptive climatic changes, new diseases, earth crust upheavals, food shortages and other cataclysms associated with global warming should increase until their causes are seriously addressed by human society. So too will the global strife created by human perceptions of differentiation. Wars and bloodshed caused by racial, ethnic and religious differences seem destined to eventually bring the human race to the brink of some great catastrophe that will force us to realize that we are all members of the same species and that we have a common need to protect our own kind from the threat of total extinction.

The seriousness of these problems will force humans to re-evaluate the basic scientific and religious philosophies that have brought them to the brink of disaster. It will force people to recognize that spiritual laws supersede those tenets of science and religion that have been the basis for modern human society. Spirituality that embraces an understanding of science and disengages from religious institutions and their dogmas will begin to flourish, as will interest in new ways to tap into the unconscious mind—such as remote viewing, hypnosis and meditation. (Indeed, this is already occurring.)

The End of Scientific Materialism

As human society undergoes a major shift in paradigm, the "Berlin Wall" of scientific materialism will come crashing down. This will make it easier for more and more mainstream scientists, government officials and respected celebrities to come forward to acknowledge their own supernatural and paranormal experiences. At some point, unimpeachable sources in the form of celebrities and public officials may reveal that they too have had alien abduction experiences. Others will make public their first-hand knowledge of covert government UFO projects. In fact, the unraveling of government UFO secrecy has already begun and will eventually be completely uncovered as public officials bend to public demand and as the reality of UFOs becomes undeniable. In this regard, the public will no doubt be shocked at the extent to which our military has been involved in the UFO mystery.

However, scientific materialism will not fall without one last determined effort to defend a material reality. For example, NASA's recent involvement in the announcement that primitive life may have existed on Mars at one time indicates that the scientific/government community is trying to gain control over the dissemination of information relating to ETs. Perhaps seeing the inevitability of public awareness of extraterrestrial life, our government and mainstream scientists are moving to position themselves as the primary authorities on the subject. The current rush to send probes to Mars in search of further evidence of life seems to some a well orchestrated effort to prevent outsiders from co-opting the scientific authorities.

For years, independent researchers have loudly proclaimed that there is evidence that Mars was once home to advanced civilizations, pointing to NASA's own photos taken in 1976 during the Viking Mars mission.[1] Those remarkable photos show what appear to be a sphinx-like face carved out of a mountain and several pyramids in a region of Mars known as Cydonia. Until recently, NASA and other mainstream scientists have scoffed at the idea that the objects are anything more than optical illusions and natural formations. But recently there has been some indications that the official position is changing. Even Carl Sagan seemed to reverse his previously rigid statements on the photos by saying that study of the photos is "solid science." Many observers within the UFO research community believe that NASA has long known that the photos depict ancient relics of a lost ET civilization.

As the paradigm shift progresses, the reigning institutions of power will no doubt begin to feel even more threatened. It might be worthwhile to speculate on how far they might go to protect their hold on knowledge and information. In this regard, it serves us well to remember that history is full of examples of the desperate measures to which institutions have stooped to defend their power base. When the high priests of the Hebrews and officials of the Roman Empire felt threatened by the radical ideas of Jesus, they had him put to death. When the high priests of the Christian Church felt threatened by new scientific views, they did not hesitate to murder Giordano Bruno and others who believed that life could exist elsewhere in the universe. Galileo was imprisoned for his view that the Earth revolved around the sun and was released only after he recanted.

Today, the high priests of science use the government classification system as an excuse to hide UFO and ET information in the name of national security. By doing so for the past 50 or so years, they have been successful in controlling our perceptions about the nature of reality, the nature of the beings who are interacting with the human race and about the true origins and nature of the human species. Their hold on this information is severely threatened by a new paradigm in which we learn that each one of us has the power to communicate directly with ETs, with the dead, or even with Jesus. They tremble at the thought of a public that might suddenly regain its psychic abilities and begin remote-viewing covert government operations such as activities at Area 51 in Nevada or the Roswell incident. Religious institutions would also be threatened if people realized that they didn't need a

---

1. Hoagland, 1987.

church to find God. If people realized their full psychic potential, they would simply see the church as an unnecessary middleman in their quest for spiritual enlightenment. Just as science's hold on power depends on our continued belief in a material world, the church's hold on power depends on our continued belief that God is outside of us and that the church controls access to Him. A new science that preaches interconnectedness and personal power then is a danger to the foundations of modern society. No wonder science has been slow to embrace the findings of quantum physics or to promote the concept of the holographic universe.

Because of this, both science and religion will urge the public to see the ET presence as a threat. Science will try hard to depict aliens in material terms and as a threat to national security, while religions will use fear of demonic forces to keep their flocks close to the fold. As with the Spanish inquisition, there will be efforts by both science and religion to discredit those who step over the line. A good example is the recent efforts by the faculty of the department of psychiatry at Harvard Medical School to fire Dr. John Mack after his book on alien abductions was published. Only a massive letter-writing campaign by other physicians and academicians persuaded the faculty to drop their complaint. With regard to remote viewing, the CIA has already attempted to discredit the success of the psychics in the top-secret military program. The CIA's assertion that the project was a failure is most certainly disingenuous. Several of the project's participants are now on record saying that remote viewing is highly accurate when used correctly. It is no secret that intelligence agencies are continuing to use the remote viewing services of private companies.

A similar campaign is being waged by the American Medical Association against practitioners of hypnotherapy. Much public attention has been called to the so-called "false-memory syndrome," implying that incompetent hypnotherapists implant ideas in the minds of unsuspecting clients. In some states there are efforts to place legal restrictions on the use of hypnosis, allowing only physicians to practice what in reality is only a mind relaxation technique.

On a more sinister note, some people believe that intelligence agencies are developing or are already using technology that can interrupt human brain waves and interfere with or destroy a person's psychic abilities. Those in the military remote-viewing program have made public statements to the effect that the military is seeking ways to use psychic powers as a weapon to disable or kill enemy agents. It is also believed that advanced technology might have also yielded electro-magnetic weapons capable of transmitting low frequency waves that disrupt human brain functions over large portions of the Earth's surface. Although such technology might be developed under the guise of national defense, its actual use would be conducted in absolute secrecy and would be impossible for us or our elected public officials to monitor. [2]

Further revelations regarding advanced ancient civilizations here on Earth are likely to come to light with new archeological discoveries. But just as with the Dead Sea Scrolls, this information is being controlled by zealots dedicated to the preservation of the status quo. In Egypt, where archeologists have discovered new hidden chambers within the great pyramid and beneath the sphinx, the Egyptian authorities are attempting to maintain secrecy over these important findings and prevent those with new-science perspectives from examining the evidence. New evidence about the origins of these monuments will no doubt cause a growing realization among mainstream scientists that they have been terribly wrong about the history and origins of the human race.

Archeological discoveries will continue to reveal that much of what the Bible says is based on fact. New evidence for the existence of historical figures such as Moses and Jesus is likely to be found. Religious institutions will at some point find it necessary to make official public statements regarding the nature of flying saucers and their relationship to religious beliefs and the Bible. The issue of how to deal with the reality of extraterrestrials will become the most burning issue for both science and religion in the future.

As science is transformed from its "nuts-and-bolts" view of reality and begins to accept the holographic nature of the universe, it will spawn quantum technology that will make present science seem primitive. This "future science" will, by today's standards, seem miraculous and will, in fact, make humans seem more like gods. A good example of this is the breakthrough in cloning technology announced by Scottish scientists in February, 1997. Using the holographic princi-

---

2. Begich, 1995.

ple of nonlocality, they successfully cloned the first mammal, a sheep named Dolly, and set the stage for the eventual and inevitable cloning of human beings.[3] The announcement touched off a fire storm of ethical and religious debate regarding our intrusion upon a domain which had always been reserved for God. In New York, state senator John Marchi immediately submitted a bill outlawing human cloning because "we ought not to permit a cottage industry in the God business."[4]

Yet, as we know from the study of UFOs, cloning of sentient beings may be a very ancient science indeed. Today's breakthroughs in quantum technology make it easier for us to understand how the many "miracles" reported in the ancient texts might have been accomplished. Such things as virgin births, creation of new species (even our own), aerial phenomena and angelic apparitions lose their mystery when they are understood to have been caused by beings who possess highly advanced quantum technology.

And, finally, the debate over whether UFOs and aliens represent the forces of good or evil is certain to escalate, within both scientific and religious communities. Religious fundamentalists will no doubt lead the chorus of those who see only the work of Satan in the mystery of the flying saucer. An example of this occurred in February, 1997, when *Times of London* religious correspondent, Ruth Gledhill, reported that a former head of the British armed forces, Admiral of the Fleet Lord Hill-Knowlton, helped found a citizen's group called UFO Concern, out of worry that some UFO encounters are "definitely antithetical to orthodox Christian belief." The Rev. Paul Inglesby, a sub-deacon in an orthodox church was quoted as saying: "It is what they (UFOs) do, and the messages that come from them that are anti-Christian, or demonic."[5]

It will take the calming voices of those who are able to embrace the grander perspective, that the universe is paradoxical, to help prevent an overreaction and panic. Humanity's natural tendency to react in fear will be severely tested. For those with a broader perspective, who can see that good and evil are only human perceptions of the natural

3. *USA Today,* Feb. 25, 1997.
4. Associated Press, March 2, 1997.
5. Gledhill, 1997.

forces of positive and negative and are, in fact, just part of the evolutionary process, the ET presence can have a positive result. Public awareness of the existence of ETs will jolt humanity's understanding of its true place in the pecking order of life, and will most certainly cause a sober introspective evaluation of its self worth. Differences that seem great today, such as those between Christian, Jew and Muslim or between races of different colors, will wane in comparison to the shock of an alien presence. Humans will, for the first time, begin to see themselves as brothers and sisters of the same species and as Earthlings, rather than as members of particular nations or ethnic groups. The shock of learning the truth about who we are and how we got here will cause a total transformation in human thinking and force us to begin searching for new answers to the world's problems. In the end, we will discover that the answers lie within ourselves and that we share a common spirituality that allows us to transcend our differences and take our first, tentative step into that long-awaited golden age of peace foretold by the prophets of ancient times.

As scientists and theologians struggle to integrate this new paradigm into their existing view of reality, each will inevitably be driven toward a middle ground where reality is not so simply defined in black and white, but rather in an uncomfortable shade of gray (no pun intended). Even now, there are signs that each side is groping for a hand hold in this middle territory. In October of 1996, in an address to the Pontifical Academy of Sciences, a lay organization, Pope John Paul II declared that Darwin's theory of evolution is sound as long as it takes into account that creation was the work of God. Attempting to move the Church a step closer toward accepted scientific consensus, the Pope insisted that faith and science can mix together. He told his audience that new knowledge has confirmed that Darwin's theory of evolution is "more than a hypothesis."[6]

Ironically, the Pope's attempt to merge science and theology comes at a time when the theory of evolution is being challenged, even by some mainstream scientists. Rather than demonstrating how open-minded the Church can be, this belated effort only shows how behind the times theologians are in understanding the implications of the leading edge of scientific thinking. More than ever before, there is a

---

6. Associated Press, Oct. 25, 1996.

sound scientific basis for understanding the human soul and the concept of God as embodied in a conscious and living universe. It is this message that theologians should be pouncing on and conveying to the public. But it seems that this middle ground between science and religion, at least for now, is the domain of the new breed of independent thinkers who are beginning to capture the attention of the general public. As this ground swell of public demand for a new scientific/spiritual paradigm bursts forth into the new millennium, it will be these independent thinkers who lead the way toward a new understanding that is finally free of the old dogmas of science and religion.

The Holographic Metaphor

The message of the God hypothesis as proposed here, which is based on the scientific understanding that the universe is holographic in nature, is that all things in the universe are interconnected at the quantum level. This scientific/spiritual knowledge teaches us that physical reality is but an illusion that makes it appear that we are separate from God and from all other things. In this regard, we can see the holographic image as a metaphor for the entire universe. If we study the diagrams depicting the creation of the holographic image (See Figure 2 on page 67 and Figure 3 on page 68), we see that the image on the photographic plate is nothing but a series of concentric circles, bearing no resemblance whatsoever to the object photographed. The photographic film represents the material world in which everything seems separate. No two places on the photographic plate seem the same—it is a perfect example of differentiation. Yet, when we learn how to unlock its mystery by shining a beam of light at the film, a beautiful image appears, floating in mid air, like a spirit from another reality. That image, floating in a mysterious dimension, free of the constraints of time and space that bind our reality, represents the quantum dimension—the nonphysical world. This paradox assaults our senses and challenges us to consider the question of which is more real. Is the image of the concentric circles on the film more real than the image of the apple floating in space? It is tempting to answer in the affirmative because we can touch the film, but we can't touch the apple. Yet those may not be sound criteria upon which to base our conclusion. It may be, in fact, that the apple is more real and that the image of the circles is the illusion. Or we might conclude that they are both equally real and that the true nature of the universe is that it is paradoxical. This last conclusion may be closest to the truth. Good and evil, light and dark, physical and nonphysical are all, in fact, the same. From God's perspective, there are no differences.

If we can learn this lesson, then we can see that the physical world is a place where our senses are confused into believing in separation and that it is our task to see through the illusion. When we are able to do so, all those differences we saw before dissolve before our eyes, like a mirage. It is our challenge to learn to see from God's perspective and to love unconditionally, as God loves. This can only be achieved through an understanding that we are all one.

The physical world presents us with constant tests to see if we are learning. Humans are constantly confronted with a barrage of things that are easy to fear and to hate: people of different colors and beliefs, people who hurt our feelings or who cheat us, people who hurt us or who hurt our loved ones, or even hideous beings who take us away in the night. Each is a test that provides us with an opportunity to demonstrate that we can love and respect all living things as the Creator does—equally and without prejudice. When we can do that, we are ready to leave this illusory world of the physical domain forever and advance in our journey toward the oneness of God.

ABOUT THE AUTHOR

FIGURE 19. *Francisco J. (Joe) Lewels*

Francisco J. (Joe) Lewels is an independent researcher and free lance writer whose interests in religion and science led to an intense study of the UFO phenomenon. He holds a Ph.D. in journalism and mass communication from the University of Missouri, and is the author of the book, *Uses of the Media by the Chicano Movement,* as well as many scholarly articles.

He served for ten years as associate professor and chairman of the departments of journalism and mass communication at the University of Texas at El Paso where he specialized in media law, freedom of the press and the social impact of the mass media. He served as a communication consultant at the U.S. Department of Justice, Community Relations Service; as editor of the *Freedom of Information Digest* and as assistant to the chief editor of the U.S. Army *Aviation Digest.* As a captain in the U.S. Army while in the Republic of Vietnam, he served as a reconnaissance pilot and as the public information officer for the 17th Aviation Group. He holds the Bronze Star and the Air Medal with oak leaf cluster. He may be reached through the publisher.

ACKNOWLEDGEMENTS

This book could never have been written without the help of the following people whose inspiration and/or assistance I sincerely appreciate.

For his tireless pursuit of scientific truth and for his eloquent and articulate writings, I wish to thank Michael Talbot. Although we never met, his influence on me has been great. For his courageous work in the field of alien abductions and for his willingness to risk his formidable reputation, I wish to thank Dr. John Mack. His example should serve as an inspiration to all men and women of science to courageously accept the findings of their research, regardless of the consequences. For helping us see the Bible through the modern eyes of a scientist/theologian and for demonstrating to all that science and religion are not incompatible, I thank Dr. Barry Downing.

For her willingness to risk her professional reputation and for volunteering untold hours in pursuit of knowledge, I wish to thank Dr. Roberta Fennig, without whom this book could never have been a reality. For their unselfish dedication to the pursuit of truth, their strict adherence to sound principles of scientific investigation, and for their friendship, I thank Linda Moulton Howe and John Carpenter. For his valuable help and guidance and for his persistence in his search for truth, I wish to thank Walt Andrus.

For their willingness to share their most intimate and private experiences, their wisdom and their knowledge, I thank the many "abductees" who have cooperated in this work. First and foremost among them is Rita Perregrino, whose courage in facing her worst nightmares has been an inspiration to all around her. Her friendship and opinion is highly valued. Although there are too many others to name here, I wish to acknowledge the help of the following persons who have shared with me their experiences and insights: "Rebecca Grant," Shona Bear Clark, Linda Seebach, Marika, Sharon, Debbie and Anita A. Also: Sabrina, John, Joan, Anita O., Mary, Lucy, Clarisse, Debra, Greg, Deanna, Diana, Joe, Craig, Bob, Jack, Sandy, Toni and many others.

For his expert guidance into the fields of spirituality and religion through his capacity as a former Catholic priest, and for his friendship and assistance as a master hypnotherapist in helping me learn about the mysteries of the human mind, I wish to acknowledge Dr. Romeo Di Benedetto. For his valuable insights into the nature and variety of alien life forms and for his graciousness in allowing me to use several of his fine illustrations, I wish to thank David W. Chace.

And for their courageous perseverance in the face of ridicule and personal attacks, I thank the pioneers of UFO research and all UFO investigators everywhere.

REFERENCES

- Arvey, Michael. *The End of the World*. San Diego, CA: Greenhaven Press, 1992.
- Ashpole, Edward. *The Search for Extraterrestrial Intelligence*. London: Blandford Press, 1989.
- Associated Press. "Climate Study Details Threat to Asian Area." *El Paso Times*, August 12, 1994, p. 2B.
- —. "Humans Are Guilty of Causing Global Warming, Panel Convinced." *El Paso Times*, September 11, 1995, p. 1B.
- —. "Meteorite Suggests Primitive Life on Mars." *El Paso Times*, August 7, 1996, p. 1A.
- —. "Pope: God, Evolution can Co-exist." *El Paso Times*, October 25, 1996, p. 6A.
- —. "Theory of the Universe Proves an Elusive Concept." *El Paso Times*, June 13, 1996, p. 1B.
- —. "World Will Run Short of Food, Report Warns." *El Paso Times*, January 16, 1994, p. 1B.
- —. "UN Backs Nuclear Test Ban Treaty." *El Paso Times*, September 11, 1996, p. 12A.
- —. "Dolly the Sheep Stirs Hopes, Fears Worldwide." *Spartanburg Herald-Journal*, March 2, 1997, p. A19.
- Barnstone, Willis, ed. *The Other Bible*. San Francisco, CA: Harper, 1984.
- Begich, Nick, and Jeane Manning. *Angels Don't Play This HAARP*. Anchorage, AK: Earthpulse Press, 1995.
- Blum, Howard. *Out There*. New York: Simon and Schuster, 1990.
- Bohm, David. *Quantum Theory*. Englewood Cliffs, NJ: Prentice-Hall, Inc., 1951.
- —. *Unfolding Meaning*. London: Ark Paperbacks, 1987.

- *The Book*. Wheaton, IL: Tyndale House Publishers, Inc., 1986.
- Boulay, R.A. *Flying Serpents and Dragons*. Clearwater, FL: Galaxy Books, 1990.
- Boulay, R.A. *Dragon Power*. Clearwater, FL: Galaxy Books, 1992.
- Bramley, William. *The Gods of Eden*. San Jose, CA: Dahlin Family Press, 1989.
- Brookesmith, Peter. *UFO: The Complete Sightings*. New York: Barnes and Nobles Books, 1995.
- Brown, Courtney. *Cosmic Voyage*. New York: Dutton Books, 1996.
- Bruce, F.F. *Paul, Apostle of the Heart Set Free*. Exeter, NH: The Paternoster Press, 1977.
- Bullard, Thomas E. *UFO Abductees: The Measure of a Mystery*. Mt. Rainier, MD: Fund for UFO Research, 1987.
- Carpenter, John. "Reptilians and other Unmentionables." *MUFON UFO Journal*, April, 1993, pp. 10-11.
- Chase, David. *A Visual Guide to Alien Beings*. Seattle, WA: David Chace, 1995.
- Chopra, Deepak. *Ageless Body, Timeless Mind*. New York: Harmony Books, 1993.
- Colburn, Theo, Diane Dumanoski and John Peterson Meyers. *Our Stolen Future*. New York: Dutton Books, 1996.
- Couliano, Ioan P. *The Tree of Gnosis*. San Francisco, CA: Harper, 1990.
- Cremo, Michael A. and Richard L. Thompson. *The Hidden History of the Human Race*. Badger, CA: Govardhan Hill Publishing, 1994.
- Crichton, Michael. *Jurassic Park*. New York: Alfred A. Knopf, 1990.
- Crick, Francis. *Life Itself*. New York: Simon and Schuster, 1981.
- Crossen, Cynthia. "Clamorous Pro and Con Campaigns Herald Book's Launch." *The Wall Street Journal*, March 7, 1996, p. 1B.
- Crowder, David. "Mars Meteorite Excites Many, Raises Questions." *El Paso Times*, August 8, 1966, p. A1.
- Davies, Paul. "The Harmony of the Spheres." *Time*, February 5, 1996, p. 58.

318

- Deardorff, James W. *Celestial Teachings*. Mill Spring, NC: Wild Flower Press, 1990.
- Deardorff, James W. *Jesus in India: A Reexamination of Jesus' Asian Traditions in the Light of Evidence Supporting Reincarnation*. Bethesda, MD: International Scholars Publications: 1994.
- de Duve, Christian. *Vital Dust: The Origin and Evolution of Life on Earth*. New York: Basic Books, 1995.
- Dibitonto, Giorgio. *UFO Contact From Angels in Starships*. Oakridge, OR: Factbooks, 1990.
- Downing, Barry H. *The Bible and Flying Saucers*. Philadelphia, PA: J.B. Lippencott Co., 1968.
- —. "The God Hypothesis." *MUFON UFO Journal*, No. 245, October, 1988.
- —. "The Rock of Ages Principle." *MUFON UFO Journal*, May 1990, pp. 10-12.
- —. "ET Contact: The Religious Dimension." *MUFON Symposium Proceedings*, July 1990, pp. 45-60.
- —. "UFOs and Religion: Of Things Visible and Invisible." *MUFON Symposium Proceedings*, July 1993, pp. 33-48.
- —. "Exodus as a Paradigm of UFO Strategy." *MUFON UFO Journal*, October 1994, pp. 8-11.
- Eisenman, Robert and Michael Wise. *The Dead Sea Scrolls Uncovered*. Rockport, MA: Element, 1992.
- "Evolution's Big Bang." *Time*. December 4, 1995, pp. 68-72.
- Fowler, Raymond E. *The Watchers*. New York: Bantam Books, 1990.
- —. *The Andreasson Affair*. Mill Spring, NC: Wild Flower Press, 1994. Reprint.
- —. *The Watchers II*. Mill Spring, NC: Wild Flower Press, 1995.
- Fuller, John G. *The Interrupted Journey*. New York: Dell Publishing Co., 1967.
- Funk, Robert W. and Roy W. Hoover. *The Five Gospels*. New York: McMillan, 1993.
- Gannett News Service, "Odds Against Sperm Grow More Daunting." *El Paso Times*, March 25, 1996, p.4D.

- Garrett, Laurie. *The Coming Plague*. New York: Farrar, Straus and Giroux, 1994.
- Gledhill, Ruth. "Defense Chief Warns of 'Satanic UFOs'", AUFORA Update, March 1, 1997.
- Grof, Stanislav. *The Holotropic Mind*. San Francisco, CA: Harper, 1992.
- Hancock, Graham. *Fingerprints of the Gods*. New York: Crown Publishers Inc., 1995.
- Hapgood, Charles H. *The Earth's Shifting Crust*. Philadelphia, PA: Chilton, 1958.
- Hoagland, Richard C. *The Monuments of Mars: A City on the Edge of Forever*. Berkeley, CA: North Atlantic Books, 1987.
- Hopkins, Budd. *Intruders*. New York: Ballantine Books, 1987.
- —. *Missing Time*. New York: Ballantine Books, 1981.
- Huyghe, Patrick. "Antimatter." *Omni*, October 1994, p. 101.
- Hyndman, Roy D. "Giant Earthquakes of the Pacific Northwest." *Scientific American*, December 1995, pp. 66-75.
- Jacobs, David M. *Secret Life*. New York: Simon and Schuster, 1992.
- Jung, C.G. *Flying Saucers: A Modern Myth of Things Seen in the Skies*. New York, The New American Library, A Signet Book, 1959.
- Keyhoe, Donald. *The Flying Saucer Conspiracy*. New York: Henry Holt & Co., 1955.
- Knight-Ridder News Service, "Experts: Global Warming For Real." *El Paso Times*, November 30, 1995, p. A1.
- Krasner, A. M. *The Wizard Within*. Santa Ana, CA: American Board of Hypnotherapy Press, 1990.
- Kulp, Thomas. "UFOs A Demonic Conspiracy." *Fate*, April 1996, pp. 32-35.
- Lachica, Eduardo. "Asia Faces Increasing Pressure to Act as Global Warming Threatens its Coasts." *The Wall Street Journal*, August 23, 1994, p. 1A.
- Lambert, W. G. and A. R. Millard. *Atra-Hasis, The Babylonian Story of the Flood, With the Sumerian Flood Story*. Oxford: The Clarendon Press, 1969.

- Lamsa, George M. *Holy Bible: From the Ancient Eastern Text.* New York: Harper, 1985.
- Lawlor, Robert. *Voices of the First Day.* Rochester, VT: Inner Traditions International, Ltd., 1991.
- Leatherberry, Keith. *UFOs Exposed in Scripture.* Midvale, UT: NW Publishers, 1995.
- Leedom, Tim C., ed. *The Book Your Church Doesn't Want You to Read.* Dubuque, Iowa: Kendall/Hunt Publishing Co., 1993.
- Lemonick, Michael D.. "The Killers All Around." *Time,* September 12, 1994, pp. 62-70.
- —. "Not So Fertile Ground." *Time,* September 19, 1994, pp. 68-70.
- —. "One Big, Bad Iceberg." *Time,* March 20, 1995, p. 65.
- —. "Are the Bible Stories True?" *Time,* December 18, 1995, pp. 63-70.
- Lewels, Joe. "Over the Rainbow: Quantum Physics Discovers the Holographic Universe." *MUFON Symposium Proceedings,* July 1995, pp. 119-134.
- —. "The Reptilians: Humanity's Historical Link to the Serpent Race." *Fate,* June 1996, pp. 48-52.
- Linden, Eugene. "Burned By Warming." *Time,* March 14, 1994, p. 79.
- Lorenzen, Coral and Jim Lorenzen. *Abducted! Confontations with Beings From Outer Space.* New York: Berkley, 1977.
- Mack, John E. *Abduction: Human Encounters With Aliens.* New York: Ballentine, 1995.
- Macvey, John W. *Time Travel.* Chelsea, MI: Scarborough House, 1990.
- Marais, E. *The Soul of the White Ant.* London: Cape, 1971.
- Meier, Eduard et. al. *The Talmud of Jmmanuel: The Original Gospel of Matthew.* Mill Spring, NC: Wild Flower Press, 1989.
- Miley, Michael. "Remote Viewing and Alien Targets." *UFO.* Vol. II, No. 3. 1996, pp.34-42.
- Milik, Joseph, ed. *The Books of Enoch.* Oxford: Clarendon Press, 1976.
- Mills, Stephen. "Last Chance for the First Peoples." *Omni,* August, 1994, pp. 63-67.

- Milner, Richard. *The Encyclopedia of Evolution*. New York: Facts on File, Inc., 1990.
- Moody, Raymond. *Life After Life*. New York: Bantam Books, 1976.
- Morris, Richard. *The Edges of Science*. New York: Prentice Hall, 1990.
- Moulton Howe, Linda. *An Alien Harvest*. Littleton, CO: Linda Moulton Howe Productions, 1989.
- —. *Glimpses of Other Realities*. Huntingdon Valley, PA: LMH Productions, 1993.
- *The New American Bible*. (St. Joseph Edition.). New York: Catholic Book Publishing Co., 1970.
- Pacheco, Nelson and Tommy Blann. *Unmasking the Enemy,* Arlington, VA: Bendan Press, 1994.
- Pagels, Elaine. *The Gnostic Gospels*. New York: Random House, 1979.
- "Paranormal Borderline." Interview with Gordon Cooper. UPN Television Network, May 7, 1996.
- Peat, David. *Synchronicity: The Bridge Between Matter and Mind*. New York: Bantam Books, 1987.
- Pottenger, Doris. *UFOs, Aliens or Demons?* Middleton, ID: CHJ Publishers, 1990.
- Pribram, Karl. *Languages of the Brain*. Monterrey, CA: Wadsworth Publishing, 1977.
- Pritchard, Andrea; David E. Pritchard, John E. Mack, Pam Kasey and Claudia Yapp, eds. *Alien Discussions: Proceedings of the Abduction Study Conference held at MIT*. Cambridge, MA: North Cambridge Press, 1994.
- Quinn, Daniel. *Ishmael*. New York: Bantam/Turner Books, 1992.
- Ring, Kenneth. *The Omega Project*. New York: William Morrow and Co., 1992.
- Roper Poll. "Unusual Personal Experiences." Bigelow Foundation, 1992.
- Russell, D. S. *The Old Testament Pseudepigrapha*. Philadelphia, PA: Fortress Press, 1987.
- Sagan, Carl. *The Dragons of Eden*. New York: Ballantine Books, 1977.

- Schellhorn, Cope G. *Extraterrestrials in Biblical Prophecy*. Madison, WI: Horus House Press, 1989.
- Schnabel, Jim. "Psi Files: The Real X Files." The Discovery Channel, Skywatch series, August 1995.
- Sheldrake, Ruppert. *A New Science of Life*. London: Blond and Briggs, 1981.
- Silva, Jose. *The Silva Mind Control Method*. New York: Pocket Books, 1977.
- — and Robert B.Stone. *You the Healer*. Tiburon, CA: H.J. Kramer Inc., 1994.
- Sitchin, Zechariah. *Genesis Revisited*. New York: Avon Books, 1990.
- —. "The 12th Planet--Key to the UFO Enigma." *MUFON Symposium Proceedings*, July 1991, pp. 15-28.
- —. *The Wars of Gods and Men*. New York: Avon Books, 1985.
- —. *When Time Began*. Santa Fe, N.M: Bear and Co.,1993.
- Strieber, Whitley. *Communion*. New York: Beech Tree Books, 1987.
- —. *Transformation*. New York: Beech Tree Books, 1988.
- —. *Breakthrough*. New York: Harper Collins, 1995.
- —. *The Secret School*. New York: Beech Tree Books, 1996.
- Swann, Ingo. *Everybody's Guide to Natural ESP*. Los Angeles: Jeremy P. Tarcher, 1991.
- —. *Your Nostradamus Factor*. New York: A Fireside Book, 1993.
- Talbot, Michael. *Beyond the Quantum*. New York: Bantam Books, 1988.
- —. *Mysticism and the New Physics*. New York: Penguin Books, 1981.
- —. "Synchronicity and the Holographic Universe." Thinking Allowed Productions, 1992.
- —. *The Holographic Universe*. New York: Harper Perennial, 1991.
- The Jesus Seminar. *The Five Gospels*. New York: HarperCollins, 1996.
- Thompson, Richard L. *Alien Identities*. San Diego, CA: Govardhan Hill Inc., 1993.
- Turner, Karla. *Masquerade of Angels*. Roland, AK: Kelt Works, 1994.

- *Unusual Personal Experiences.* Las Vegas, NV: Bigelow Holding Corp., 1992.
- *USA Today.* "Human Cloning: Unsettling and Now Perhaps Inevitable."February 25, 1997, p. 14A.
- Vallée, Jacques. *Dimensions: A Casebook of Alien Contact.* New York: Ballantine Books, 1988.
- —. *Passport to Magonia.* Chicago, IL: Regnery, 1969.
- Van Biema, David. "The Gospel Truth?" *Time,* April 8, 1996, pp. 52-56.
- Van der Post, Laurens. *Lost World of the Kalahari.* Orlando, FL: Harcourt, Brace, Jovanovich, Publishers, 1986.
- Waldholz, Michael. "Scientists Debate Future Threat of Common Chemicals." *The Wall Street Journal,* March 7, 1996.
- Walters, Ed. *The Gulf Breeze Sightings.* New York: William Morrow and Co., 1990.
- Watson, Lyle. *Beyond Supernature.* New York: Bantam Books, 1987.
- Weiss, Brian L. *Many Lives, Many Masters.* New York: A Fire Side Book, 1988.
- —. *Through Time Into Healing.* New York: A Fire Side Book, 1992.
- Weldon, John and Zola Levitt. *UFOs: What on Earth is Happening?* Ft. Lauderdale, FL: TSELF, 1975.
- White, John. "Aliens Among Us--A UFO Conspiracy Hypothesis in a Religious Mode." *MUFON UFO Journal,* February 1992, pp. 7-13.
- —. *The Meeting of Science and Spirit.* New York: Paragon, 1990.
- Woodward, Kenneth L. "A Vindication of God." *Newsweek,* August 19, 1996, p. 58.
- Wright, Dan. "Commonalities and Disparities: Findings of the MUFON Abduction Transcription Project." *MUFON Symposium Proceedings,* July 1995, pp. 164-203.
- —. "The Entities: Initial Findings of the Abduction Transcription Project." *MUFON UFO Journal,* February 1994, pp. 3-12.

FIGURES

INDEX

Mayans 51
meditation 93
Meier, Billy 116, 152-153
memory 74, 105, 121–123, 154, 191, 201
mental block 155
Mesopotamia (*see* ancient civilizations)
meteors 214
Middle East 7
Midwayers 96
mind control 122-123
miracles 18
missing time 64, 119-120, 127, 133, 152, 156, 158, 188
Mitchell, Edgar 47
Mohammed 19
Monroe Institute 92
Moody, Raymond 47, 78
Mormon Church 19
morphogenic fields 76, 78
Morris, Richard 101
Morse, Melvin 78
Moses 236, 239–256, 264-265, 307
MUFON El Paso 184, 196
MUFON Journal 20
Mutual UFO Network (MUFON) 18, 21, 116, 124-125, 127, 141, 147, 150, 158-159, 183, 196
MUFON Symposium 159

N

Nag Hammadi Texts 219
Nagas 223
National Aeronautics and Space Administration (NASA) 3, 33
National Investigations Committee on Aerial Phenomenon (NICAP) 154
National Science Foundation 56
National Security Agency (NSA) 87, 219
Native Americans 196, 288
near-death experiences (NDEs) 46, 78, 81, 166-168, 178, 200
negative forces 21, 101–105, 107, 111-112, 242
Nephilim 226, 232, 238
Neteru 224
neurophysiology 6
new science 111, 113
New York Times (newspaper) 157
Newton, Isaac 72, 212
Noah 226, 230, 232
nonlocality 69, 73-75, 78, 81-82, 85, 101
nonphysical dimensions 5, 44, 66, 73, 75, 77-78, 81, 93-94, 96, 104-105, 109, 111, 165, 168-169, 262, 277
North American Aerospace Command (NORAD) 89
North American Treaty Organization (NATO) 137–138
North, Oliver 88
Nostradamus 279

O

O'Leary, Brian 47
Omega Project 166, 170
Orion 7, 14
out-of-body experiences (OBEs) 17, 49, 64, 76, 78, 81, 92, 96, 124, 162, 163, 175, 192, 200, 204
overpopulation 48, 230, 285
Ozark UFO Conference 115, 125

P

Panspermia 213-214
paradox 102, 112, 309, 311
Parallel Universe Theory 15
paralysis 128
paranormal phenomena 6, 50, 73, 88, 120, 136, 142, 152, 157, 162, 165
    mental telepathy 7, 11, 74, 130, 152, 160-161, 167, 175, 183, 188
    out-of-body experiences 6
    precognitive visions 6, 74
past-life memories (*see* reincarnation)
past-life regression 79, 106
Paul, the apostle 261-262, 272
Paulism 262
Perregrino, Rita 126–135, 184–194, 297
Peter, the apostle 264-265, 274, 278
Phillips, Harold E. 90
phobias 127, 133, 186
photons 101
physics 6, 11
Pleiades 7, 14, 152
poltergeists 49
Pope Gregory VII 53
Pope Innocent III 53
Pope John Paul II 309
positive forces 21
post-traumatic stress 156, 185
prayer 47
praying mantis beings 132, 134, 160, 172–181, 188, 204, 242, 297
premonitions 85
Pribram, Karl 47, 73
Princeton Engineering Anomalies Research Project (PEAR) 87
Project *Aquarius* 90-91
Project *Bluebook* 27
Project *Sigma* 125-126
promised land 253, 255
prophesy 175, 266, 269, 278
protons 101
Psalms, Book of 241
psychiatry 6, 111, 156-157
psychic abilities 5, 6, 46, 86-89, 162, 169, 267, 278, 293, 298
psychokinesis (*see* paranormal phenomena)
Puthoff, Hal 87
pyramids 94

330

Blue Water Publishing

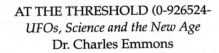

Wild Flower Press

AT THE THRESHOLD (0-926524-
UFOs, Science and the New Age
Dr. Charles Emmons

BECOMING GODS (0-926524-34-8)
Prophecies, Wisdom, Practical Advice
by Cazekiel
as received by James Gilliland

CONNECTIONS (0-926524-35-6)
Unraveling Our Alien Abduction Mystery
Beth Collings & Anna Jamerson

Swan•Raven & Co.

A MAGICAL UNIVERSE (0-926524-39-9)
The Best of Magical Blend Magazine
Michael Langevin & Jerry Snider

ANGELS & ARCHETYPES (0-926524-38-0)
An Evolutionary Map of Feminine Consciousness
Carmen Boulter

PLANT SPIRIT MEDICINE (0-926524-09-7)
Healing with the Power of Plants
Eliot Cowan

CALLING THE CIRCLE (0-9632310-8-1)
The First and Future Culture
Christina Baldwin

For a complete catalog of Swan•Raven & Co. , Wild Flower Press
or additional books that we distribute, call 800/366-0264 or write to
Blue Water Publishing, Inc.
Post Office Box 190
Mill Spring, NC 28756